Letters to Eden

DAVID HABER

SAINT DUNSTAN'S PRESS

BALTIMORE, MARYLAND

Copyright © 2015 by David Haber.

All rights reserved. No part of this publication may be reproduced, distributed or transmitted in any form or by any means, including photocopying, recording, or other electronic or mechanical methods, without the prior written permission of the publisher, except in the case of brief quotations embodied in critical reviews and certain other noncommercial uses permitted by copyright law. For permission requests, write to the publisher, addressed "Attention: Permissions Coordinator," at the address below.

Saint Dunstan's Press
P.O., Box 39221
Baltimore, MD 21212

http://www.saintdunstanspress.com/

Book Layout ©2015 BookDesignTemplates.com

Cover Design by Liz Merchant

Illustration (p.395) by Kalasea Sanchez-Fernandez

Letters to Eden/ David Haber – First Edition
ISBN 978-0-9963237-0-3 (hardcover)
ISBN 978-0-9963237-1-0 (epub)
ISBN 978-0-9963237-2-7 (paperback)

Contents

	Prelude • 1
Part I	No Sweat • 3
Part II	New Muscles, Old Aches • 19
Part III	An Interlude • 67
Part IV	Food and Drink • 77
Part V	An Interlude • 125
Part VI	Touching Fire • 137
Part VIII	Alternate Routes • 177
Part IX	Second Wind Hymns • 193
Part X	An Interlude • 243
Part XI	Repairs and Roadblocks • 252
Part XII	An Interlude • 322
Part XIII	Elementary Nature • 328
Part XIV	Down from the Mountain • 372
Part XV	The Trunk of Our Olive Tree • 392

ACKNOWLEDGMENTS

All journeys (whether by bicycle or by pen) are defined, not by the road travelled, but by the people met along the way. And it is to those many people that I wish to express my sincere gratitude. Without them, this adventure would never have happened, and my life would be substantially different.

A special thanks to Julie Meadows for slogging through early drafts of the manuscript and keeping me focused on the important bits; to Rodney Atkins, copyeditor extraordinaire, whose eye for detail keeps me in a perpetual state of amazement; to Marc Johnston for inspiring me to complete the journey of writing by a single courageous and somewhat insane act; to Regina—I mean—Liz Merchant for capturing the essence of my story within the perfect cover design; and to Ella and Caleb, my two mischievous children, who know how to keep secrets when necessary and prod the sloth when needed. Thank you all.

And finally, I would very much like to thank Mary, whose touch is in everything I do. In everything I write. In every moment I live.

For Mary and Oma
Bound together as grass and dew

Prelude

Dear Reader,

I am not the letter writer that my brother is. I wish I was, but not many of us are. The art is fading, dying, being replaced by hastily typed texts and status updates tweeting from Twitter.

When he was younger, he terrified me as he skulked around the house like a ghost; he was more stranger than brother, fenced off from us, his family, by a barrier of his own creation. It may have been the years separating us, but for me, it was as if I didn't have a brother. We had no real relationship.

Until he randomly sent me a note during his Junior year of college, I never recognized the powerful combination of fear and shyness pushing my brother away. In that short note, he revealed more of himself than in my previous sixteen years.

He admitted his aloofness openly. He acknowledged being ill-equipped for the role of a proper older brother. He confessed a new-found love. My brother in love. Imagine that. His note was illuminating to me in so many ways, and I began to understand something of his anti-social behavior. I also began to see how his letters (whether to me or to others) were a needed layer of protection, a set of training wheels latched to his life; without them, I realized, he felt no balance. But to live and act through one's own written constructs—wooing without talking, loving without living—he was not going to get very far. Especially when a woman crashed into his life.

For a woman who conquered the wilds of Kenya like Mary, this behavior just wouldn't do. She needed the stimulation of change, of newness, of conversation. She was the explorer of Africa, the connoisseur of still-squirming sushi, the solitary adventurer restrained by nothing but her own daring.

Mary and my brother were so different, and everyone could see that their relationship, no matter how we may have wished it otherwise, would not last. How they survived the summer of the accident and rediscovered love, I can't describe. Everything changed during his journey across America, though, and my brother's letters grew into something new.

But I'll let his letters do the talking.

Sara Haber

PART I

....

NO SWEAT

TELLING JOKES

September 15
College Creek
Annapolis, Maryland

Dear Mary,

When it comes right down to it, adventures seem to involve a great deal of labor, and frankly, I don't like hard work. Look at your African expedition. You spent months preparing, getting vaccinated, buying equipment, finagling cheap airfare. With that trip so far a success, I am filled with two conflicting emotions—the first being incredible pride. That's my woman in Kenya, bravely unaccompanied in a foreign land, ready for anything. Nothing can stop her, not even my own clinging love.

Then I begin to feel the shame. Alone here in Annapolis, I'm painfully aware that I'm letting you down; I've been left behind to watch and wait.

I have dreams, too. I have ideas for my own spectacular enterprises, exploits that would make you proud. The Appalachian Trail. Tap dancing. Rock climbing. Jet skiing. Winter camping. Surprising you in Nairobi.

At the thought of such feats, though, fear freezes me. I tell myself that it's just the work necessary in planning such quests that keeps me iced to the couch. Sure, I could hitchhike to Alaska—if I *wanted to*. I could pack up my one pair of good pants and strike out on my own. To make money, I could construct a parachute from old tube socks and become a fire jumper, saving the national forests from raging summer blazes.

But I don't. Instead I sit and wait and exaggerate my dreams into absurd jokes. It's all I know. So, my joke today is:

Why did the sloth cross the road?

Three days ago, Oma asked me to help her pull a weathered log from Lake Ogleton. We had been watching its progress for about a week as it bobbed and swirled with the currents. After eating dinner on the sun porch, she would measure its distance from the shore and nod. Predicting when the water-beaten branch would strike land became our nightly ritual, filling the time while dessert digested and before the *Wheel of Fortune* started. When the driftwood finally lodged between the dock and our rowboat, she turned to me and said, "Tomorrow we should haul that wood out to the mailbox. I think it will make a nice dragon sculpture to protect the flowers. Like a scarecrow."

I doubt she really needed my help. I imagine she just wanted company. I used to think you embellished that story about her wiry arms swinging an axe scant months after the hip replacement surgery. Seeing her calf-deep in water the next morning, reaching for the log just as a heron stoops to catch pike, I am now a believer. Her amber eyes carry more life than mine ever will. Unless I do something. Unless I act on a dream instead of telling another joke.

In the waters at the end of Eden Lane, yanking at a tree trunk alongside your grandmother, I began to chuckle.

"Oma, do you happen to have a bike I could borrow?"

"There may be a bicycle in the garage." Her nose crinkled at the thought. "I haven't ridden in years."

"Would it be okay if I borrowed it?"

"I don't see why it wouldn't be. You'll need to inflate the tires and put oil on the chain." She cleared her throat and twisted a few strands of white hair that had escaped her bun. "Why do you want it? Is the Volkswagen giving you trouble again? I can drive you somewhere if you need."

"The Rabbit's doing fine...it's just an urge, I guess. To ride around. Maybe to Baltimore."

"Baltimore is a long way down the road." She stretched, unknotting her time-twisted spine. "But there is that new bike path that's supposed to be quite nice."

Yesterday, while wobbling atop Oma's ancient Raleigh, the spring-loaded saddle tenderizing my rear, I couldn't out-pedal my desire. Baltimore is not enough. I do want to see the world, despite my fear of interacting with strangers. I need to stop living through others, relying on their strength. It's time to become the man that complements you as a woman. I want an adventure.

I wonder if I could I bike across the country?

Definitely not on Oma's bike, of course. Riding that bike is impossible. It's too big in some places and far too small in others. Pedaling along the bike path, I felt like a one-legged stork balancing in a strong wind. To be honest, there was a point at which I just wanted to get home, dump the damn bike, strip down, and lay spread-eagled on the living room floor. When actually home and collapsed on the sofa though, I couldn't stop thinking about the road, about passion, about what you said before you left.

"Find what you love."

To bike across America.

I wish somebody would laugh these terrifying thoughts away. Even now, part of me is cackling at the absurdity of it all. I now understand why you didn't press me to come to Africa. I was—am—afraid; I tell jokes about life, and you actually live life. We're on a mountain, you on the top and me lost in foothills. If I'm not careful, you'll return home with a dowry of twenty oxen, towing a gallant husband who bears a strong resemblance to Michael Jordan.

To San Francisco by bicycle it must be.

Here is my chance to ride off into the sunset, alone and free, finally the man I was raised to be. Brave, courageous, conquering the world. Nothing can stop me. Well, nothing except for the small problem of not having a bicycle, a map, or any idea of what the hell I'm getting myself into.

With her old Raleigh, Oma has pointed a way west toward the Pacific Ocean. There is no derision, no laughter at what should be a ridiculous joke.

The sloth doesn't cross the road, see; he just thinks about it. But I'm done thinking. That punch line is no longer amusing. I did in fact ride to Baltimore. The world holds an adventure for me on the highways of America. I feel it. The sloth has risen, and now he needs to find a pair of padded cycling shorts.

Love,
David

David Haber

....

SITTING ON THE TOILET

January 26
City Dock Café
Annapolis, Maryland

Dear Mary,

    I completely understand your frustration. I noticed your annoyed looks before you left to visit grad schools last week. I know you fear that this ride to the West Coast may never happen—that my motivation may be waning.

I'm well aware that I need to buy a bike. It just has to be the right one. If I choose poorly, who knows what might happen. That's why I spend hours studying catalogs of state-of-the-art equipment. I think Oma is becoming rather perturbed by this tendency. Since you left, the catalogs have migrated everywhere: crumbled beneath sofa cushions, strewn across the coffee table, wedged between the washer and dryer. Of course, nowhere is there a larger pile than where my most creative thinking occurs: the bathroom.

But alas! Only so many minutes can be spent in the bathroom. Just as Don Quixote must saddle Rozinante, so too, must I buy that green touring bike I've been talking so much about. The time has come to let action seal my plans.

There are many doubts, though. After spending hours studying books and trying in vain to locate equipment lists on the Internet, I still don't feel like an informed shopper. How can I trust that I'll purchase the proper gear? It would be wonderful if someone could just tell me exactly what I need, what I'm to face, for what disasters I should prepare.

While sitting on the toilet, I hear Ted, our local bike mechanic, whisper in my imagination's ear, "Word on the street is you're biking across America…

"See that bike on page sixteen? That's the T1000. It's bombproof. It's perfect for an African expedition. For you though, that's way too much bike. Go for the T700. It's got upgraded wheels that will stay true over the roughest roads. With a relaxed geometry and a longer frame, it's a mule, man…

"Yeah, some people prefer steel, but if you want aluminum, and I can tell that you do, then go for the Cadillac of aluminum bicycles and try this one. It's even got three water bottle holders so you never have to worry about running out of water."

Ted leans close, cupping his mouth behind a grease-stained hand. "Now, the standard seat on this bike is absolute crap. Since you're gonna be on this puppy for eight hours or more a day, I recommend a leather saddle. Sure, it may look hard as hell, but when riding long distances, the Brookes B-17 is the best. The seat actually shapes itself to your butt. Show me a gel saddle that does that!

"You'll need bags, too. We only sell treated nylon saddle-bags in the shop, but if you go online, you can find some really sweet gear. I've heard about these high-tech, virtually indestructible, completely waterproof panniers made out of old astronaut suits or something. You can submerge them in a river, and not a thing will get wet. And let me tell you, there's nothing worse than wet socks in the morning…"

In reality though, our bathroom is empty but for the countless, moisture-curled catalogs stacked in the tub; Ted isn't talking.

And all I hear is the flushing toilet.

Love,
David

DEPARTURE'S EVE

> May 14
> The Sun Porch, Eden Lane
> Annapolis, Maryland

Dear Mary,

It's late, and you're dreaming upstairs. We just made love for the last time in what will be months, and as much as I want to—as much as I need to—I can't sleep.

Tomorrow I leave Eden Lane.

I've never told you this before, but when Oma first suggested that we save our money by moving into her home after graduation, I was a bit...reluctant. The only roommate I desired was you. I didn't want to live with an eighty-three-year-old woman, especially since you were related to her. Her house was large enough, sure, but would there be enough emotional space for us to figure things out? How could we argue and make up with Oma shuffling around downstairs?

To my absolute surprise, this house on Eden Lane became our home because of her presence. Our relationship lasted through difficult times because of the calmness of her age. Her amber eyes laughed away my worries, and I came to love this home we all share.

To me, the house's layout is its charm—with the stove and kitchen cabinets stashed in the butler's pantry; the dishwasher, sink, and microwave hidden in the laundry room behind ten years' worth of carefully stacked Styrofoam egg cartons; and the toaster, coffee maker, and silverware completely across the house here on the sun porch beside the propane grill.

In the coming months, each night that I hunch over my grasshopper-like blowtorch that backpackers call a stove, I will miss the aerobic workout of cooking dinner at Eden Lane. I will miss tripping over the abundant bundles of yellowing papers heaped in the vestibule while scurrying to the sink to drain spaghetti before it becomes mush. I will miss trying to slice onions among the many peaked mountains of Burger King ketchup packets collecting on the counter. I will miss Oma. I will miss you. I will miss our home.

Did you feel such dread when you left for Africa? Because I'm terrified, Mary. Beneath all the excitement is pure fear. That some of our friends tell me I'm crazy doesn't help matters. I should go change my route and travel west to east, they say. The prevailing winds will push me home, they claim, and make riding that much easier. I should definitely cycle in a group, they advise. I shouldn't attempt to tackle the entire country, but rather go on smaller, more manageable trips. According to them, I need to bring a cell phone or, better yet, a rather large pistol. And sometimes, in what can only be spite, they arch an eyebrow, smirk, and remain silent, prodding the scab of my greatest fear: failure.

I can read their glances as well as anyone. *You can't finish. Your legs will wear down. Angry drivers will torment you. You'll get lost. Fifteen feet of snow will strand you in the Rockies. You'll get kidnapped by a radical Mormon warning of the end times. You're better off staying home. You won't make it to San Francisco.*

With such words and looks, scattered doubts coalesce in my stomach, and my imagination ignites. I see myself adrift tomorrow. Despite my plans to travel on a bike path for most of the day, I feel I will lose myself in suburban Maryland. I won't be able to reach the campground. I will make a terrible mistake. I see a huge stop sign marking the spot...

> Beneath a rumbling overpass, the shadows between the base of Old Lawyers' Hill and River Road lengthen. About three hundred yards past the sign, the road ends at a locked gate. To the left, Old Lawyers' Hill, which must be the only hill in central Maryland, rises steadily toward nowhere. There is no campground; my maps are wrong; my tire leaks air. As my head swivels from gate to hill and back again, I will be struck dumb by the realization that I'm lost, alone, and have no idea in which direction the Pacific crashes...

I'm a goofball, Mary, not an adventurer. I have no inkling what I'm getting myself into. I keep telling myself that pedaling six thousand miles will be no sweat, but really, who the hell am I kidding? I've never ridden farther than thirty miles—with frequent breaks. Combined with the eighty pounds of extra weight draped about the frame like misshapen floatation devices, my bike resembles the haphazard collection of oddities stored in Oma's garage rather than a respectable mode of transportation that's supposed to carry me to the Pacific.

I thought I had been selective, but even my few possessions weigh a ton. Steering reminds me of Esau wrestling with Jacob—no matter what, I lose because he cheats. When I want to drift left, the bike veers wildly right. When I want to turn sharply right, my bike balks. Tomorrow is going to be difficult. And the mountains...well, getting my bike over the Rockies will be like coercing a mule to plow forty acres backward in a blizzard.

But I can't worry about snow. I must do this. I must reach San Francisco. Just as you went to discover yourself in Africa, I must untwist myself on the highways of America. It's too late now to do anything else. I've quit my job and sold my power tools. Cabinetmaking is in my past. Another carpenter in Annapolis can struggle with the demands of unrealistic customers. I'm tired of it and have more important things to do. I've glimpsed what a life without you would feel like, Mary.

To be with you, I must leave and grow.

I need to suffer the newness of the unknown. I want to experience the wonder of meeting you all over again, swapping late-night stories until the sun cracks the darkness.

You're the foundation on which this odyssey will be built, and despite the miles that will separate us, our lives are connected. That connection will only grow stronger as I approach the Pacific.

Tomorrow, I may get lost. I may puncture a tire. But I will not be alone. I will feel your breath in the wind; I will sense your touch with each drop of rain; I will see your eyes within each setting sun. Mary, you are both the beginning and end of this journey—my Dulcinea spurring me onward and my Penelope in whose arms I will eventually rest.

Love Always,
David

PART II

....

NEW MUSCLES, OLD ACHES

From Reisterstown, Maryland,
to Poughkeepsie, New York

DAY 1

THE DANGERS OF RAMEN NOODLES

May 15,
Scenic Hills Motel
Reisterstown, Maryland

Dear Mary,

At this moment, I no longer have eyebrows. My attempt at boiling water has singed them off and in the process scorched a small section of burgundy shag near the bed in my motel room. So many cigarette butts have scarred the carpet that I don't think the manager will notice another charred section, despite its being a good six inches in diameter. I knew I shouldn't have attempted to cook ramen noodles within this coffin of a room.

If my little adventure had been progressing as envisioned, I wouldn't have paid seventy dollars for this closet in the first place. I wouldn't have been trembling with hunger while priming my Whisperlite stove, which caused the tiny explosion burning the hair from my face and forced me to devour a meal of tap water-heated, still-crunchy ramen. This first day of riding has wandered far afield of my plans.

Leaving Annapolis at ten o'clock didn't help. Neither did forgetting to make reservations at the campground. When I arrived and found a Park Ranger, he informed me that the campground has been closed for the past six months because of a contaminated water supply. If I had made a simple phone call to reserve a site—as you had suggested—I could have planned accordingly.

But I didn't, and I was forced to exceed my first-day mileage limit. I rode sixty-five miles, which is farther than I have ever ridden before. My legs feel like melted fudge. My shoulders and neck are as stiff as an overstarched shirt. My fingers are numb; my toes tingle. And the damn lumps in this bed poke and jostle any hope for a relaxed evening.

To be honest though, I enjoyed much of the ride despite my current state. My *own* muscles carried me past Baltimore today. I can't explain how that makes me feel—how free—how alive. The first thirty-five miles were spectacular. Along the B&A Trail, other riders pushed me on with head nods, encouraging words, and gifts of PowerBars. A woman stopped me at one point and grilled me for almost twenty minutes about my experience so far. Being only seven miles into the journey made answering her questions difficult, but her curiosity was invigorating.

I never thought I would be the center of attention on a bike trail, yet everyone acknowledged me. Cyclists are a friendly lot, I guess, and seeing my loaded bike made me a rolling marvel. Kids were particularly captivated. They didn't seem to understand how all my bags remained attached. While stopped at the ranger's station—being informed that the campground was closed—a little girl decided to test how securely the panniers were fastened to the racks by hanging off them like a jungle gym. Before I noticed, my bike tumbled over and drove her to the ground. Her parents were faster to the scene than I was, and their tongues were even quicker as they lashed her with their displeasure. As they dragged her away, the girl glanced over her shoulder, eyes red-rimmed with guilt. I shrugged and intentionally dumped my bike on my leg, hopping around in an elaborate pantomime of extreme pain. The girl giggled. For her, the world had been made right once again.

For me, though, things started to go poorly. Despite being a bit tired, I still felt good on the saddle; so instead of finding a motel, I tried reaching a different campground. At this point, I had ridden about fifty miles. The campground, according to the Ranger, was about fifteen miles away. Thinking that those fifteen miles would be as pleasant as my first fifteen this morning was my first mistake. My tiring body, although achy, was not the main difficulty, however. I was cycling on busy roads now. Cars zipped past at speeds far exceeding what seemed prudent. I was honked at, cursed at, and more than once driven from the shoulder. At one point, a mirror grazed my elbow. Before I could fall, a dog stuck his head from the passenger side of a truck and began howling as if I had stolen his favorite bone.

Regaining my balance, I swerved onto a more secluded road and realized that fifteen miles at the end of a ride feels more like fifty. My cyclocomputer captivated me as I measured my progress against the energy reserves in my stomach, which explains how I missed a right turn and, instead of camping, rest eyebrow-less in a room with creeks of nicotine staining the walls.

Things can only improve. Right?

I mean, my eyebrows will grow back. Won't they?

Love,
David

DAY 2

....

THE LINE OF TWO ASTRONOMERS

May 16
Otter Creek Campground
Airville, Pennsylvania

Dear Mary,

I laze under the arms of a huge oak tree in Pennsylvania and am baffled. If you had told me yesterday that I would be crossing the Mason–Dixon Line today, I would have thought your sanity was vacationing in Barbados. In my imagination, the border seemed weeks away.

There's an incredible psychological effect when traversing boundaries, and as I crossed the Mason–Dixon, everything changed, including the landscape. All morning, I had been passing the generally flat pastures and horse farms of northern Maryland with their vibrant green lawns, wooden fences, and grand houses. The moment I entered Pennsylvania the terrain began to dip and rise, the fields yellowed, and what the fences lacked in wooden pickets they made up in twisted chicken wire.

I was back in the North.

As I stood taking pictures of the sign marking the historical significance of this boundary separating states, dividing regions, segregating ideologies, I felt deep in my gut there would be no going back. Already I am somehow different than yesterday. The adventure has begun.

Love,
David

DAY 3

....

THE MATHEMATICIAN

May 17
Subway
Columbia, Pennsylvania

Dear Mary,

Dawn broke drenched in profanity. That I slept so poorly didn't help matters. The campground was deserted. Every chirp and rustle added another barrier between my eyes and needed rest. And the night—it is far darker than I remember. The last time I had been camping—about three years ago—a dazzling halogen lamp, strung from the eaves of the restrooms, had made me forget that I was in the woods. The voices of other campers yapping around fires had comforted. The slamming screen door of the bathroom had provided a constant reminder that indeed I was not alone in the dark night.

By midnight, though, I had just wanted my smoky motel room back. I would have been able to bear the scorched carpet for another night if I could just wash myself under a steady stream of bright light. As much as I would like to claim that I'm an intrepid traveler of the world, afraid of nothing, willing to confront the direst circumstances, I can't. I shake whenever I think about trying to cross America alone. I shiver under visions of being stranded in a cornfield with a broken bike. And last night as doubt magnified worry within the lens of fear, I shuddered in my sleeping bag, soon becoming convinced a genetically modified fox that had discovered a keen taste for fillet-o-Dave lurked in the shadows, sharpening his sixteen-inch claws on my tent stakes.

I've always believed sleep has a special power that transforms such fears into glorious dreams and sweet forgetfulness. I wish I could tell you that those dreams came, filled with visions of cycling success and heroic glory and our spectacular reunion. But they didn't; my dreams fled with doubts fed by the night, and sleep scurried just out of reach.

Yet I did wake with the sun. I still lived. That fox had simply been a phantom created by my overactive imagination. I think. Two stakes had been worried from the rocky ground, so I will never know for sure. As I soon learned, though, it was far more difficult to contend with daylight and cycling than mutant foxes, whether imaginary or otherwise.

"Off early, are you?" Asked the campground manager as I bought a few Snickers bars for the road.

"Yeah. I feel better when I start early. Makes it seem like I'm getting somewhere."

"That candy your breakfast?" She scrunched her face with a grimace.

"Not really. I had some cold instant oatmeal. The map says there's a restaurant a few miles down the road, though. I'll probably grab something there."

Her cheeks became even more pinched, shrinking and wrinkling like fruit left in the sun for a month. "There's a pretty big hill between here and there. I don't know why so many bikers pass through here with that hill in the way. It doesn't make good sense."

"Well, that's where the bike route is. It goes right up the Atlantic coast to Bar Harbor, Maine."

"You mean, somebody decided climbing the hill to New Bridgeville on a bike was a good idea? That's just plain foolishness. You should've stayed on Rt. 74 and cut over later. Where'd you get your maps anyway?"

"I bought them from Adventure Cycling. They're specially designed for—"

"You paid money for highway maps? Why'd you go and do that? Gas stations give 'em out for free…and also can steer you away from any hills. Like the one you're heading for."

"Sometimes, though, certain roads are closed to bikers."

"You'd know better than me. All I'm saying is that you're headed for a big hill that you could've gone around if you had better maps and weren't on some cockamamie route to Bar Harbor or wherever."

"Actually, I'm trying to get to California."

"California? Well, if your maps keep guiding you up hills that you could go around instead, it's going to be impossible. That's for sure. Hey, isn't Maine up north and

California west anyway?" I nodded. "Seems like that route you're on is just plain crazy. You should just go straight west. I know I've got a map here somewhere. We can get you on an Interstate in no time."

She bent over and began rummaging beneath the counter. "Now," she mumbled between wheezes, "where'd that map make off to?"

I stood dumbfounded for a moment. Biking west along Interstates is not only illegal but also insane. Besides, didn't this woman realize that my cycling maps are comforting? The miles are precisely measured and groceries and campgrounds all carefully marked. Traveling along a well-known route—a route that others have biked before—is important. Without the relief of knowing I follow in the pedal prints of others, I would still be frozen in Annapolis banging nails at an intolerable job, coasting through life. Without my cycling maps, so much could go wrong. I could run out of water and food. I'd probably end up hog-tied by a horde of hairy militiamen garrisoned in Idaho and tossed in a ditch. Wandering the earth like Kane in *Kung Fu* simply wasn't in my future.

Leaning on the counter, the woman dragged herself upright with a wad of crinkled papers that appeared to be a Pennsylvania road map from an era when the state had only seven roads. She stroked the creases smooth while sucking in her already sunken cheeks.

"See. You're right here." She tapped a spot smeared with grime. "I think if you head north this way." She traced a path with a thick, yellowed fingernail. "You'll be able to avoid most of the hills. Although you'll still have to climb out of the valley. Then if you turn here at Brogueville and then maybe a left at the four corners by the old willow tree." She looked at my legs. "It's a shame you didn't go to a gas station. They'd have put you on a much better route. You'd have saved yourself some time."

I cleared my throat. "Thanks for the advice. But I think I may just follow my maps. The way you showed me looks awfully complex. I don't want to get lost or anything."

The woman frowned and stared at me a long time. She gathered her map in a pile. "Suit yourself." She glanced at the candy bars on the counter and grunted. Shaking whatever thoughts of my route from her head, she peeled the withered apple of her face with a tight grin. "I guess for someone biking across America, that hill shouldn't be much of a problem."

Arriving at the hill's base a few minutes later unhinged my jaw. Defying modern physics and bending classical mathematics, it rose at a ridiculous angle to partially block the early morning sun. Such angles should not be found in the natural world. Humans might be able to create them on paper, but to see such a slope with a highway riding its spine seemed impossible. Appearing to be a few degrees shy of perpendicular, this behemoth stretched skyward with no switchbacks to ease the grade, no plateaus to rest tired legs, no grassy shoulders on which to collapse in exhaustion. But even if there had been, the idea of ascending it perched atop a bike was absurd. The angle was too steep. I would be flipped from the saddle like a teenager popping wheelies on his younger brother's BMX.

I would have to walk my bike.

Yet I couldn't allow myself to trudge up this hill—no matter how ludicrous its incline. I felt that if I somehow found the strength to pedal over the top, I would never drag my bike up a hill by foot. Over the White and Green Mountains, across the Adirondacks, through the Rockies, finally to cross the Cascades, my feet would never touch the ground…

If only I could pedal to the top of this hill somewhere in Pennsylvania.

About ten feet into the climb, the profanity began.

We all have cursed friends, neighbors, opinionated campground owners, and even fate sometime in our lives, but never have such words burst from my mouth. No, that's not quite right. It wasn't the words; I have said such things countless times before. It was their source. Deep in the belly, the words brewed, each strained muscle fiber creating a fire that brought curses bubbling through my shouts. Anger and frustration and stubbornness congealed in my gut. Lactic acid molded these emotions with a hammer of agony, pounding curses from my throat to paint everything blue. It wouldn't surprise me if trees lost leaves beneath the onslaught.

What I remember next is straddling my bike—legs twitching, tears mingling with sweat—and shouting wordless until my voice folded itself into a rasp. Somehow, I had conquered this absurd angle.

And it was only 7:30 in the morning; I still had another eighty miles to go.

I wish I could say continuing was easy, but I'd be lying. My legs did not function properly. Unable to push the pedals with any sort of rhythm, I turned my cranks with the jerky movements of a marionette controlled by an alcoholic. Exhaustion shuddered my muscles with each yard forward. My bike lurched across the asphalt like a record player needle across scratched vinyl. But bone-weariness gave me hope. After conquering such a steep slope, the rest of my ride would be downhill. Surely, the universe contained only the energy necessary to create a single such hill here on Earth.

I soon discovered, however, that the net direction of the Pennsylvania highway system is up, not down. Initially, I blamed my fatigue. I thought that the activity of climbing only appeared to occur with greater frequency because of my exhaustion. The descents just seemed to be decreasing in length because the respite freed my mind to wander. Very quickly, however, I began to notice a trend: the greater the drop in altitude, the larger the next hill would be. Soon, rather than being a greatly anticipated breather, descents became a warning: BEWARE! BEWARE! Yet another mound of earth squats ahead, heaving the road heavenward.

It was in a flash, while ordering a Subway sandwich in Columbia, PA, that I made a magnificent discovery. I felt rather like Archimedes after bolting from his bathtub; except of course, I wasn't running down the streets naked shouting EUREKA! See, Mary, there's a secret mathematics governing Pennsylvania. This previously unrecorded *Law of Hill Conservation* is expressed thusly:

$$D_{down} = \sqrt{D_{up}} \div K_{Penn}$$

Let's suppose that in an afternoon I travel a total of 5,280 feet uphill (D_{up}). To determine the distance I had traveled downhill (D_{down}), you would take the square root of 5,280, which is about 72.664, and divide it by the Pennsylvania Hill Constant (K_{Penn}), which happens to be 2.2 in the southern part of the state (in Western PA, it's 6.7). So, according to my calculations, a climb of a mile would reward me with a meager thirty-foot descent. It may not seem fair, Mary, but it's a mathematical certainty.

Love,
David

DAY 3.5

....

FONZIE IN A REDCOAT

May 17
French Creek State Park
St. Peters, Pennsylvania

Dear Mary,

A DWARF SUMO WRESTLER has squatted inside my belly all afternoon. I wish I hadn't stopped at Subway and devoured that Classic Italian sub. If I hadn't stopped though, I wouldn't have felt as if Sensei Futoi was practicing his stomping exercises within my intestines. If I didn't feel as if this sensei was bum rushing my stomach acids, I wouldn't have spent time in the Subway bathroom and wouldn't have crossed the Susquehanna River when I did. If I hadn't crossed the river at that particular moment, I would never have seen the thumb raised in encouragement as a southbound car passed.

Seeing this driver's thumb lightened my spirits before I even realized how heavy they'd become. The loneliness, which I had refused to recognize earlier while climbing the hills of Pennsylvania, shattered. Just like that. He connected me with the rest of the world; he recognized what

I was doing, what I was attempting, with what I was struggling. He was my Fonzie, linking me to countless explorers and adventures, just as Chachi, Potsie, and the whole Cunningham gang were bound by two thumbs and a shout of "Aaaayy!" For a moment, I was no longer alone.

And then it happened.

The effect of a car horn is amazing on a cyclist. These horns open veins and scrub the heart in an adrenaline bath. There's more to it than simple shock: the momentary confusion—what did I do?…followed by the anger—how dare you honk at me, bastard?!…and finally the brief glimpse of death as the offending vehicle speeds by. All this is packaged and delivered to the gut in a matter of seconds. Unable to handle such bombardment, the stomach drops and transfers these feelings to the farthest reaches of the body, namely the arms or legs. So, with my legs jellied like a harvest of overripe strawberries, I swerved to keep my balance. That I didn't fall was a miracle.

While reestablishing my equilibrium, I noticed that the honking car, a green Dodge Intrepid, had pulled off the road about fifty feet ahead. My insides flipped, sumo wrestler and all. Does this have anything to do with me? Forty feet. The door opened. What did I do? Thirty feet. A man got out of the car. Should I just stop? Twenty feet. He walked to the trunk. Oh, God! What's he getting? Ten feet. He leaned against the bumper and crossed his arms. Are there any witnesses to this?

I started to drift from the shoulder, giving him plenty of room.

"Aaaayy!" Two thumbs shot into the air; a grin parted the nest of dark hair sprouting from his face. From within the crows' feet surrounding his eyes glowed hazel chips of merriment. "Where you headed?"

I didn't stop but rather stumbled off my mount in the spastic sort of way only a bicycle tourist can manage as bike tips one way, body flings the other, and we both fall down. It was in this moment that I learned about the difference between the "right-on-you-can-do-it" toot and the "get-the-hell-off-the-road" honk. But more importantly, while being pulled to my feet with a reassuring hand, I met Neale Bayly, world-renowned motorcycle adventurer.

"Easy, laddie." His accent was thick. Scottish maybe. "In a spot of bother?" One hand, tan and strong, gripped my shoulder, while the other steadied the bike. "On a wee holiday, are you?"

"I guess."

"Where's that machine leading you?"

"West."

"Brilliant. Absolutely brilliant. Those sacks there are right shiny. How long you been going at it?"

"For a few days now."

"Brilliant. Just brilliant. You hungry?" He pointed back down the road. "You want some fries from Burger King. I have some HP Sauce in the trunk. My treat."

"Sorry, but I just ate."

"You sure? A spot of brown sauce is delish, mate...bollocks. Of course you don't want food.

You said you just ate. Can't have you all bloated for the ride. How far you go on that machine in a day anyway?"

"I don't know. Maybe eighty miles if I don't get too tired climbing hills. But I just started, so I'm not a good judge of that stuff yet."

"Riding on a bike with no plans. Brilliant."

He opened his trunk.

"The first days are the toughest. Don't I know it. I'm a wee adventurer myself, and when I passed you on the bridge, I thought you might need something. I've plenty of food. Sure you don't want something?"

I shook my head.

"Anyway, have a look in here. Got these wool gloves. You may need them in the mountains. Go on take them." He stuffed them in a pocket on my handlebar bag and then started sifting through the duffel in his trunk. "Here's some HP Sauce, mate. Brown sauce is delish on tuna. It will get you through the chill nights ahead. The stuff's great in coffee, too. Better than sugar lumps."

He handed me a jar crusted around the lid and, after burying his head in a bag, yanked out a pair of fluorescent orange sweatpants. "Oh, look at these. You must take these knickers. At night, cars will be able to see you, and they'll keep you real warm, too."

"I can't take your sweats."

"I have plenty. Here. Go on."

I eyed the pants. The elastic had been stretched so thin that both Neale and I could fit in them with room to spare. "Looks a bit big for me."

He thumped his forehead with a palm. "You are a right skinny bloke. Here take these granola bars instead. If you put brown sauce on them, they'll fatten you up like a Christmas pig in no time."

He dug in his pocket, nibbling on the few unruly whiskers from his moustache.

"And here. Take this fifty-cent piece. It'll give you luck. Better than a hare's paw. This really exotic looking taxi driver—tall and part Polynesian, I think—gave it to me when I first came to the States. She fancied my looks, I guess. But that was a long time ago…"

Born in England, Neale had been adventuring since he was sixteen. Now, at thirty-seven, he had seen most of Europe, parts of Africa and South America, the outer rim of Australia, and, on a thirteen-year-old motorcycle, the back roads connecting Florida to Alaska. He had hitchhiked 3,400 miles in four days, which must be some sort of record. He had worked the black market of South America as a money changer. He'd been a shade-tree mechanic, a factory worker, and even a journalist. But more than anything, he was an adventurer—a knight most true—a modern day Percival questing after the Grail.

But what, you ask, is an adventurer of this magnitude doing in the small town of Columbia, Pennsylvania, driving a car of all things?

As with most stories, there's a simple answer and an interesting answer, and that simple answer almost always relates to money. So, the simple answer is that Neale is tracking phone lines through various towns along the East Coast. Six months ago, he had been helping a neighbor change a tire when the car slipped off the jack and rolled over him. To give his reconstructed spine a short rest from motorcycles and make a bit of cash in the process, Neale found a job with a phone company. They provided the car and a per diem; he brings the brown sauce. It's crappy work, mapping phone lines and cell towers, but within a few months, he hopes to save enough money for a motorcycle, supplies, and airfare to China.

And that's where the interesting answer begins…

Love,
David

DAY 6

OFF THE TURNPIKE

May 20
Shady Acres Campground
Portland, Pennsylvania

Dear Mary,

I have passed through the Garden State many times, but I never imagined anything more to this area than the two-mile stretch of land on either side of the New Jersey Turnpike. I remember reading at a rest stop that Governor Driscoll, the politician who first recognized the need for this superhighway in 1947, claimed the turnpike would offer "motorists new vistas of New Jersey—with its large and small industries, pleasant productive farms, rolling countryside, beautiful woods and streams, and magnificent resort areas." Personally, I've never seen a pleasant farm along the Turnpike, having only experienced its grime, smog, and ceaseless traffic. I have always thought that calling New Jersey the Garden State was a cruel marketing joke devised by an advertising firm trying to trick travelers into the toll booths of the Turnpike.

Off the Turnpike, as I crossed and recrossed the border between Pennsylvania and the Garden State this afternoon, I soon realized how blurred my image of New Jersey really was. To think the state actually borders the Delaware River on the west—a boundary free of the dams, locks, and hydroelectric plants I had expected along New Jersey's western terminus. In my youth, I had imagined the state simply fading into the coalfields of Pennsylvania about five miles west of the Turnpike.

To my shock, Jersey is not the polluted cesspool it's rumored to be by those dashing along the I-95 corridor. The residents of this state don't have three arms because of exposure to excessive amounts of radiation; not everyone can be identified by Turnpike exit. The countryside isn't a barren wasteland, scattered with overflowing landfills and polluted beaches, fit only for a highway linking big cities. New Jersey is not a concrete nursery but, indeed, an actual garden. There are trees—green, flowering, and rather beautiful. There is water—blue, clear, and rather refreshing. And, there are geese—gaggles and gaggles of geese, all hissing me north.

Rather than ruining New Jersey, maybe the Turnpike has saved it. For many, New Jersey will always be a corridor linking the huge metropolises of the northeast to the seat of power in Washington, DC. Carrying hundreds of thousands of vehicles daily, the Turnpike channels the filth and noise of these travelers along 118 miles of super highway. The rest of New Jersey remains free of transients and commuters and is saved for those wanting to live in peace.

As I bounced and rattled my way from small town to tiny village, I listened to the undammed Delaware lap its way toward the Atlantic. I saw a great blue heron dive for pike and then take to the air like a parachute opening; with its flight, I was pulled back to you, Oma, and Eden Lane.

For hours, nary a car disrupted my silence. The only distraction was the nagging pain in my knee, which has grown from a dull ache to an incredible throb accompanied by sharp needle jabs. The pain became so severe that I began pedaling with only my right leg, pushing and pulling while my left leg circled without power.

After fifteen minutes of one-legged cycling, my right knee started creaking like a two-hundred-year-old oak straining against a fierce spring gale. Perfect timing for a break, I thought, and so stopped short in the middle of the road.

"What the Hell you doing, man?" Hearing brake pads squeal, I whirled around as gravel yanked at the wheels of a fast approaching titanium bike. The rider, wearing a tie-dyed jersey with matching socks, slid forward on his saddle to plant his crotch hard on the top tube.

I burned red with mortification beneath his glare and stuttered out an apology.

"You need to pay more attention, man. You're likely to get killed. You're lucky there wasn't a car passing." Shaking his head, the man reached around to his back pocket, grabbed an aluminum packet, ripped it open with his teeth, and began guzzling some sort of mystery goo.

"Are you riding the Atlantic Coast Route?" He wadded the empty packet into a ball and tossed it to the shoulder. He began scanning the horizon as if he expected a jet to fall from the sky.

"Yeah. Up to Maine, then—"

"How long have you been riding?" The man took off his helmet and began preening. He had yet to look at me.

"About a week, I guess. Maybe a little less."

"So, you started in Georgia? You're making pretty good time." The man met my gaze with approval. His eyes were gray.

"Actually, I started in Maryland."

The racer frowned and took off his gloves. His hands were white. He began gnawing on his cuticle, eyes once again wandering. "Damn, man. You're going slow. When I did the Atlantic Coast two years ago, I made it from Key West to Bar Harbor in nineteen days."

"That's amazing."

"No. Not really. I was pacing myself. In September, I'm going to do the entire Pacific Coast in fifteen days—from the tip of Washington to Baja. It's really going to take only fourteen days, but I wanted to give myself an extra day. You know, to sightsee. So, are you going to take the Northern Route across the country or is this just a short trip?"

"That's what I'm planning. I figure it will take me a few months. I've got plenty—"

"I did that route last year. Took thirty-one days. Next year, I'll do the Southern Route. Then I'll have done the whole perimeter."

I nodded, not knowing what to say next. Although riding with a companion would have been nice, this guy just didn't seem to be my type. He shaved his legs for crying out loud. That's a far greater commitment to cycling then I'll ever have.

"I'd ride with you for a bit," he said, glancing at my legs. "But it seems like you're struggling a bit. Are your knees bothering you?"

"How'd you—"

"You really should lower your saddle. It'll take the pressure off your joints. You shouldn't be leaning forward so much either. Before you stopped, it looked like you were about to fall over your handlebars. Who fitted you for that bike anyway? It doesn't look like the right size. Jeez. The hacks out there these days. And that seat! God, I thought leather saddles went out with the Sixties. They're junk, man. You should get yourself a gel saddle like mine." He pounded on the narrow wedge he called a seat. Perhaps one of my butt cheeks could have balanced on that slice of plastic but certainly not my entire rear. "It's really light. Get one. You'll go faster. Then it won't take you a year to get across the country."

He climbed back on his bike and clipped into his pedals. "Remember to adjust your saddle height, man. Well, I'm off. Wish me luck."

Before I could say a word, he glided down the road, dancing in his pedals like Baryshnikov. I dumped my bike on the ground and limped toward the shoulder to pick up the wrapper he had tossed aside, thinking the whole time that he doesn't belong in western Jersey; he is but a commuter and must live somewhere off Exit 8, a mile from the Turnpike.

Love,
David

DAY 7

....

A BARED FOOL

May 21
Worthington State Forest
Delaware Water Gap, New Jersey

Dear Mary,

This afternoon was the first in which I wasn't in motion, and my legs were limp with glee at the respite. Having gained a black belt in laziness during high school and trained under a master sloth in college, I was well prepared for a day of idleness, cooling the burn in my knee. I wouldn't have to deal with any more arrogant cyclists disparaging my equipment, my goals, my techniques. Camped ten feet from the Delaware River, I looked forward to silence and a wonderful afternoon nap. What I hadn't expected was the nasal greeting of a young park ranger as I lay, more asleep than awake, savoring the sun against my cheek.

"Howyadoin'?"

I squinted and smiled. Stringy hair fell to his narrow shoulders. Scraggly sideburns, failing to conceal his acne, glowed blonde in the afternoon sun. His shorts, cinched around the waste with a purple rope, hung from his skinny hips as if from a clothesline.

He kicked a few loose pebbles and said, "Yeah, it's a pretty bitchin' afternoon. Reminds me of skippin' class and surfin'."

I grunted in agreement.

"Dude, you surf any?"

I shook my head.

"You got a car or anything?"

I yawned a negative.

"I didn't think so. They told me there was a biker here. Trip been cool so far?"

With thoughts of Neale fresh in my mind, two thumbs shot skyward.

"Totally rad." The surfing ranger looked to his pick-up and signaled to his comrades on latrine duty. "Yeah, so anyway, like I didn't mean to bug you and all, but I just wanted to sort of stop by, and, like, well you know, give you a heads up…'round these parts, there's been a few sightings…you know, of bears and such, so you should hang…"

There's something incredibly sobering about the word "bear," and when that word becomes plural—well, there's no need to tell you I sat up right quick.

"Bears?"

"Yeah, so, like I was sayin', I wanted to stop by, you know, and make sure you had a good place to store your food tonight. Seeing you don't have a car, and you're, like, on a bike and all, you'll probably just have to hang your food, 'cause you know, you can't be leavin' food out too long 'cause a bear's gonna smell it. Those suckers have good snouts. They say bears in these parts can smell three-day-old honey on a dirty napkin."

I glanced at the picnic table where all my food was spread out, any sort of organization the casualty of my search for a Reeses. My enthusiasm for chocolate and peanut butter stained the shirt I had been using as a pillow. I was in serious trouble, which was magnified by his next question.

"You've got rope, right?"

Of all the things to forget. Rope is to adventuring as duct tape is to repairing. How can I even pretend to compare myself to people like you and Neale?

"That sucks dude. I guess you could, you know, climb a tree and hang one of your bags with a bungee or something. You'll probably want to do it pretty soon, too. A buddy of mine — few weeks back — had a bear rummaging through his tent in the middle of the frickin' afternoon. Can you believe that? Broad daylight. He won't go anywhere near the woods anymore."

I just stared at him.

"I gotta jet. Latrine mucking calls. Good luck, though. If you, like, need help or anything, I'll be close by. Later, dude."

I crammed my food into a pannier and shimmied up a tree to hang my pack. For more than a half an hour, I struggled with my bag and two bungee cords. A cool breeze blew from the west to muffle the laughter of the ranger and his buddies while they pretended to clean the latrines a few sites away. And, let me tell you, there's nothing more amusing than seeing a shirtless fellow in biker shorts as he dangles fifteen feet from the ground, one hand balancing an over-stuffed bag, the other trying to toss, tie, and secure a bungee, all the while attempting to maintain a grip on a flimsy tree limb.

It was not a pretty sight.

Somehow, perhaps by summoning the powers of my contortionist ancestors, I did manage the feat. But Mary, I don't want to talk about it right now; my teeth still ache.

Love,
David

DAY 8

....

SCHOOLED BY THE PROFESSOR

May 22
Ottisville Campground
Ottisville, New York

Dear Mary,

There is nothing quite like waking to the gentle rustle of tent's rainfly as the late morning sun, tinted blue by nylon, warms the skin after a day of relaxation. What's even better is when you realize that, at least for a night, the bears of New Jersey have left you alone. With such reassurance, how could I be expected not to go back to sleep?

Yesterday, I had envisioned all my gear packed by sunrise, fifty miles under my wheels by noon, and my tired legs resting in Poughkeepsie by 7:00 p.m. That would mean riding over a hundred miles (114 to be precise), which is something I've never done before. After an afternoon on my back watching the clouds for shapes and the woods for bears, I believed I could do anything. My legs would be fresh; my knee wouldn't burn; my spirits would be lifted. Nothing could stop me; once I clambered from my sleeping bag and climbed onto my bike.

When I finally climbed the hill leading from the campground—it was far closer to noon than to dawn—I still believed I could reach Poughkeepsie. That is until my knee started to throb. For the next six minutes I fought for every foot, scraped for every inch, struggled with every rotation of the crank. I wasn't going to make it. I should turn around and rest. Poughkeepsie and my childhood home would have to wait a few days.

"Jeepers, you're packed heavy. Are you headed to China with that set-up?"

He had appeared out of thin air, right beside me, astride a touring bike the same shade of green as my own—matching my cadence, breathing easy, bike humming beneath him like a live wire. He was no arrogant tied-dyed racer, with clean-shaven legs and muscles bunching with effort. He was paper thin, all sinew and bone, and matched my slow speed without complaint. His close-cropped gray beard and wire-rimmed glasses contrasted harshly with the blue-striped spandex bib hugging his torso; he seemed more suited for a suede-patched tweed coat, surrounded by smoke rings puffed from a pipe. He made his bike seem as comfortable as a leather swivel chair. The woods were his office, the leaves his books, the branches his shelves. Since I can't remember his first name—it was Harry or Henry or Harold or something equally ordinary—I'll just call him the Professor.

The lessons began when he started asking me about my knee, where it hurt, whether it burned or throbbed, whether the pain was localized or diffuse. He didn't mock me; he didn't make me feel like an idiot. He actually wanted to help, and after questioning me, he made suggestions about my riding position, seat height, and most importantly pedaling cadence. In any other situation, a conversation about cadence would have had the appeal of boiled bacon.

As we talked though, as I watched him glide up inclines and then coast down, I began to understand that climbing hills didn't have to be a knee-straining battle between geography and my will. There was a serious flaw in the mathematics I derived the other day in Pennsylvania. There was no need to scratch and snarl my way to the top of every rise; I would get there when I got there. It's not like either me or the hill had anywhere in particular to be for the next few days. With that realization, the *Law of Hill Conservation* was amended, and I began shifting down and spinning my way up.

"Dave, why do you pedal downhill?"

"What do you mean?"

"I don't mean to lecture, but according to the various laws of nature, of which I am intimately aware—being a physics and math professor—what goes up will freely come down again."

"Okay"

"And, as you probably already know, we're going down a hill right now."

"That's true."

"Yet you seem to be pedaling. Why do that when there's the wonderfully mysterious force called gravity?"

"Good point."

"It would be a shame to wear your knee out. Pedaling downhill doesn't create that much extra speed anyway. It's not worth the energy expended. Let gravity do the work. You've got thousands of miles to go yet. Just out of curiosity, how's your knee doing?"

"It feels pretty good. Still hurts a bit. But I feel good."

"Conversation is a magnificent distraction. If the knee keeps bothering you though, try some shark cartilage or chondroitin and glucosamine. They work wonders. Like gravity."

For the next few miles, we continued through the Delaware Water Gap in relative silence. I tried hard to mimic the Professor's cadence, but he was a far better rider than I. Naturally, he reached the top of each climb well before I did, but despite my fears of being abandoned, he was always circling the top, waiting for me and smiling.

"Watch yourself down this next descent. The Old Mine Road can be tricky at times. You'll probably be going faster than you've ridden before. There's a pretty sharp turn about halfway down where gravel collects. Make sure you aren't going so fast that when you apply your brakes, you fly into a tree and break your back. Speaking from experience, riding with a broken back is not a hurdle you need to be worrying about right now. That sore knee is enough."

"You rode with a broken back? Are you nuts?"

"Psshh. Broken backs are overrated. If you're flexible and in good shape, your body will heal itself. The real problem wasn't the inevitability of broken bones, but rather the moral dilemma I faced right before the crash. Do I collide with a pedestrian who had misjudged my speed or sacrifice my body for another and smash into a pile of garbage cans?"

"And you chose?"

"Neither. I slammed on the brakes, soared above the gentleman and landed flat on my rear."

"That had to hurt."

"Actually I didn't feel a thing when I wiped out. After I rode home though, my muscles stiffened up severely, and my wife dragged me to the hospital, where I learned I'd cracked a few lower vertebrae. As you can imagine, my wife was a bit perturbed by the whole event. I tried explaining how all moral dilemmas can be avoided by picking a third choice, but she would hear none of it."

At that, he took off down the hill.

I had ridden twenty mph before. Yesterday, I may have even reached twenty-nine. When I hit thirty-five today, I was shocked. When I broke forty-five mph, I remembered when I was learning how to drive and would only take small roads home because I was afraid of being unable to stop. As I approached fifty mph, adrenalized joy peeled my face to reveal a grin.

"Watch yourself." The Professor pointed ahead where the road seemed to disappear into a forest. I slammed on my brakes…

...And almost shattered a few of my own vertebrae before regaining control of my shimmying bike.

"Gently. Pump your breaks. You don't want to burn up the pads and lose control. Alternate between the front and back. Feather them. Don't bear down. You'll be fine."

He coasted past, vanishing around the bend.

I relaxed a bit and managed not to impale myself on a tree.

"Damn fun, huh?"

I wiped the grit from around my eyes. "You know, you're pretty freakin' crazy for a math professor who just broke his back."

"Books can get boring sometimes; even professors need a little excitement, and this is my first ride in awhile. Hey, you getting hungry? There's a sandwich shop up in Layton that makes a mean ham and cheese. Lunch is on me."

A few minutes later we pulled up to an ancient Victorian house that had been converted into a deli. About fifteen bikes were parked around it. We found the back of the line.

"Lots of riders here. They must make good sandwiches."

"It gets like this on the weekends. People come for miles to ride the Old Mine Road."

"There're mines around here?"

"Used to be. The road we've been riding connected them all. Some say the Old Mine Road is the oldest commercial highway in the United States. When the Dutch first moved into this area in the mid-1600s, this road was constructed to haul copper ore to Kingston, where it was ferried along the Hudson to New York City."

We had reached the counter. The Professor ordered a ham and cheese. Bombarded with endless choices, I ignored past experience and risked ordering a hoagie dripping with oil and vinegar, inevitably stirring Sensei Futoi. We found an open table on the porch.

"It's beautiful here. Doesn't seem like mine country. So peaceful."

"That's because in the late 1800s, the mines ran dry. Soon developers moved in and created summer resorts for folks exhausted by city life. Trains stations appeared; steamboats filled the Delaware. At the turn of the century, even a few silent movies were filmed in the Gap. Later, after the Depression hit, this area was forgotten by most."

"That's a shame."

"Not really, if you think about it. Look, being forgotten isn't the worst thing that can happen to a place... When I was kid, some genius in the Army Corps of Engineers decided the Delaware needed a dam and this valley would make a wonderful lake. My parents and our neighbors fought hard against the Tocks Island Dam Project. If it weren't for the fact that General Gates secretly marched troops along the Old Mine Road to aide Washington during the Revolutionary War, this deli probably would be under twenty feet of water right now."

"Really? How so?"

"Well, someone was able to convince the government that this area was historic, and the Army abandoned the dam idea."

"It seems like a good thing then that not everybody forgot about the area."

"Yes and no. That a monstrous dam never flooded the Gap is a blessing. But if our ancestors hadn't stolen the land in the first place, the Lenni Lenape Indians might still be around, living as they had for thousands of years."

"The Lenny Le Nappy?"

"Len-e Lun-NAH-pay. It's the tribe that lived here before the Europeans came. This whole valley on both the Pennsylvania and New Jersey side was prized by the Lenape; it was their summer hunting grounds. When fine land is discovered, however, leave it to us to find a way to acquire it, even if the inhabitants had been occupying it for centuries."

"Another case of outright theft?"

"Right you are, Dave-O. It ranks right up there with Peter Minuit's purchase of Manhattan for sixty guilders, a shiny oyster shell, and a broken copper necklace. Of course, good old Mr. Minuit bought Manhattan from the wrong tribe and ended up the swindled rather than the swindler—maybe there is a bit of justice in the world…Anyway, legend has it, when Chief Teedyuscung lost the Delaware Water Gap to our ancestors, his face materialized in the side of a mountain to remind the settlers of their treacherous past. It's a long sad story, but if you want to get to Port Jervis while there's still daylight, I'll tell it to you as we ride."

For the next three hours, as we rode through the Delaware Water Gap, not only did the Professor give me constant pointers about my riding habits, but he also passed the miles by revealing a bit of our swindling heritage.

It began with a walk.

To understand this walk, we must first look back to when William Penn came to the New World and settled the land that would eventually become the city of Philadelphia and Chester and Buck counties. To acquire this territory, he struck many bargains and signed countless treaties with the Lenape Indians. While he lived in America, overseeing his dream of religious tolerance and brotherhood, the agreements made by Penn were respected and honored, and those treaties were never broken. Or so legend says.

Penn eventually returned to England, leaving his holdings in the charge of his sons and various deputies. Money flowed like Liquid Plumr down a clogged drain, and soon the Penn family found themselves close to bankruptcy. Because of their need to pay growing crowds of nefarious creditors, his sons began selling off their diverse holdings and were soon forced to contrive new ways in which to acquire more territory. In 1735, a mysterious treaty appeared ceding Penn's family the rights to even more tribal land. This treaty had supposedly been lost seventy years earlier, only to magically appear exactly when the sons needed more property.

This document granted Penn's decedents the right of what the Lenape called a Walking Purchase. According to the treaty, the Penns were to walk north from a set point and, after a day and a half of traveling, would be given all the land due east from where they halted to the Delaware. To the Lenape, walk meant amble along, hunt a bit, rest for a while, smoke from a pipe, mosey a bit farther, and sleep for the night. To the Penns, walk meant hire professional runners to haul ass for as long and as fast as they could.

On September 19, 1737, three runners left from beneath a chestnut tree outside of the village of Wrightstown heading north. The next day at noon, after two of the runners had collapsed, the final "walker," one Edward Marshall, arrived at the town now called Jim Thorpe, some sixty-five miles away. The Lenape were slightly perturbed at this point. The spirit of the treaty had been shredded. But their anger only grew, when, to the tribe's absolute astonishment, the "impartial" surveyors decided that east did not mean due east but rather northeast, all the way to Lachawaxen, a town about thirty miles north of Port Jervis. From this crooked walk, the Penns claimed the Delaware Water Gap and more, a landmass equal in size to Rhode Island. Check a map, Mary. You'll be amazed.

The Professor's story concluded as we arrived in Port Jervis. He may have had many more tales but had to return home before dusk. A part of me wishes he had been able to continue with me. Another part, realizes how absurd that wish is. New people will drift in and out of my life each day. I can't just stop and latch onto strangers.

Right now, though, alone with my thoughts, I feel so incomplete. I need more teaching. There are many lessons to be learned. I crave to be the apprentice of a master, to study living from someone like Neale or the Professor full-time. But I can't stop moving north and then west, across this stolen land.

I have nowhere else to go.

David

DAY 9

....

WET-SHOE WISDOM

May 23
Mom's House
Poughkeepsie, New York

Dear Mary,

 I tried calling this afternoon. Oma said you were off on a run and a swim. It's good to hear you're still training hard. The big race will be here before you know it. Soon you'll find yourself amid a pack of sweaty and limping triathletes, wondering, as spears of pain shoot through your calves and stitches tighten your sides with cramps, why the hell you're doing what you're doing. It's a familiar train of thought; I wonder that very same thing every morning when I awake in a tent far from you.

 I'm sure Oma has already told you that I reached Poughkeepsie safe and relatively sound, although a tad disappointed. Arriving to an empty house is a bit disheartening when expecting oodles of praise and loud trumpets of fanfare after cycling over four hundred miles. Talking with Oma, however, quickly banished any disappointment I felt. We laughed quite a bit, and that was good. I believe she thinks I'm insane—biking all those miles when a perfectly good car could have carried me equally as far in eight hours rather than eight days. Nevertheless, I want to believe she sees something of the forces pulling and pushing me onward. And I need to believe she respects me for facing those forces.

I so want her approval, Mary. Of our relationship—of our life together. Her opinion matters so much—more than anybody's, I think. It's so strange because she's your kin, your grandmother; I'm really just a stranger to her. Yet when she hugged me as I left Eden Lane, I felt a warmth through her delicate, bird-like angles that I didn't expect—a warmth I again experienced today, bubbling with laughter, as I told her of the rain.

It began so gently this morning. At first, I wasn't quite sure what the sound was. When the drops began splattering my face through the open mesh, I knew I'd have to shed my pajamas of laziness and either muster the colossal amount of energy necessary to break camp or scrape together the minimal, simply zip the fly, and wait out the storm—more than likely falling asleep in the interim.

Sleep is an ever-attractive option. Especially when there is a hypnotic drizzle strumming nylon walls. The problem is that when you shift to get a bit more comfortable, water has a tendency to seep into the tent. To my mind, warmth is great, morning heaviness wonderful; wet covers, not so much. Knowing I would have access to a dryer in the evening if I could reach Poughkeepsie finally pushed me from my cocoon.

Any remnants of laziness were shocked from my system soon after I wiggled from my sleeping bag, only to have the damn fly decide it was a gutter and my bare back was a downspout. In that instant, as I rocketed naked from my tent, I rediscovered a hidden and long-forgotten truth about rain. Much to my satisfaction, Oma agreed when I told her:

Once you're wet, you can't get any wetter.

It's only when you're dry or beginning to become dry that you can get wetter. If you're already wet—embracing that wetness like I embrace my laziness in the mornings—there's no possible way to get wetter.

Remember when you were a kid and wore those canvas Keds that seemed to draw you toward every puddle? You must recall that squishy warmness of wet socks—that magnetic lure of feet to puddle, positive and negative getting closer, until unification with a…

Splash!

In childhood, your feet felt this truth of rain and wetness, defying fathers and mothers and what many call common sense by traipsing from puddle to puddle and, in so doing, blocking the discomfort of dryness with constant, beautiful wetness.

The wisdom of adults is so very different from the wisdom of children, and the wisdom of children is extremely close to the wisdom of cycling tourists. I never really understood that before. Having wet shoes is about being carefree, about being so joyous that you just want to sing.

Boy, did I want to sing.

Remembering how to make music isn't easy though, and wet-shoe wisdom is tricky to hold. It's always been difficult for me to sing; I've felt that I never knew how, so I couldn't really try without humiliating myself. Even alone, in the shower for example, I blush at the sound of my own voice, squelching those warbling sounds before they can root within my ears.

So, when a soft hum escaped, it isn't surprising that I quickly turned to verify that I was indeed alone on the highway. I certainly couldn't have anyone hear my notes. That would be far too embarrassing. For the next few miles, I halted all humming when I heard that distinct slurping of a speeding car on wet pavement. As the vehicle passed, I would strain to pierce the smoky windshields. Did the driver hear me? Was he laughing?

Totally irrational behavior, I admit, and far from carefree. But I couldn't allow anyone to eavesdrop. Considering the riotous cacophony created by water on steel, rubber through puddle, and wiper across windshield, it was ridiculous to think someone could actually overhear my songs from their passing cars. Old habits die hard, though, and this trip is revealing that so many of my thoughts and reactions are governed by habits years in the making. I am a cycling marionette, trying to pull free of his strings. And today's storm has weakened them.

Once the rain strengthened, shyness was forgotten, and my humming discovered shape in words. Those words, first meaningless strings of formless verse, soon found a pattern, acquired substance and meter, and actually rose in volume to silence the rain beating upon the drum of my helmet. I remember neither verse nor chorus, although I have the distinct impression that I sang ballads of love, far away and growing more distant with each passing mile. What I do know, though, is that I sang long and loud, making a joyful noise as the heavens rained down.

Love,
David

PART III

AN INTERLUDE

Poughkeepsie, New York

DAY 13

....

HUNG OUT TO DRY ON THE WALLS OF JERICHO

May 23
Spackenkill High School
Poughkeepsie, New York

Dear Mary,

Thank you for deciding to come up to Poughkeepsie this weekend. I'm both grateful and excited, even if that means staying with my parents for another week. I miss you so much and crave your calming presence desperately.

I'm just so frustrated right now.

I am sitting outside my old high school like a beggar outside the walls of Jericho, waiting for the arrival of Joshua and his mighty ram's horn to tumble all barriers with a ringing blast. This morning I had decided that today was the perfect day to visit my alma mater. Little did I realize that security has increased to such an absurd level. I still can't believe that the secretary, a woman who has known me since I was eight years old, would not let me in—as if I were hiding a Beretta in my biker shorts and a grenade beneath my helmet.

I understand that everyone is up in arms about the recent violence in schools, but by not allowing older graduates to come back and drop in on classes, the students lose a very important part of their education—a vision of who they could become in those who have gone before. When I was a freshman, I remember the cafeteria being visited by ex-varsity soccer players or Harvard attendees. These graduates always inspired me. I was filled with pride. I would emulate their superior play on the field; I would attend the very best colleges. I, like those before me, would make my high school proud. Then, I too would return with honors and laurels to be an inspiration to those younger.

Today, I fulfilled that obligation and returned to tell the beginning of an adventure—a story no one before had ever dared imagine from within the walls of Spackenkill High School—a story I need to share yet am unable to. According to new policies, written permission is required to visit teachers during the day. I can't get in otherwise. But to get said permission, I must first speak with the teachers I would like to visit, which I'm barred from doing because I can't get into the school. I have to wait until the students are dismissed, which defeats the whole purpose.

God damn it! I just want some attention.

My journey is not easy, and I want to share my struggles and my joy. I can be an example. I can inspire. Fear is not the only governing force. There's also the courage of Neale, the honor of the Professor, and the glory of trying to be a good man. I could have shared that with the students. What better lessons are there?

Instead, with helmet as a pillow, I rest in the sun, waiting for school to let out with the ringing of a bell.

Yours,
David

David Haber

DAY 17

....

SQUARE DANCE

May 31
44 Scenic Drive
Poughkeepsie, New York

Dear Mary,

Although we made overtures toward reconciliation before you left, still I must ask: Need we fight?

I'm not going to see you again for months. This tension between us, although hibernating as the miles grow and time passes, will awake when we reunite, whenever and wherever that may be. The fight will begin again.

Do you remember that story Oma told us about square dancing? Three days a week for the length of their marriage she and her husband would bow to their corner and do-si-do. Everyone has bits of disagreement, she said. But that frustration can't last during a square dance. You're too busy trying to bow and swing, down the center, and split the ring. So, before I'm once again to confront my fears on the road, I will try to confront my fear of losing you. Right down the center.

I was inconsiderate on our brief ride through my old neighborhood yesterday. I was a jerk. I was like that damn tie-dyed racer. All I needed was to shave my legs. I was oblivious to your concerns when I rode ahead as we biked on roads unknown to you. There's no excuse for leaving you behind, nor will I try to make one. I completely understand your anger as I pulled ahead, your mounting frustration as I didn't respond, and your increasing terror as I disappeared around a corner. I am sorry.

I couldn't say this the other day because I shut down and became defensive when you questioned me about my behavior. I built a barricade of mud bricks until I could build no higher, protecting my kingdom with a wall of silence…and, in some strange way, of love.

Don't think I'm being deluded by the sound and fury of our argument. What happened as we biked together is no longer relevant. As with all our fights, the causes are soon forgotten because of the infuriating (to you) pattern we (I) fall into. Usually, it works like this:

1. I say or do something absurd.
2. You get angry and ask me what the hell I was thinking?
3. I immediately get defensive and start building structures of silence.
4. The frustration mounts on both sides.
5. You think our relationship is about to end and demand some glimmer of emotion.
6. I clamp down and remain silent to the brink.

I'm just so frightened, and that fear makes me silent. I have to remain in control; I can't allow myself to feel what I should be feeling because what could happen is completely unpredictable. If I allow emotion to swallow my reason, I fear I will become something you've never seen, something that will scare you back to the safety of friendship, something that will frighten me back to the irresponsibility of youth.

Therefore, I build. I construct with silence in a muddy attempt to love. I build my Tower of anti-Babel until I can reach no higher. This castle will protect us both from ourselves, from our anger, from our emotions. The promenade is forgotten, and we can't dance the squares.

It seems fitting that over the past few days I've spent more time than expected with my father. Like most, my parents have shaped me more than I typically admit. A core of arrogance resides within me, a spark that shouts: I am the sculptor of myself. I have taken shape through the sometimes delicate and often times clumsy touch of *my* chisel and *my* hammer.

After this week though, I have begun to see shades of both my father and mother within me: his emotion and her supreme confidence, his fears about living and her constant struggle with perfection, his skulking insanity and her ubiquitous frustration. I feel their touch distinctly on my every act, my every outburst, and my every moment of silence before the ocean of feeling that at times overwhelms me. As the tide rises, the gift of my mother's rationalism begins to build sandbank walls to contain the flood. And, so begins the cycle of silence—the birthright of my mother battling the emotionalism of my father.

In that struggle is born my every act.

I know I need to try harder to be honest with you. I want to let you in. I need to let you in, and I think the bike is teaching me how to be open. We must remember, despite my lapses of communication and your increasing frustration with them, that we are indeed

In love,
David

PART IV

....

FOOD AND DRINK

From Rhinebeck, New York,
to Surry, Maine

DAY 18

'CEPT WITH DUST IN THEIR EYES

June 1
Interlake Campground
Rhinebeck, New York

Dear Mary,

As everyone knows, real men don't cry, 'cept with dust in their eyes, and boy the pollen is thick today. Everything I own is coated with yellow dust—my bags, my bike, my deeper parts.

Your return to Annapolis has made me lonely something fierce, and as I pedaled from Poughkeepsie this morning, I couldn't keep the tears from cutting tracks down my cheeks. I have really left you, and when we next hug, I will be different. Will I feel the same? Will I be the same? Will you even recognize this new person who chose to leave behind the woman he cared for more than anything to pedal across America?

From the moment I climbed atop my bicycle, I felt a deep emptiness materialize in sobs, which have yet to stop. I hate crying; it makes me feel so helpless, so out of control. Why am I so forlorn now? Why didn't I feel this loneliness when I left Annapolis?

I'm going to be gone for three more months. These emotions will only become stronger. If I keep leaking like this, I will either have to buy another water bottle or fail in the struggle to keep my body properly hydrated. I can't help but question whether I am man enough to face the challenges ahead.

Remember the couple who sat in front of us when we saw *Titanic*—how after the movie, the woman quickly gathered her briefcase-like purse and tried to drag her boyfriend from his seat as tears rolled from his eyes like the credits on the screen? Her frustration and impatience, her embarrassment, were painfully apparent. Sitting here writing this letter, I see myself as both that crying man and his mortified lover. I feel frail and ashamed at that very frailty. I just need to forget about this awful day. That's why I cling to my noble lie. These tears are making me doubt my own strength. So repeat after me…

…Real men don't cry, 'cept with dust in their eyes…

And boy, the pollen is thick today.

Love,
David

DAY 19

....

FILL 'ER UP

June 2
Farmington River
Pleasant Valley, Connecticut

Dear Mary,

I awoke thinking that the universe was plotting my demise by accelerating the laws of entropy. The dishes from my dinner the night before were still dirty, and my tongue and teeth felt fuzzy, as if they needed a good waxing. My belongings were scattered haphazardly around my tent; my panniers, once a shining example of organizational genius, were in such a sorry state that it took me twenty minutes to find matches. My bag of spare parts is even missing, more than likely left forgotten in some dark corner of my mother's house. The past week of sitting on the couch has completely scratched away the routine I had established, and any discipline I once knew lazes back in Poughkeepsie, resting next to my lost bag o' parts. Just pray that I don't get a flat before my patch kit and tubes are found and sent ahead to me.

For an hour this morning, I was adrift in the campground, avoiding the disaster of my site by wandering around the Loop—that ubiquitous circuit required by either the federal government or the campground gods when granting permission to create an RV Park. By the fourth Loop, after I had resigned myself to stuffing my crap in my bags to sort out later (maybe tomorrow but definitely the next day), I met Butch.

I think the name shapes the person in a very special way. In what profession other than football could you find such characters as the huge linebacker Bruno Nagurski, the bruising running back Larry Czonka, and the graceful, silky-smooth receiver Lynn Swann? In what profession other than baseball could you find a pitcher named Rollie Fingers and the catcher Johnny Bench? And let's not forget about Iggy Pop, Grace Kelly, Mick Jagger, and Fred Astaire—all people whose characters and names are like socks to toes. With his gapped-tooth, loose-lipped grin, Butch was no exception, tattoos snaking over farmer-tanned arms and light-blue polyester bowling shirt straining to contain a volcanic belly.

He was vacationing from the literal grind of making small parts for large engines—jet engines in fact. Every year at about this time he would get fed up with trying to make the monthly quota and take a two-week vacation to a place he had never been, the picking of which involved a map, his red "good-vibe" bandana, a dart, and a case of Coors.

According to Butch, these trips—determined by the tip of a dull dart aimed with drunken precision—refill his spiritual tank just enough to give him the resilience to stand in front of a CNC lathe for another year. The winter months, he explained, with their shortened days and chill winds, were always the most difficult—especially February. Despite being shortened by two days, the production schedule would remain the same. This means that, in twenty-eight days, Butch and his night-shift counterpart have to produce six thousand parts. On a good day, when everything is running smoothly, Butch and his buddy can mill two hundred parts between them; but that rarely happens. There's always a brief fire or a chipped tool.

Nevertheless, assuming the company has employed people willing to work through the weekend without a break, this machine shop will still be short by four hundred parts on March 1—which further assumes there wasn't a shortfall during the previous month. None of these assumptions are valid though. Poor Butch is constantly working from a deficit. For him to last on a single two-week vacation, Butch must have one hell of a spiritual tank.

I asked him how, and more importantly why, he would do such a thing with his life.

"Planes gotta fly, suppose. Somebody gotta do it. If not me, then some other sucker. Planes just gotta fly. Ya know? It's like I tell my little 'uns. It's not what ya do at work that's important, but what ya do after that matters. That's life. 'Cause planes still gotta fly, even if the work sucks…the work, that don't matter. It's after the job. It's here…"

He gestured around the campground. His belly button winked as his shirt lifted and stretched across his stomach.

"Let me tell ya somethin'. About ten years back, I used to be real ornery. Just plain mean. Cranky, not carin' about nothin', drinkin' real hard, hollerin' at the kids, hollerin' at the wife. Real ornery, ya know? But then, for some reason or 'nother, I figured it was time to get away and go fishin' in Jersey."

Butch paused to scratch his wide back.

"Man, I never even been fishin' before then. I don't even like fish really. Don't know why I did it, but damn if I didn't catch the biggest trout ever…I was livin'. Really livin'. Since catchin' that rascal, though, I've stopped drinking, 'cept on Wednesdays. I stopped bein' so ornery. 'Cept in February. But that's okay. Ya know how it is. The tank's runnin' low."

"But doesn't it get to you? Standing in front of a machine knowing there'll always be more parts to grind."

"Yeah, it gets pretty bad…Look, I'd be lyin' to you if I told you I liked work. But this is how we gotta live to survive. It's hard. It's borin'…But no matter what people may be thinkin' about what I do, I know what I *am* is good. My kids know it; the wife knows it. They know I ain't wasting what I was given. My work ain't me."

He cleared his throat noisily and spit.

"Hey, look at my gut." His hands massaged circles on his stomach. "Most people think I'm just some over-weight hick who drinks too much and's goin' die by sixty. Shoot! Eleven years ago, I weighed a good 312 pounds. Since goin' to Jersey though, I started exercisin' with my eldest. I've been doin' push-ups and sit-ups every mornin', except two, for the past seventeen months. I'm up to ninety-four sit-ups. Every mornin'. Just by lookin' at me, would you guess?"

It was then that I decided to pull this adventure and my life with it back on track. If Butch could do it by catching a fish of all things, then so could I. If he could do sit-ups and push-ups every morning, then so would I. If he could love life, then so will I. From this moment forward, Mary, I have taken a vow of discipline, a vow of dart-determined vacations, a vow of living.

After Butch and I swapped addresses, I hurried back to my site, did ten push-ups and ten sit-ups, brushed my nasty teeth, and then began the process of organizing my things. I left later than I would have liked, but I left with my spirits high.

My tank is full, Mary, and February is a long way off.

Love,
David

DAY 21

....

"STILL EATIN'?"

June 4
Crystal Springs Campground
Bolton, Massachusetts

Dear Mary,

I was sitting under a tree and eating my second breakfast of the morning, finally having reached the conclusion that it wasn't the rolling hills but rather the wicked winds whipping out of the north that was making the ride so difficult, when this wiry, wispy, willow branch of a fellow shuffled toward me with a young girl sitting on his shoulders. She was eating an ice cream cone and trying (but failing) not to drip the melting treat on his Boston Red Sox cap.

"That your bike ovah theyah?"

"Yup."

The man nodded and bounced his weight from one foot to the other.

"Wicked hot. Ain't it?"

As he looked at the sun, a brown drop of ice cream missed the brim and landed square on his nose. The girl, mouth slathered with chocolate, grinned.

"Yup. It's pretty darn hot."

"Been eatin'?"

I took another bite of egg sandwich.

"Tryin' to."

"Ayuh. How's the ridin' been?"

"Today it's tough. I think it's windy or something."

He peered skeptically at the sky through the still branches.

"Ayuh. Wind's a tough nut to crack, but so is heat…I bike, too. Even raced a time or two. Nothin' more than a hobby, 'course. Wicked fun. Casey heyah likes watching." The girl slumped her shoulders at the mention of her name and started giggling.

I took another bite of my second breakfast.

"You sure you're eatin' enough?"

"I eat when I'm hungry. That's probably enough right?"

"Ayuh…Do you eat when you're not quite hungry though? 'Cause, you know, I rode from my parents' house in Bucks Hahbor, up north in Maine, down apiece to Bahston, and damn if I didn't lose thirty pounds. I wasn't eatin' right, see. And if you don't eat right, you'll bonk."

"Bonk? What's that?"

"It's when youah tank runs wicked low. You've got no energy. You can't pedal. You just wanna sleep. Forevah. Haven't felt that way yet?"

"I don't think so. Somedays I sleep till nine thirty. But that's because…well, I sort of like sleeping and don't feel like packing. No energy though? I don't think I've felt that."

"From the looks of things, you've been real lucky. You gotta be real careful and constantly eat. The way you look, if you go about losing even five pounds—poof! You'll up and disappeah. People will start wondering where you're at, and you'll be right in front of them, too skinny to see."

I finished off the sandwich and started in on a Cliff bar.

"Well, me and Casey are off to scalp some Sawx tickets. Just be sure to keep eating enough. I don't want to heyah any stories about the skinny bikah who passed out because he forgot to eat right."

He studied me for a long moment.

"You sure you aren't still hungry?"

I shook my head.

"Heyah take this fivah and get yourself something more to eat anyway. You gotta still be hungry. Damn, it's wicked hot and not even ten."

He walked to his car; I went back into the convenience store and bought another egg sandwich.

Three breakfasts can't hurt.

About an hour and a half later and some twenty miles away while I sat at a picnic table devouring my first lunch and feeling every bit the hobbit, a car pulled up to the corner and honked.

A peanut butter sandwich half in my mouth, I looked up and saw the Boston Red Sox cap. The man rolled down his window.

"You still eatin'?"

I waved my sandwich.

"Well, it doesn't look like it. Heyah. Take this ten. Get yourself some pistachio ice cream. Best in the state right ovah theyah. It's too damn hot not to be eatin' ice cream."

I walked to the idling car and accepted his gift.

"Thanks. I guess you didn't make the game?"

"We couldn't get tickets. Feckin' Yankees are in town. 'Sides, it's wicked hot."

"Ayuh, wicked hot," his daughter shouted from her car seat.

"Ayuh. We'll go home and watch the game in the air conditioning. The food's cheapah that way, and boy, am I stahving. Good ridin'. Ya still look hungry, though. Keep eatin'."

Even now, as I write this letter nibbling at my second dinner of pizza and coke, I'm still eating...

You wouldn't want me to disappear now would you?

Love,
David

David Haber

DAY 23

....

DE-BONK-TION

June 6
Camp Eaton
York Harbor, Maine

DEAR MARY,
 THIS AFTERNOON I CROSSED into Maine and saw the Atlantic. For a while, I didn't think I was going to make it. This far north I had mistakenly expected mild temperatures. By noon, the air had become thick and heavy. But the heat was far from the only problem. I also had forgotten the advice of the Boston Red Sox fan and hadn't been eating well enough.

 One minute, I was riding fine, and in the next, a great heaviness pressed down upon my entire body. Even wiggling my toes became a chore. My skin seemed to puddle around my pedals, reflecting Dali's most twisted visions. My pores were exhausted and unable to produce sweat. Blinking became more difficult than taking out the trash on a Saturday morning. I had bonked. Utterly and completely.

 You'd think that two packets of oatmeal, two rolls smothered with peanut butter, five cereal bars, three eggs and a side of bacon, two twenty-four-ounce bottles of Gatorade, two hotdogs, a vanilla milkshake, a fourteen-inch pizza, some fries, a Coke, an iced tea, a can of beans, about five bottles of water, and a handful of various vitamins tossed in for good measure would have been enough to deflect the bonking blues. But the cumulative effect of my less than stellar diet over the past few days had drained me, and I was forced to find a spot to rest earlier than I would have liked.

"You look like you could use some shade," said the manager of the campground as I stumbled into his air-conditioned office and flopped across the counter. "You're in luck. I've got the perfect spot. Plenty of trees. How's site thirty-four sound?"

I pulled myself mostly vertical, leaving a stain of sweat and grit on a stack of brochures. "Sounds good to me. How much is it a night?"

"Normally, sixty bucks." I frowned. "But I saw you pull up on a bike, right?" I nodded. "Since you've got about a tenth of the stuff some campers who claim they're roughing it have, I'll give you the site for six bucks. And, you can have as much ice as you need. Fair enough?"

Even piled high with three bags of ice, I left the office substantially lighter.

Circling the campground on my bike, I began to understand why this place was so expensive. These so-called "campers" probably used megawatts, maybe even gigawatts, of electricity with all the gadgets they had brought. Christmas lights, which had been strung around awning poles, blinked constantly, even in the middle of the day. Compressors chugged while inflating air mattresses. Huge antennas pulled signals from the air, filling the campground with the sound of televised gunfights, car crashes, and cheers at a Red Sox victory. Astroturf blanketed the ground of some sites, while other campers had decided a more natural look was appropriate and had planted elaborate flower gardens around their motor homes. One enterprising camper created an actual lawn in a box made of two-by-fours. Now, why anyone would go camping and pack a weed whacker is beyond me.

The hum of electrical appliances faded when I crossed a wooden bridge into the tenting area. This was more to my taste. Instead of being cleared to fit the unwieldy girth of mobile homes, the trees were permitted to grow and wrestle with one another. Some sites were so thick with tangled limbs that pitching anything but the smallest of tents would be impossible. This would do quite nicely, I thought as I coasted toward site thirty-four.

A black Lab tore from the underbrush. With its hackles raised, the dog sunk to a crouch and began howling and pawing at the ground. He started frothing as if I had just stolen his prized London broil. I leaped from my saddle, hoping to ease some of the tension. The dog inched forward still barking.

"Mattie! Hey, Mattie!" A man whistled. "No barking."

The dog backed off and sauntered to an approaching man who walked with a slight limp and carried his head cocked to the left as if he were perpetually listening to faint music. His black hair was slicked back tight to his scalp like a swim cap.

"Don't worry. Mattie won't hurt you or anything. This is his way of introducing us, since I'm a bit shy around new people. My name's Doug."

He smiled crookedly, slumping his left shoulder and pulling at his dark goatee.

"Nice to meet you, Doug. Mattie's an awfully pretty dog. Must be smart, too, introducing shy people and all."

"He sure is. I found him when he was a puppy in Willow Creek, California. He's been with me ever since, helping me meet people as I drive around. If it weren't for him, I would probably still be staring at you, wondering about the dude who just rode in on a bike that was almost as heavily packed as my truck."

"And, if Mattie weren't around, I would be wondering whether that dude who was staring at me from across the campground was a stalker and whether I should switch sites."

"Yeah, thankfully, Mattie's around." Doug grinned, and I started laughing.

If I had stopped for a moment to weigh the odds of meeting Doug, a person who not only was a needed and willing companion in conversation but also seemed so similar to me, I would have arrived at the conclusion that there was indeed a grand scheme to the universe, that there was some single thought thinking itself, that there was a Something out there nudging us when we needed nudging. But that would happen later. For now, I was swept away with the sweetness of a human voice.

"Where you headed on a bike packed like that anyway?"

"California."

"No way, dude. I just came from L.A. Well, sort of. Long story. Hey, you want to come over to my site? I've got some Bud Light."

Yeah, I know, Mary. I don't like beer, and Bud Light is only a few notches above Schlitz. But I am on an adventure after all, and what could be more adventurous than having a Bud with some dude from L.A. after an exhausting day?

What first struck me about Doug's site was its lack of a tent. He had the standard picnic table and small fire pit but not an ounce of camping gear. It looked like he just backed his truck up and decided that his diagonal parking job was good enough for him.

"How long you been camping here?" I asked.

"I don't know. A few days now. I kinda like this place. It's quiet."

"Don't have a tent?"

"No. I've got a tent. Two in fact. Come here. Check this out." Doug tossed me a beer from the cooler by his bumper and opened the tailgate.

I had never seen anything quite like his setup. I thought I had accomplished an amazing feat by packing everything I might need on my bike, but it paled in comparison with what he had managed to do with his truck. An entire apartment's worth of stuff was arranged within the bed of his pick-up like the results of a perfectly played game of Tetris. Boxes and bags, sacks and suitcase were wedged in every nook and cranny like jam spread on an English muffin, leaving about a two-foot gap between his things and the ceiling of his truck's bed cap.

"Damn. There's a queen mattress in there!"

"Yup. I certainly wasn't going to get rid of it. Besides, I need somewhere to sleep. That space there is just big enough for me and Mattie. Everything I own is in there, including my tents. Buried somewhere is even a bike. The rear wheel got stolen in Spokane though, so I haven't taken it out since."

"You should go into business as a mover."

"I did that in L.A. for a bit. How do you think I got so good at this? Let me tell you, the dude who trained me—well, he was one serious packing mo' fo'. He could pack an entire house in about two hours. No wasted space on the truck either. He sweat and stank like you wouldn't believe. But that dude could haul other people's crap. Being a mover wore me down though. My back couldn't handle all the lifting. So, I did the most logical thing."

"Which was?"

"Became an oxygen bartender."

"What the heck's that?"

He took a long sip from his beer and sat on the tailgate.

"Well, you know how L.A. is—all those rich celebrities willing to try anything and everything to improve their complexion, their boobs, their brains. We had hits of oxygen for every ailment you could imagine. Feeling down and need a pick me up? Well, try the O_2 Breeze. Want to enlarge various body parts? Try our Triple-Hit Tornado.

Want to lose weight? Try a Double-Shot Hurricane with a lemon wedge."

He grinned like an insurance salesman, offering me an invisible oxygen mask after he took an imaginary hit.

"But the most requested blast of O_2 was the one hundred percent pure, ten-minute MindWind chased by triple-infused dihydrogen carbonic acid—you known, soda water. We also sold special pills called the Brain Dewrinkler, which was a standard capsule of ginseng and ginkgo. That went for eighty bucks and was supposed to sharpen the mind and increase memory."

"That's insane. Our lungs aren't even designed to take pure oxygen. It's a total waste. People just can't be that stupid."

"Sure they can. Just give someone hope, and they leap at it. We're all looking for quick wisdom and instant gratification. At least that's why I eat Chinese food, tasty enough and the fortune cookies are enlightening. Who cares if I'll be hungry in an hour?"

"So, how long did you push air to those asthmatic junkies?"

"Oh, not that long. Maybe two weeks. I started to feel guilty. People were coming in two, three times a day to suck down some wind. It was amazing. Those rich cats really knew how to tip, too. I lived for two months without steady work on the tips alone."

"I still can't believe you actually had customers."

"We're talking about L.A. here. In California, almost anything is possible. It's a breeding ground for weirdness.

Between gulping down O_2 at eighty bucks a puff, getting pores sucked at local spas, and fluffing auras to remove stress, you sort of forget real people exist. Everyone is either a waiter waiting on their next big break or a has-been dreaming of past success. You ever see that old movie *Sunset Boulevard?*"

"Nope."

"Well, see it. Captures L.A. perfectly...I couldn't take it any longer, dude. I was one burned out oxygen bartender."

"So, you left then?"

"Not for about six months. You're not going to believe what finally drove me away." He flung back his head and chugged the last of his beer. "I reviewed foot-fetish movies, summarizing the plots for catalogs and such."

"Those movies have plots? You're joking right?"

"Someone needs to describe the movies, and for a few months, that someone was me. If I don't see another stiletto-heeled foot or fishnet-wrapped toe in my life, you won't see me crying about it. You want another beer?"

"Not yet. So, you actually had to watch all the movies?"

"Dude, I couldn't just make up the stuff out of thin air. I couldn't just say that the hot action in *Miss Legs USA* involved the shapely toes of Asian imports fresh from the mainland when the movie was really about a beautiful thigh contest happening in Las Vegas. The cats who buy this stuff—most of them live in Indiana by the way—well, these middle-American pervs wouldn't be too pleased when they bought a movie expecting Chinese toes and got a flick filled with good old American thighs. So, I had to at least make an attempt to watch snippets. What I would usually do is just put the tape on fast forward and begin writing."

"I guess Foot-Fetish Movie Reviewer will not be included on your resume."

"Probably not. Anyway, like I was saying, it's a bit strange seeing legs wiggling to-and-fro at about sixty mph, but it beat actually watching the flicks at regular speed and being subjected to some of the worst dialog ever written. What's amazing is that people pay money for the stuff."

"Well, people buy blasts of air. Porn at least has some sort of purpose."

"Sure it does. But it would be one thing if there was a sense of seduction, of passion, of something even the least bit alluring… hey, maybe even a coherent story rather than the usual Betty greets mailman and immediately begins doing her thing—mailman leaves—Betty suns herself by pool and is surprised by Julio the pool man—they start getting busy—a construction worker passes—Betty becomes really, really busy—yada…yada…yada. Of course, decent actors and actresses might help, but you can't have everything. Shoot, *Star Wars* survived on story alone, so why can't something like *Sex Wars*?"

"I think that flick has already been made."

"Well, you know what I mean. More than once, I wanted to gouge my eyes out. I was so completely bored—bored with L.A.—bored with floating around without any real passion. I was a ghost. I was tired. I was lonely. At twenty-nine, I didn't have a single goal. I was a dried-out corn husk about to be swept away in the gutter."

He patted the tailgate.

"Until I saw this puppy parked at a Toyota dealership. Dude, I don't know about you, but sometimes the simple act of consumerism can lift the deepest and darkest funks."

"I hear ya. In college, my thing was books. I must have spent about five grand on books. Old books. New books. Thick books. Thin books—"

"One book. Two book. Red book. Blue book."

"Very funny. You know, if it had pages and words and I was feeling down, I'd buy it. I think it had something do with the smell. It was just so comforting."

"Well, I'll tell you something. There was nothing more comforting than the smell of this truck when I first drove her around the freeways and made my first L.A. left turn. It was great."

Doug tossed me a beer.

"Don't go thinking I'm some materialistic glutton single-handedly turning the wheels of commerce. I don't regularly buy new stuff. I'd rather be in a Salvation Army store than at the GAP. It's just that sometimes—well, sometimes you have to be a hypocrite, succumb to the pressures, and buy yuppie. All I can tell you is that something pulled me to that truck."

He swilled the last of his beer and grabbed another can.

"If my friends from high school knew I had a brand new pickup, they would be flabbergasted. I was the one voted most likely to tie himself to a tree in front of a lumberjack, the one who was going to be the first Green party president, the one who scorned all those preppy, feathered-hair, Members' Only-wearing, Don Johnson look-alikes. I had big dreams. I was going to save the world. Then I went to UCLA, when I should've gone to Reed."

We fell into a long silence.

Mary, I read somewhere that a conversation, any conversation at all, can only sustain itself for eleven minutes, after which there's either the uncomfortable "first-meeting" dread of the eternal silence of that infinite space between two people or the "I-am-comfortable-and-contemplating" lull where you unconsciously hum to cricket music before beginning anew. All I could hear was our duet...

We punctuated that melody by swapping stories of adventure well into the night—he told me about the spirit and unity he felt with the forests of the West Coast, about the great food and conversation at small Midwestern cafés, about his meandering drive from L.A. to perhaps Nashua, New Hampshire (but who can tell for sure where he'll end up)—and I tried to paint pictures of singed eyebrows and sore knees, of insatiable hunger and the gift of brown sauce, of the happiness and loneliness of biking across America.

As I sit here in my tent, flashlight between teeth, writing this letter to you, my heart is still shaking at something he said. I would have completely dismissed it as New Age crap if the words had come at any other time. But tonight was different; his companionship has fortified my psyche against an emotional bonk.

I know I will mangle the idea with trite words, making it too easy, too Californian, too much like fetish-film dialogue. But I am afraid I'll forget—already I am forgetting—so…

…He told me to put the dream out there, to just send it off. People will hear. People will help, and I as a dreamer will also help the imaginings of others awake as they embark on their own pilgrimages.

Of course, those are my words tainting his ideas with ink. I don't know. I just don't want to forget the moment. The words really mean nothing anyway. They're only shadows.

Just listen hard, Mary. Can you hear the melody of two adventurers sharing living dreams, sipping Bud Light?

Love,
David

David Haber

DAY 27

....

THE TANKS OF BELFAST

June 10
The Moorings Campground
Belfast, Maine

DEAR MARY,
THE TANKS HAVE ROLLED IN, and Belfast is under siege. Will there never be a ceasefire?

The campground owner had warned me, but I didn't fully comprehend the sheer magnitude of the invasion until I found myself nose-to-tire with the largest motor home I had ever seen. I peered to my left. Another house on wheels stretched across two sites. And beyond that yet another. And another and another.

I was surrounded.

Splashed with swirled blues, greens, and purples, many of these beasts stretched for more than forty feet. They had hydraulic leveling systems, satellite televisions, huge awnings, and even double slide-out units making the behemoths even larger.

"Hey, is that a mountain bike you riding?"

Squinting into the late afternoon sun, I peered at the nearsighted retiree leaning from the driver-side window of a Unihome. His ten remaining hairs appeared to have been systematically placed to break the glare reflecting off his forehead.

"No, it's a road bi—"

"Can't be. Look how beefy it is." He pushed his glasses higher up on the bridge of his nose. "The top tube slants down just like a mountain bike. And I know bikes."

Great. Another know-it-all. Just what I need—a geriatric techie with his finger on the pulse of the latest enhancements in cycling technology.

"It's aluminum so the tubes are fatter for stiffness, and I guess the slope is some sort of design feature. It's a touring bike, though."

"Uh-huh. Sure it is. Still looks like a mountain bike to me. They must have seen you coming."

"Well, it's gotten me this far."

He grunted. "So, where are you touring to?"

I so wanted to say China.

"San Francisco."

"Where are you coming from?"

How's Timbuktu sound?

"Maryland."

"Nice ride. I rode from Anacortes a few years back on my seventieth birthday." Seventieth birthday, my ass. Rode in that motor home, maybe. But on a bike? No way. "You do realize, of course, that you're headed in the wrong direction? West is that way." He pointed in the general direction of south.

"I'm heading to Bar Harbor first. I always wanted to go, and it seemed as good a time as any."

"Makes sense. Hey, what are you doing for dinner?"

Filet mignon, asparagus drizzled with hollandaise sauce, and a nice glass of Chianti.

"Noodles, probably. Maybe with some chopped up peppers and whatever else I've got stashed in my bags."

"Well, then today's your lucky day, son! My life partner just went to the store to pick up some more meat and vegetables, so we'll have plenty. Go get yourself cleaned up and come on over. While we're waiting, we can compare notes. I'm working on a book about my ride, and I'll show you the manuscript and pictures from my trip. Do I have some stories for you."

Did I really want to eat with these people? Was I that lonely? Was I that hungry?

"My name's Richard, by the way. See you in a bit."

It was the best shower in my life—a true sensual experience as liquid heat massaged sore muscles and kneaded away my sarcastic tendencies. Rather than building the standard cinder block box with toilets and showers, the owner of this campground converted his basement into a bathroom walled in cedar and frosted glass. He spared no expense, from the radiant heat floor to a bench in the shower. And let me tell you, all showers should have benches.

As I sat in effigy to Rodin's Thinker, steam building to hold the heavy scent of cedar, I wondered what it was about certain tones that triggered my sarcastic self. Am I such a prisoner of first impressions that I would give up free food and conversation just because someone turned me off by the way he showed curiosity? Am I nuts? We're talking free food here. No matter how much someone may appear to be a jerk, food is still food, and conversation is still music to lonely ears no matter who's talking and who's serving. All people have something to offer.

Refreshed and relaxed, I knocked on Richard's camper.

"Come on in, son. You're just in time for my afternoon pick-me-up."

Richard was a bit bow-legged and more than a bit thick in the belly. For seventy-plus years, he had a full-fleshed vitality that I pray for when I collect retirement fifty years hence. "You want a beer? Or do you want a shot?" He waddled to a cabinet and put a tall thin glass etched with a bare-breasted mermaid next to a bottle of Hennessy Paradis Rare Cognac. "The beer is probably better. You need all the carbs you can get."

He reached down to a stainless steel refrigerator.

"I'll try a smidgen of what you're drinking."

He turned to me and peered over his bifocals.

"You sure, son? Carbs are the most important thing. Cold beer after a long ride—there's nothing better. Besides, what I'm drinking..." He shook the bottle. "...Is quite an acquired taste. You probably won't like it much."

"I'll try it."

Yes, Mary, I know what you're thinking. Cognac? Since when? First, a Bud with Doug and now a shot of $300 liquor. I guess I'm just becoming a lush.

Dick carefully poured the Hennessy to the left nipple of the etching on his glass and then looked at me again.

"You sure, now?"

I nodded, and he grabbed a mug from the sink, wiped it out with a napkin, threw in a cube of ice, and splashed it with a bit of amber.

He handed me the mug. The fumes tickled my nose.

He slowly took a sip, held the liquor in his mouth a moment, smacked his lips, and slammed down the rest in one gulp. "Damn that's good. Now drink up."

I took a sip and went blind.

"Holy shi—"

"Good. Isn't it?"

"Uh…sure."

"That's my secret to getting through the night. Everyday at five for the past twenty years or so. It gives me something to look forward to. I know with cognac on my lips, there's no way I'm going to die in the night." He started laughing and slapped me on the shoulder. "Hey, I've got something to show you."

Richard grabbed a binder and passed it to me.

"I haven't come up with a title yet. But I've got a friend of a friend who said he might be interested." I opened the cover and glanced at the first page.

CHAPTER 1. *As I learned from a bent-over Mrs. Brubaker who had been weeding in what had to be the most fragrant garden in the fifty states, all good things start with a "Hello." So, "Hello..."*

"Here. Go to the middle. That's where the pictures are." Richard reached across the table and hurriedly flipped the pages.

"That's me and my life partner next to our red rockets in Anacortes. We had road bikes, probably a bit lighter than your ride." Next to a slightly slimmer Richard was an attractive woman, freckles coloring her face and dimples bracketing her smile. She looked about forty.

"Your life partner? You mean your daughter right?"

"No, no. She was my life partner, until I found Evelyn, my new life partner. Marjorie just couldn't keep up. Anyway that was the morning we left. It took us sixty-three days. Pretty good, I must say. The key is resting and Advil. We would ride for exactly fifty minutes and break for ten. No matter where we were or what time it was. It kept us refreshed. That's the key. Food and rest. Rest and food.

"Eastern Mountain Sports gave us a bunch of those freeze-dried meals. They were pretty good. In fact, EMS was really good to us. We received a free tent, sleeping bag, and all sorts of things. All I had to do was advertise by putting a sticker on my helmet."

"Not too bad."

"No it certainly wasn't. Do you have any sponsors?"

"Nah, I didn't really think about that. Anyway, I want to do it alone. No attachments. You know."

"To each his own. But free stuff is free stuff. And those meals were pretty good, too. I hope you're eating well?"

"Well enough, I guess."

"You'll eat really well tonight, but you should definitely check out those EMS meals. They are rather tasty. But you'll do what you do, I know how it is. People always giving advice, trying to help out. It's human nature, I guess. Shoot. I'm doing the same thing right now. It's just another way of remembering, I suppose.

"People are going to offer you all kinds of things. Dinners. Snacks. Stories. And who knows what else. They all want a bit of what you have and don't begrudge them an ounce. It's your duty. Sheriffs will show you safe places to sleep. Congregations will open their churches for rest. If you're lucky, women may even offer you a bit of—well, you're young." His eyes danced.

"I actually have a girl—"

"Be that as it may, just remember that with each inch of pavement conquered, you will change. You will grow. People need to see that and will want to experience it as well. You are a living river. As you splash over the pebbles of the road, those will become a part of you, flavoring your water with the minerals that give life. Don't forget to share it, son."

A car pulled up.

"Enough talk. We better start cutting vegetables. Evelyn's back."

Richard tossed me a few potatoes and a peeler just as the door opened.

"Hi, honey. I'd like you to meet our new friend. He's having dinner with us. I hope that's okay."

"That's fine, Richard. Could you help me with the groceries? It's hot as hay out there today. To think we're in Maine."

"No problem, honey." He stood up and wrapped Evelyn in a bear hug. "Could you do me a favor, son, and get my life partner here a glass of water?"

So it came to pass, that with a toast of water, the treaty of Belfast was signed.

Love,
David

David Haber

DAY 28

....

STILL STORIES RUN DEEP

June 11
Patten Pond Campground
Surry, Maine

Dear Mary,

You want a beer?

Lately, that question has led me to places I never before expected, especially for someone who does not drink. When I was younger, I wouldn't allow a drop of liquor to reach my liver; my body was a shrine to the soccer lords, and I needed their blessings to fulfill my dreamed destiny as the next white Pelé. I had to remain completely pure and free of all toxins, except for the occasional Big Mac.

Something has changed, however. Admittedly, I don't suddenly have an insatiable desire for liquor. I don't wake up with cravings so fierce that I stash Nyquil in my front pannier to keep the edge off. Yet I now recognize its importance, how it breaks barriers and reveals truth—perhaps not the whole truth—but something of an emotional truth hard to touch when one is sober and in control.

Which brings me to the Outlaw Indian.

"Who is that?" You ask.

His name is Earl, and his story is beyond belief, part Jerry Springer, part *Crime and Punishment*, all suffering and despair. It all started with that simple question.

"Chief. Ya wanna bee-ah?"

I have to admit that this fellow was more than a tad frightening. With his swayed back, short legs, and muscled arms, he seemed on the verge of a brawl. In the wee hours of the morning, I would not have wanted to be the bartender who had to tell him it was "last call." Perhaps it was the wraparound sunglasses as the sun set. Or maybe it was the thick drooping moustache scratching his chin. It may have been the ripped pink tank top, dirty jeans, and scuffed work boots. There was something, though—something that leaked sadness.

If it had been any other day, I would have suffered through the twenty-five miles to Bar Harbor. My instincts had shouted for me to stop, though, to get a good night's sleep, hit Mount Desert Island early in the morning, and arrive in Bar Harbor to get my mail at the post office before it closed. So for a change, I listened and camped early. My instincts have yet to fail when I actually listen. Was he the reason I was listening?

"So what'll it be?"

The man was pitched a few sites away. Earlier I had noticed that he didn't have much of a tent, just some Wal-Mart special that probably couldn't survive a steady breeze. Empty cans littered the grass. Another man slouched on a cooler by the fire and hadn't moved in about an hour.

I had already set up my tent and boiled noodles for dinner; the evening was young, and I was lonely, so...

"Why not."

Was I crazy? It must be the persuasive power of the sing-song rhythms of the slowly spoken Down East dialect, transforming cars into cahs, Mainer into Mainah, as well as stretching many single syllable words (there) into two (they-ah).

"Come on oveah. Name's Earl."

We walked over to his site.

"Everybody calls me the Outlaw. Earl 'The Outlaw Indian' Stooppahr. That's me. Right Jim? Have a seat." Earl kicked me a log and tossed me a Schlitz. "That's my brothah, Jim."

Silent, Jim looked up at me through the fire and simply stared.

"Don't pay him no mind. He don't talk much. My dad dropped him a couple too many times. Always been a bit gawmy. Ya know, little numb in the head. Be back in a sec." Earl dashed into the woods. He sounded like a confused moose with all the crashing and crunching. I watched Jim watch the fire.

A few moments later, the Outlaw came back with a log under one arm and what looked like an entire tree slung over a shoulder. "Had to go back apiece. Find me somethin' to rest on and a bit more wood."

"Damn, man. You sure that's going to be enough? I mean, we might want to burn down the entire campground instead of just this field."

He choked out a laugh and tore off a branch the diameter of my calf, splitting it over his thigh as if he were a baseball player who was angry at an inferior bat.

"Ayuh. Should be enough. Theyah's always more. Maine's known for her forests." He finished off his beer in a gulp, and Jim tossed him a can. "Thanks. Ya want anothah?"

"No thanks."

Earl pulled his log up next to mine. "Just gimme a holler if ya want more." We stared into the fire. "So, wheah ya going on that theyah bike? Ya not a Mainah, for sure. Gotta be from away."

"I'm traveling a bit here and there. Maybe to San Francisco."

"Out there in Californier? Ayuh. Well, Maine's got some wicked forests anyway. Got tons. I've worked most of 'em."

"Are you a lumberjack then?"

"Ha...Ayuh that's me. Paul Bunyan. Right, Jim?" Jim grabbed another beer. "They say he's from 'round these pahts, ya know."

"I thought he was born up in Minnesota."

"The real forest was always in Maine, not out west and whatnot. 'Sides, my granddaddy would read me stories writ way back 'bout him. Ayuh, he's gotta be from 'round heyah Down East." Earl cracked his knuckles. "'Fore the accident, I worked the dray, huffin' logs all damn day. But I took a wicked diggah and a log rolled me. My grapple-skiddah busted in two. Damn near killed me." Jim tossed me and Earl a beer. "Drink up. Workin' the forests was good, though. Maine had the finest kind of forests. Green and thick. Now, they ain't so great."

"They look pretty spectacular to me."

"Ayuh, to them tourists just passin' through, it looks real pretty. But if you fly somewheres, you know, by plane or somethin', ya can see the huge clearings. Hundreds of acres cleared naked like a woman. 'Bout a hundred feet on either side of the roads, the forests is gone. It's sad, Chief. Soon, theyah won't be nothin'."

In a sudden flurry, Jim smashed his can and pitched it into the woods. Earl and I listened to clatter. A bird squawked and took flight. Jim grabbed another can from the cooler. The crackling of flamed pine continued undisturbed.

"Chief, you see any moose, yet?"

"No. I thought I saw some prints this morning along the shoulder and tried to follow them. But they got swallowed up in my own tire tracks. I don't think I'm much of a tracker."

"Figures. Them's tricky crittahs. Same with the crunchahs. Let me tell you. I was workin' one day 'while back, stumblin' and fumblin', makin' a gawd awful racket, and then…" Earl whipped his head around and leaned toward me, our noses but millimeters apart. "I was this close, Chief. Freaked me out somethin' wicked, it did. That swampdonkey stood stock still, with them honkin' eyes, not movin'. They say if them moose don't want ya to see 'em, they can be even this close." Stale breath washed over my face.

"But them eyes…They looked like my girl's, from way back." Earl stood and began pacing around the fire. "Was 'round '81. She was wicked cunning and right nice, if ya know what I mean. Met her at Capt'n Tom's Bug Hut—they got the cheapest bee-ah and the finest kind of chowdah ya'll ever taste. Ya should go sometime, it's just down the road apiece. Well, after a bit, she done got knocked-up. Bitch didn't go 'bout tellin' me for six months, though. Just figured she was gettin' a bit chunky. Ya know how women are when they like ya."

"Um…sure."

"Ayuh, once they get ya, they don't gotta keep up with theyah looks. So I figured. But damn she was still cunning even if a bit honkin' 'round the hips. Looked like that actress, what's her face? Jim, ya 'membah?"

Jim grunted and kicked a stick into the fire.

"Ayah. That's right. From *Pretty Woman*. Julie Robaire."

"You mean Julia Roberts?"

"Whatevah. But her brotha…That bastahd!" Earl grabbed a log, lifted it above his head, and hurled it into the fire with a shout. Sparks shot toward the stars to burn out long before the journey was complete. "I should have killed the fawkah when I had the chance."

Jim grunted and took another sip of beer.

"Ya got any idea of what's it like, Chief? Any at all?"

I remained silent as Earl stood and circled the fire, flames reflecting off his mirrored lenses.

"I loved her well 'nough. We was gonna be married. Then my buddy showed up with this tape he just bought.

'Check it out,' he says. 'Good flick,' he says. 'Ya'll love it,' he says. So I put it in. Seemed like a good enough flick at first. Ya know. Two people, gruntin' and groanin', really enjoyin' themselves, makin' real good love. The woman on top really takin' control, just like I like…Fawkin' bastahd. Gawd damn fawkah!"

"Bastahd." I heard Jim barely mumble.

"Ayuh, Jim! Bastahds. All of 'em." Earl shouted and collapsed next to me.

"Ya know what's it like, Chief? Ya understand?"

I didn't say a word.

"Chief, I watched that whole damned video. The whole show. Her lookin' back and smilin'. The laughter comin' from behind the camera. I watched it all. Fawkahs! See, it was fawkin' me and my girl in that video. Her bastahd brothah was filmin' us from the closet and went and sold it. Can ya b'lieve that sheit? Fawkah went and sold it. Jesus! Just plain common. Shouldn't be doin' that sheit. It's just not right, Chief. Not right at all."

Jim threw another beer across the fire.

"Thanks." He popped the top and chugged, foam collecting on his moustache to drip down the front of his shirt. "I didn't say nothin' to nobody. Nothin' at all. I just went to all the video stores I knew and bought every one of those damn tapes I found. 'Bout fifteen of 'em. Took 'em to my girl's house with some gas and made a wicked fire on her lawn.

"'What the hell ya doin'?' she says when she heyahs all the ruckus outside. 'Burnin' stuff,' I says. She was watchin' those plastic cases melt into globs. 'Are they videos?' She says. What the hell she think they was! 'Yup.' I says. 'Is that my video?' She says."

Earl turned toward me, lips twisted.

"*Her* video. Her fawkin' video. She knew about the video. She fawkin' knew. Her and her bastahd brothah both! They was killin' me on the inside. I was dyin'. I could feel it…Bastahds."

Earl snorted.

"Ya know what she says to me, Chief? Ya know what? She says its her fawkin' video and I got no right to burn 'em up like that. No right at all. That's when I tell her she got no right to makin' the damn thing in the first place. And ya know what? She started to laugh right in my face. She tells me she can do whatevah she wanted 'cause she and her brothah needed the money—for the new kid and all. That I should be providin' bettah. That it was her body. That I was lucky that it was me in that video and not some other guy. And, ya know what? That common bitch reached right in the fire to grab her videos…

"I smacked her then. Smacked her real hard till she fell on the ground. I knew I shouldn't with her carryin' my baby and all. But I didn't know what to do. I couldn't help it. I just didn't know what to do. I was real sorry. Real sorry. I nevah hit no woman before. Not evah. I just couldn't stop…

"She started shoutin' and cryin' and screamin'. 'I'm tellin' my brothah. And, he's gonna kill ya. He's gonna kill ya dead!' 'Fore all the ruckus drew the cops, I left and went to The Hut for a few bee-ahs to cool off. I was fumin' at my girl, at her bastahd brothah."

"Then that bastahd brothah come in." Jim spoke without even moving his lips, more a hiss than actual vocalized words.

"Ayuh, Jim. That he did. Screamin' and howlin' somethin' fierce. Wavin' a gun back and forth. The bar cleared right quick, let me tell ya…it was just me and him. Alone. And ya know I took care of business real good. It was a wicked fight…He gave me this…" Earl pulled the fabric of his shirt to the side revealing the puckered scar of a bullet wound. "…But I poked him in the belly sumpin' fierce. With my knife."

Jim picked up a stick and began fencing with the flame, hooting and grunting, a look of extreme concentration balling his face.

"Jim, I think it's dead." Jim whistled the branch through the fire again. "'Nough. Cut it." His brother settled back on the cooler. "Well, that bastahd learned not to fawk with the Outlaw. Shoulda killed him. Had it comin', that's for sure. But I was 'fraid the cops would show up any minute, so I took off. Lived out in the willie-wacks, ya know, 'til things settled down a bit…missed my kid's birth even."

"You mean the cops didn't arrest you for anything?"

Earl laughed.

"I outsmahted 'em all. See, I was thinkin' ahead. My girl and her brothah never knew my name. They thought

I was Mark Gruber. That poor sap died 'bout five years 'fore any a this evah happened."

"But what about the people at…what was it…The Hut?"

"Sheit, Tom's the bartender and his son, Lawrence is my best friend. We're blood brothahs. Both Penobscot Indians. He's full-blooded and I'm just a quarter, 'course. But still blood. So no one was talkin' any at the bar. Sheit! They all knew that bastahd had it comin' anyway." He paused. "But that don't matter no more. Nothin' much matters."

It was quiet for some time. This story was completely unbelievable. And, if I chose to find it believable, I should immediately pack my things and move as far as possible from this psychopath and his slightly off brother.

Earl stirred beside me. His cheeks were wet.

"See, Chief. My girl's dead. My daughter's dead. Beaten dead with a bat. Cops found 'em back behind ol' man Chestah's barn. If only I nevah hit my girl. I didn't mean nothin' by it. I was right pissed, ayuh. But that's no excuse…I loved her the best I was able…

"If that damn video hadn't nevah been made, my girl and me would still be togethah. I know it. After it all went down with the fire and stabbin' and hittin', she nevah talked to me again. Don't blame her any. I wouldn't want see me neithah. But she wouldn't even let me see my own little girl. My own blood."

My heart froze as the headlights of a truck turned into the site. Earl took off his sunglasses, shielded his eyes with an arm, and continued.

"I wasn't theyah for 'em. I shoulda never got mad. But it's too late. She shacked up with some bum to support herself and my kid, my kin, and the fawkah turned out worse than her bastahd brothah. The cops found him with a bloody bat in his trunk, tryin' to get to Canada."

The Outlaw's mouth distorted into a sort of maniacal grin. "If that fawkah ever gets out of prison though, he's gonna have to find himself a new house 'cause I burned the fawkah to the ground. It was a wicked fire!"

He stood as the headlights of the truck were killed, and the doors opened.

"Ayah, Jim. Audrey and Lawrence are finally heyah with more bee-ah!"

Jim turned around and smiled, the first real smile I had seen all evening. Two people, a man and woman, approached the site carrying a couple brown paper bags. The man was dark and short, but walked like a king, chin high, back straight, legs a bit stiff. For every three steps he took, the woman took one. She was an Amazon and towered above the man—like an oak protecting violets. They made quite a pair.

"Hey, Jim, catch any big'uns?"

"Audrey!" Jim wobbled to his feet and grabbed the woman and hugged her. He snatched one of the bags and brought it to his side of the fire, where he proceeded to carefully remove the cans from their plastic handcuffs and gently set them in the cooler.

"Earl, you make a friend?" The man eyed me carefully.

"Ayah, Lawrence, he's fine. Chief heyah is bikin' 'cross county to Californier."

"Really?" Audrey pulled up a log next to me. "I've nevah been outside Maine."

"Come on, 'Drey," Lawrence said, sitting down next to Earl, studying me the whole time. "That's not true. When you turned twenty-one, I took you to the big city for a wicked glass of beer."

"Lawrence, that was ovah seven years ago. And Providence, Rhode Island, isn't much of a big city. Not like New York. Or Californier."

Lawrence's laughter, pure and clear, danced with the flames. "Hon, Californiar ain't no city. It's a state like Maine."

Blushing, she grinned and threw a beer at Lawrence. Like lightning, Earl grabbed the beer, popped the top, and started drinking.

"Thanks, Audrey. I needed that. My throat was dry with all the stories I been tellin'."

Audrey and Lawrence briefly made eye contact and slid their gaze toward me. I didn't say a word. After a moment, he sighed and nodded. "So, where's this bike of yours? What you riding anyway? Kowasaki? Honda? I always wanted to do a trip like that on a Harley."

"Oh. I'm not—"

"Sheit, Lawrence. He ain't ridin' no motor bike. He's ridin' a bi-cycle. Ya b'lieve that sheit? Chief here is crazier than me." Earl choked out another laugh and ran into the forest to get more wood.

"You're ridin' a pedal bike?"

"Yeah. It's right over there."

Lawrence turned around. Audrey looked up at me, eyes large.

"Really? On a pedal bike? Aren't you scared of loonies and such? I mean, 'round heyah everyone's pretty all right. But in those cities…people are just plain crazy."

I laughed.

"People are people. They're all friendly enough."

Jim looked up and hissed. "Not Doreen's bastahd brothah."

Audrey shot up and hurried to Jim's side. Lawrence looked to the woods where Earl was making enough noise to scare all the moose for miles around. Audrey patted Jim on the thigh.

"Jim, you know we don't talk about them. It's sad and we don't like being sad." She glanced at me and looked back at Jim. "You didn't tell me. How was fishin'?"

Jim looked at Audrey and smiled. "Wicked hot. Didn't catch nothin'."

A tree smashed to the ground in the forest.

Lawrence turned back toward me, shaking his head. "There was a time, before Doreen and her brother, when Earl could move as silent as wind. Me and him were like Davy Crockett and Daniel Boone. Our folks taught us to love the woods. And we did. But since—well, since it all happened, Earl just wants noise. I think it keeps his brain quiet. I can only imagine what all he told you—so, please…" His words faded into the song of the fire. "We're the only family he's got left."

Earl came stomping from the woods, a twenty-five foot tree dragging behind him, soil still clinging to the web of its roots. Earl smiled proudly. "Got more wood. Reminds me of the good ol' days yankin' the scoot along."

"I don't know why you liked the scoot so much, Earl. It damn near killed you. More than once, too."

"Sheit. Ya know me. Livin' on the edge. That's why they call me the Outlaw." Earl smirked. "'Membah that time when we was helpin' Audrey's dad—"

"—Dig Mrs. Schmidt's well." Lawrence finished, rising to stand and circle the fire.

Earl sat on the ground beside me. "Sit back, Chief. Lawrence got the blood of shaman in his veins. Nobody tells stories like him 'round these pahts." Audrey crossed her arms and settled against Jim's legs. I could see Jim visibly relax atop the cooler. I watched rapt as Lawrence shuffled around the fire, kicking up dust with his small steps. Flame and shadow tangoed across his features, changing him as he spoke, slumping his shoulders, thickening his waist, cracking his hands with age, enlarging joints with rheumatism.

As he spoke, Lawrence became a doppelganger to Audrey's mad-scientist father, who decided, when he couldn't get his gas-powered auger working properly, to enlist the aid of a few sticks of dynamite. His hands worked elaborate patterns in the air as he told how Audrey's father ran the fuses so that he could hide behind his pickup. He looked up with shock, then joy, as he explained how pleasantly surprised Audrey's father was when he heard his six-year-old son approach on a too small bicycle bouncing from one training wheel to another.

With the fire internalized in some magical way, Lawrence collapsed into himself, and yet somehow expanded like a cornered kitten, to lose about thirty years and transform into a slightly overweight and pudgy son supplying his dad with his favorite sandwiches: peanut butter, banana, and mayonnaise. Tricked by flame, it looked as if Lawrence's right hand, small and plump, passed his left hand, calloused and gnarled, a sandwich.

Suddenly, with a croak and a flap, it appeared as if Lawrence's nose grew and sharpened. His hair became ruffled feathers as a hungry crow pecked and hovered and pecked again, trying and succeeding to steal the morsel. In the confused and frantic scuffle between father, bird, and son, somehow the fuse wires were crossed…

Boom!

Dirt shot to the heavens. The earth groaned and trembled. Mrs. Schmidt's barn shook itself to the ground. Glancing out her kitchen window after all the racket, she found, not a well, but rather a wicked cool pond running as deep as the stories told on this night.

Love,
David

PART V

AN INTERLUDE

Bar Harbor, Maine

DAY 29

....

GHOSTS OF ANNAPOLIS

June 12
Mount Desert Island Hostel
Bar Harbor, Maine

Dear Mary,

I don't think I care for Bar Harbor. It's haunted, see? The ghosts lurk everywhere. I'm sure I could enjoy the town, but the problem is that it resembles Annapolis too much. Flocks of people wander about in crowds, waiting to be watched by an expert people watcher. Tan legs and blonde hair are everywhere. Boats, masts rising from the water like their southern sisters, clog the harbor.

The architecture is different, of course, and obviously, the scenery is far from similar, with Cadillac Mountain guarding the harbor under its rocky gaze and the Thunder Caves roaring in the distance. But still, the heavy smell of brine and fish and sun haunt the island with the ghosts of Annapolis.

The place is surely hexed. Fear and homesickness feed my heart with a thick soup of longing and dread. Semi-familiar faces hover just out of sight. I constantly twist and turn and wrench in search of an overheard voice, recognized, yet misplaced in Maine. Just ten minutes ago, I swore I heard Oma ordering an Arch Deluxe at McDonald's; I am just as positive I saw you walking toward me, all smiles and eyes, arms wide for a hug. Everywhere I look, hints of you and Oma tickle the periphery. Yet the moment is gone before I know it. That dreamed Oma turned out to be but a stooped grandmother buying a hamburger, and that Mary, loved so fiercely for an instant, blurred with the focusing of my eyes.

How could I leave you, Mary? You should be here with me, exploring this Annapolis of the North.

Each day, we are growing and changing, and as the literal miles stretch between us, a more figurative void swells amid our hearts. I've come more than a thousand miles—one-sixth of the distance that will eventually separate us. If I feel isolation six times greater than what is afflicting me now, I'm doomed. There will be no way for me to continue. This odyssey will be over. What's scary is that I'm accustomed to the Northeast. I'm familiar with New England. These sites are known factors in an unknown adventure. Home has never seemed far, and despite the ghosts of Annapolis—or perhaps because of them—you have seemed, if not close, then at least near enough. I know it will only get worse. Soon, I venture west into mystery. I will hear and see things alien to my familiar cradle in the East. I fear being tossed from that crib and forced to sleep in an adult bed.

I need silence. I need to be far from this place disturbed by shades of my own creation. I don't want to sleep here. I don't want to explore this town without you. Bar Harbor should be discovered with you beside me, Mary. We should climb Cadillac Mountain and lose ourselves along its miles of carriage paths. Together. We should be kissed by mist at the mouth of the Thunder Caves. Together. We should devour lobster rolls and clams while being eaten raw by black flies. Together. So I will find a place to camp far from the Harbor, saving the memories for a future made with you.

Love,
David

David Haber

DAY 30

....

SWIMMING POOLS
ON THE ATLANTIC

June 13
Bar Harbor Campground
Hulls Cove, Maine

Dear Mary,

How strange it is to be resting beside a swimming pool with the Atlantic crashing just few hundred yards away. Although it seems a bit at odds with my beach-loving self, this pool offered the perfect combination of sun and shade, close enough to my tent for an afternoon nap yet far enough away from my bike to keep all thoughts of riding from my mind. I parked the green steed behind a tree on the edge of my site and pointedly ignored the dust and grime speckling her frame. There will be another day for cleaning and polishing.

I even refused to ride to the store a few miles away, deciding instead to eat at a restaurant around the corner. By dinner, I figure Simone, the saucy waitress who served me both breakfast and lunch, will recognize me as a regular and have my Coke and apple pie ready. Such recognition is what I crave: to be a regular somewhere, to have people know me, to be able to waltz up to a counter and say, "Hi, Simone. I'll have the usual." I hope she smiles at me during dinner. I hope she adds some extra whipped cream to my pie. I hope she remembers me.

Sometimes I feel like a lone cloud drifting across a perfect sky. My friends and relatives are making storms across the Atlantic, banging with thunder and pelting with rain, but somehow I have strayed and am missing the party. I hover low in flawless fields of blue, drifting aimlessly, a single cloud that just wants to be noticed. I feel as lonely as that cloud—even now surrounded by twenty people lounging beside a swimming pool a hundred yards from the Atlantic.

In this pool, a boy named Forrest splashes wildly as his father teaches him to swim. A gigantic life jacket is clasped around his waist, which makes his attempts at kicking and paddling that much more amusing. He is like a cork with limbs. When an arm or leg strikes the water, he is momentarily upended, his neck stretches like a tortoise, and he giggles uncontrollably. Smiles float around the poolside like a volleyed badminton birdie as we all watch Forrest learn to swim with the support and advice of his older sister—a sister actually helping without an ounce of jealousy. Shocking. That's no sister I have ever known. No ultra-competitive screams of "Daddy, look at me. I'm a better swimmer, Daddy. See? I can even dive. Look, Daddy. No. Look at me! Not him! Me, Daddy!"

Rather, Forrest is being coaxed to brave the deep by his sister with encouraging murmurs of "You can do it, Forrest.

That's it. Don't forget to kick now. Okay. That's better. No, Forrest, don't breathe in the water. Don't be scared. I have you…Look, no hands. You're doing it. You're swimming, Forrest."

That is me, Mary. Different pools, perhaps, but I too am trying to swim. My only hope is that after my lap across America I will be surrounded by love in the same way that Forrest and his sister are now wrapped together in an oversized Snoopy beach towel, sharing that special watery tiredness of accomplishment beneath cloudless skies.

Love,
David

DAY 31

....

BOTTLED BITS

June 14
The Atlantic Shore
Bar Harbor, Maine

Dear Mary,

The tire is dipped, the beach is bottled, and so begins my western journey with an ancient ritual known the world round by generations of explorers: the taking of the familiar into the unknown. Soldiers, for example, carry pictures of loved ones or favorite playing cards in the bands on their helmets. With a scribbled piece of scripture taped to the instrument panel, astronauts comfort themselves. According to Arthurian Legend, when knights would go a-questing, they clutched a token given by their Lady—a scented scarf or glove that in times of need would remind of the familiar. I read that Odysseus, on being cured of his feigned madness and convinced to journey to Troy, bottled a bit of Ithaca's rocky soil in a flask to remind him of Penelope and all things of home.

This morning I had returned to Bar Harbor to take piece of the Atlantic with me across the country. On a bench overlooking the docks, bike propped against a tree, I watched the mist strangle the tall masts of a lonely clipper as a strengthening sun came to the rescue with a soft but insistent touch. An old woman, skirts tied about her knees, walked along the black, stony shore, bending every so often to pick up a shell or pebble that caught her attention. Perhaps sixty, she walked alone. She stopped to watch a short-billed dowitcher peck at pebbles. A moment later, she tiptoed around the rising tide, tossing unwanted bits back to the sea like a child skipping stones.

Quiet and lonely was this morning. The silence was broken only by the moored clipper rocking with the tide and a few gulls squawking their discontent. I wished the old woman would wander this way, notice the bike, and let curiosity invade the stillness of the morning. My wish remained unheard, and she continued along the shore lost within her own thoughts.

It was time to mount up. But there were two things left to do. With the town still drowsy beneath its comfortable sheets, I rolled my bike toward the ocean to christen my tire with the Atlantic's touch. As my tires popped and crackled over fragmented shells and dried sea pods, I wondered how other cross-country cyclists performed the rite of wheel dipping without looking like idiots. I had enough trouble riding the damn bike down the road; guiding it into the ocean without appearing as foolish as I had while dangling upside down from that tree in the Delaware Water Gap seemed impossible. Organized with a touch of Seussian genius, the four green balloon-like bags pulled and shifted with a gravity all their own. The sleeve of my fleece shirt, which was buckled loosely to the front pannier, trailed along the wet sand and, when not absorbing frothy beards of sea foam, threatened to entangle itself in my front tire. As I drew nearer to the ocean, my dinner-crusted pot rattled against the rack, an annoying syncopated rhythm at odds with the pounding surf.

The tide swirled around my front tire. My fleece was soaked. I skipped around the surging sea and, in the process, lost my grip on the handlebars. My bike tumbled into the ocean. The seagulls laughed.

I scanned the town to see if there were any other creatures besides birds lurking about. The woman had disappeared, and Bar Harbor slept on. Reaching down, I dragged my bike to its wheels and rested it against my hip. The tide covered the tops of my shoes. Shrugging, I bent down and filled an empty film canister with a bit of beach, seaweed, and ocean. Not having wax to properly fasten the lid as ancient mariners once had, I used the next best thing: duct tape. That would surely keep my miniature Atlantic coast safe and sealed within my handlebar bag.

With front tire dipped and my entire bike baptized, the journey continues west, propelled by wet shoes and the memories held in a bottled bit of sea.

Love,
David

PART VI

....

TOUCHING FIRE

From Conway, New Hampshire,
to North Hudson, New York

DAY 34

....

IN LOVE

June 17
White Mountains Hostel
Conway, New Hampshire

Dear Mary,

On a porch between the toes of the White Mountains, I felt God in another. Her name is Sally. She is one of the hostel managers. Our conversation was incredible. The moments spent together exquisite. But more than anything, I felt connected, grounded, at home.

She introduced herself while I sat Indian style in a wicker rocker, transfixed by the expanding storm. Immediately, I sensed...something.

"Do you mind if I have a seat? I love watching the clouds when a storm is coming." I motioned to the porch swing, and Sally settled into it with a sigh. The swing hung three feet above the floor; her toes couldn't touch the blue-painted planks. As she folded her legs beneath her, the chains protested with grumpy creaks. She brushed her humidity-curled hair from her brow, nibbled on a thumbnail, and turned to the fragile dusk.

Broken by the lumpy mountains rising around us, maroon clouds stretched to purple. Angry streaks of dark orange shot between the gaps before the clouds reformed into a mass of gloom. The heavens turned green. The wind howled and then subsided. The sky spit three drops of rain onto the planks of the porch. The clouds lightened to gray and opened. Water poured from the sky like roiling seas flooding a torpedo-pierced ship. A car passed, flaring the sodden air red with brake lights. With a crack, the heavens trembled. I flinched. Sally touched my arm, and my stomach dropped. Lightening was not the only form of electricity crackling the air.

I glanced at her fingers on my arm. Her nails were worry bitten. An Indian ink daisy tattooed her hand at the seat of her thumb. Her calloused palm tickled the hairs on my forearm, setting my stomach to flutter. The wicker groaned as I shifted in the rocker. The rain slowed to a drizzle.

"You're going up that road tomorrow." Sally lifted her hand from my wrist and pointed toward a highway snaking up the White Mountains. My arm felt naked. "It leads to the Kancamagus Pass."

I turned from the fading storm and studied her profile. Her nose was long, hatchet-like. Her cheeks were round, almost plump, waiting to be dimpled by a smile. Her neck was flushed red from being in the sun too long.

"To be honest, I've been dreading the ride. My maps had a cross-sectional view of the terrain through the mountains, and it looks like the EKG of a cheerleader opening a creaky door in some kind of horror movie."

Sally chuckled and then folded me into her amber eyes, Oma's eyes.

"It is a long ride up the pass. That's true. Twenty-two miles, I think. The grade is steep. But be patient. You'll get to the top."

"Have you ridden it before?"

"No. I row. A woman's eight." She watched the remaining wisps of the storm drift south. A squirrel shook water from the leaves of an oak tree. "I wish my life could always be this quiet."

I nodded. She touched my arm again and asked, "Why do you think it takes a storm to remind me what colors look like? Green is never so green as it is after the rain."

The squirrel, bored with rustling leaves, leaped to a telephone wire and scurried onto the roof of the hostel. On wild wings, a bat chased insects. A mosquito landed on my calf. I swiped at it and started to rise from the rocker.

"Stay a bit. Help me look for the Man in the Moon."

I sat back and looked at Sally. Her eyes never left the night sky, and her fingers never left my wrist. It didn't matter that the temperature was dropping. I no longer cared that the insects were feasting. I forgot the difficult ride tomorrow. I felt like I was home, despite Eden Lane being more than a thousand miles south. The galaxy poured its milk across the sky as starlight, and the crescent moon rose…and set. We sat, watching silent, simply being. The world touched me with life, and beside me, so did Sally.

If I had experienced this moment with a man—Neale or Dan or the Professor, hell even Lawrence or Earl—I don't think I would feel so confused right now. Yet as I wrestle with sleep on this hostel cot, I can't shake my turmoil. Sally's touch still burns my wrist, still tingles my heart. And it is solely because she is a woman.

We shared a special evening and are only friends. Yet…

Wait a minute. The words "only" and "friends" should never be grouped together. It doesn't seem proper to bind friendship with an "only" moniker as if it were not deserving of love. It is worthy of love. Even now, I feel the honest joy of that love when I picture the rocker, the storm, and Sally.

I don't want you to misinterpret me. This is not some Dear Jane letter. Don't think that my brain is filled with sordid sexual fantasies. These emotions are not about sex. They are about openness and nakedness. My heart should be able to love without shame. There is room enough in there for many. I never realized that before. I don't need to fill my every emotional need from a single person by clinging like a leech to your heels. Such behavior will drag us both back. Our relationship will never become what we both hope it will be. And the reality is that by my loving Sally this night, our own love has only strengthened, grown, and deepened.

To fall into love in a single moment reminds me of its special power—the grace of it all. The excitement I feel is the excitement of life. And the most amazing thing of all is that these feelings have carried your spirit to the foot of the White Mountains. Love has brought you to me for the night, and in that darkness, I see a vision us—two lovers entwined in love, growing old, growing young, growing beautiful.

Being with Sally has only affirmed our own love and commitment. I love you, Mary. And, I love Sally.

I simply love.

David

David Haber

DAY 35

....

THE HIGH COURT
OF A LACONIC KING

June 18
Big Rock Campground
6 mi. E. of Lincoln, New Hampshire

D<small>EAR</small> M<small>ARY</small>,
 C<small>LIMBING BY BICYCLE IS</small> a strange combination of concentration and distraction. The spirit must be focused, yet preferably not on the climb itself. Patience is required, as is silence, for the nerves and mind both.
 Which brings me to automobiles. Roaring cars drive the mind toward impatience. They bring unbalancing images of twisted metal and broken bones, transforming climbs into a battle between the armies of poise and strength and the cohorts of fear and weakness. When attacking a mountain, it's best to start as early as possible, while cars still sleep in garages wrapped in the morning's silence.
 So, up I went before the sun rose. Tendrils of mist snaked heavenward, reverse rain falling from trees to clouds. Like steaming loaves of freshly baked bread, the mountains heaved about me. On that sight I feasted,

nourishing my ascent with nature's finest. Neither car nor truck disturbed me, and higher still I climbed.

For many miles I pedaled, fixing upon a loose pebble or a fallen feather in the distance. I mused on its existence until the next thing caught my attention. Silence reigned, and I continued higher.

BRRRRRRRRRRMMMMMMMMMMMM!

My concentration shattered as the silence cracked. Three Harley's grumbled by. I took a deep breath, collected my heart from my throat, and continued. Not two minutes later, four more motorcycles burped past. Two Honda Gold Wings followed, trailed by a large group of leather-clad Hell's Angels. There was not a single car on the road. Motorcycles ruled, and I was invading their kingdom.

After the initial shock, I soon learned to brace my teeth against the skull-rattling roar and simply pedal. Many riders would slow to wave or shout, encouraging me higher, their iron horses neighing, recognizing a kindred spirit.

My mule and I reached the pass, some 2,855 feet above the Atlantic, just before noon. I leaned my bike against a sign. Perfect timing for lunch.

"Hey, we passed you climbing the hill and were wondering if you'd do an interview. My wife and I are making a documentary about motorcycle festivals…you know, Laconia, Sturgis, and Daytona Bike Week…and figured you'd have an interesting perspective."

"There's a festival going on?"

"Yeah, man. It's Laconia Motorcycle Week. Best rally on the East Coast, if you ask me. The oldest of the Big Three."

"Guess that would explain all the Harleys."

"Damn straight, bro. So, man, want to do an interview?"

For the next few minutes, I answered questions of all shapes and sizes as the camera rolled. What was my name? Where was I from? How did I like the festival? Have I ever ridden a Hog? How far did I ride in a day? How far was I going today? How far did I plan on going in all? Do I stay in motels? Any jerks on the road? Do I like ice cream? Cops ever bug me? How about small-town folk? Do I like America? Is she going in the right direction? Do they make leather chaps for bicycle riders?

The questions kept coming, falling like manna. If only it had been manna. I was getting hungrier by the minute. My answers became shorter, despite my desire to elaborate. Finally, with an unruly stomach shouting to the point of rudeness, the interview ended, as did my fifteen minutes.

Or so I thought, until I looked up to see a horde of bikers circled around my bicycle talking. Some gestured passionately, confusion clear with their shrugged shoulders and bobbing heads. Others pointed to various parts of my bike and appeared to be explaining something. Voices were raised.

I tentatively approached.

They turned as a group, clapping, hollering, and whistling. Very soon, I found myself surrounded by a gang of surly-looking Bandidos, showering me with yet more questions.

After posing for a few pictures, they left...only to be followed by a charter of Hells' Angels from New Jersey, who crowded around, pumped me full of further questions, and again captured the moment on film. This went on for well over an hour, and I fed off the attention. Me holding court in my light blue cycling shorts surrounded by leather-wearing, bikini-clad, tattoo-painted bikers must have been a sight fit for the ages.

They were of all shapes and sizes: conservative weekend warriors, who replaced their work uniforms of ties and blue suits with cracked chaps and ripped shirts; young speed demons encased in brightly colored leather suits astride crotch rockets or Jap-scrap; murdering and marauding one-percenters riding grunting hogs, stripped-down choppers with ape-hanging, high handle bars, or chromed garbage wagons heavy with saddlebags. It seemed the entire rally at Laconia sought an audience, had a question, requested a picture. Upon how many rival charter house walls will I find myself looking goofy and out of place, I will never know.

But high atop the Kancamagus Highway, I was sustained by my subjects, king for day.

Love,
David

David Haber

DAY 36

....

THE ROADSIDE ENTREPRENEUR

June 19
Thetford Hill State Park
Thetford Hill, Vermont

Dear Mary,

What's wonderful about mountains is that, if the proper location is picked for camping (last night it was), your morning will begin with a long, pleasant descent to a feast of bacon and eggs and pancakes and toast and sausages and gravy and biscuits and hash browns and orange juice and coffee. The crowds overflowing from the festival at Laconia only added to this meal, flavoring my rather large breakfast with gruff yet comforting voices.

The bikers were with me throughout the day, but by now I had acclimated myself to the rumble, the wave, and request for a picture. Such appeals weren't as frequent as on the pass, yet whenever I stopped for a break, it was not long before I was being grabbed, praised, and photographed.

I was still the center of attention, and it felt great. Despite the sun jabbing the back of my neck with smoldering fingers, my emotions soared. I felt connected to something bigger than my bike ride. The other day, Sally had pried my heart ajar, and the rough Laconia revelers have kept it wedged open. The world is still amazingly green, and new friends seem to fall like rain dripping from wet leaves rustled by the wake of my speeding bike.

"Boy, mister. You pedal fast!"

I squeezed the brakes. A boy of about eight, reddish hair flopping across his eyes, squinted up at me. He stood behind an old green card table piled high with plastic cups. A tin pitcher sweated beside them. In careful print, a poster read:

Hey Bikers!
Best Lemonade in New Hampshire.
Try Connor's finest. Not as good as beer...
But Yummy enough for thirsty tummies.
All proceeds go toward The Connor Harley Fund
(or a new set of LEGOs, depending on business)

"Not so fast that I can't stop for some lemonade. How much for a cup?"

"Cool. You're my first customer. Is fifty cents too much?"

I smiled and shook my head, tossing him the fifty-cent piece Neale had given me.

"Wow. Awesome! Harley here I come. I got cookies, too. My Nana's making them. They're a quarter. But they aren't done, yet. You wanna wait?"

He handed me a large plastic cup. I chugged down the syrupy juice, instantly freezing my brain. I collapsed beside Connor on the grass; my bike sprawled on the shoulder like a sleeping hound.

"You musta been real thirsty. Biking on a two wheeler's hard work. Maybe you need another cup."

I grinned and passed over a five-dollar bill.

"I don't have enough change yet, mister. Do you—"

"Don't worry about it, Connor. Pedaling's thirsty business. I'll have a couple more cups."

"Really?"

The garage door groaned open; an older woman strode toward us carrying a plate of tinfoil wrapped goodies. A big-stoned turquoise necklace jangled around her neck. Gray roots peeked through a sea of dyed orange hair atop her head.

"Nana! Nana! Look! This mister here gave me five whole dollars. Can you b'lieve it, Nana? Five bucks! I can already buy the LEGOs. Shoot. I'm gonna get a Harley in no time!" He clutched the bill over his head in two-handed triumph.

His grandmother smiled.

"Connor, remember what I told you. Don't discuss your profits while customers are around. It's not a good for business."

"Sorry Nana. I forgot."

Connor glanced at me sheepishly and buried his hands in his pockets, rocking from foot to foot.

"That's a pretty fancy contraption there. Been riding long?"

"Not too long, Ma'am. About a month now."

"A whole month!" Connor banged a hand against his head. "Nana, did you hear that? A whole month. That's longer than camp."

Connor walked to my bike and stretched for the handlebars.

"Don't touch that!" His grandmother warned. "That's not yours. You should never touch someone's things without asking first. Especially when they're your customers."

"It's all right. He didn't do any harm."

Connor sulked back behind the table.

"Hey, Connor. You want to sit on my bike?"

"Can I? Really can I? Nana is it okay? I won't fall. Promise. Please, Nana."

His grandmother nodded, took a cookie, and passed me one.

"My bike's a bit big for you," I explained around the cookie wedged in my mouth. "So you can't actually ride. But I'll hold her steady while you climb on."

I lugged the bike upright and spun the pedals so that Connor could easily climb atop. He tapped the leather seat dubiously as he prepared to mount.

"That's really hard. Doesn't it hurt?"

"No. It's really comfortable. Try it." I grabbed the collar of his shirt and helped him up. His feet dangled six inches from the pedals.

"Look, Nana! I'm ridin'!" He glanced over his shoulder. "Wow. Your seat isn't too hard at all. This is way more funner than riding a Harley!"

I rocked the bike, one hand around his waist the other beneath the seat. Cranking his wrist for a burst of imagined speed, he made zooming noises and bounced on the saddle as we pretended to corner around a hairpin turn.

"Nana, I wanna get one of these. Forget the Harley. This is cool."

Tour de France won, he leaped from the bike and poured me another cup of lemonade.

"Mister, you think I can ever ride a bike like that by myself?"

"Don't see why not. If I can do it, you can for sure."

"Nana, you hear that? I'm gonna get me a two-wheeler just like his and ride it all the way to China by myself. I'm gonna, Nana. I really am… You b'lieve me, right Nana? You think I can do it?"

"Connor." His grandmother smiled as she licked chocolate from her fingers. "You have always done everything you ever said you were going to do, and I don't expect you to stop anytime soon. Now, give this gentleman another cup of lemonade for the road."

"Yes, ma'am." He poured me a final cup. "Do you think I can bike to China, mister?"

"It's like your Nana says, Connor. If you put your mind to something, you can do anything at all. I mean, look at me."

Indeed, Mary, look at me!

Love,
David

DAY 37

....

NOONER

June 20
Sipping a McDonald's Milkshake
Bethel, Vermont

Dear Mary,

It is harder than I ever imagined riding with an erection.

Various parts keep getting in the way, and even my leather saddle is uncomfortable. Maybe I should have gotten a seat with a hole in it.

This whole situation is not my fault. If the campground hadn't been full, I wouldn't have been forced to camp in the overflow lot beside Mr. Sunset Sex and Mrs. Dawn Coitus. The whole night his moans and her shrieks kept the raccoons away. Although it was nice not worrying about hanging my food, there comes a point when such eavesdropping becomes painful to the lonely traveler.

Despite my best efforts, that ache was with me all morning and is still with me even now. I hope it can be cooled by this vanilla shake. Otherwise, my imagination will be distracted by visions of your belly pressed against me, your warm breath in my ear, your arms squeezing me as I sink deeper into your embrace…

Soon, Mary, I will reach San Francisco. We will be together. I will be home.

But first I think I need another milkshake.

Love,
David

DAY 37, PART II

....

ALMOST BEEF

June 20
The Rochester Bandstand
Rochester, Vermont

Dear Mary,
    While I napped in a covered bandstand, recovering from the two milkshakes I drank earlier in the day, a group of kids surrounded me and began whispering.
 "Do you think he's okay?"
 "He doesn't look too good."
 "You think we should talk to him?"
 "You have the stuff right?"
 "Yeah."
 "Well, go on. Wake him up…"
 I cracked an eye. Five boys were circled around me, ranging in age from six to about twelve, grass staining their knobby knees and dirt collecting on their elbows. The boys all had the same bowl haircut. One wore a pair of thick plastic glasses. The tallest held an aluminum-wrapped plate fogged with warmth even on this hot day.

"Our dad saw you pull up," began the shortest boy. He was missing his two front teeth.

"Yeah," interrupted the tallest, "and I thought—"

"No you didn't," said the boy wearing glasses. "We all asked Dad."

"Yeah. We all did."

The tall boy cleared his throat. "Anyway, we had some leftovers at lunch, and we all thought you might want them."

"Dad said it would be okay," piped in the small boy.

"We figured you'd get mighty hungry riding that bike, so Dad and me—" The boys glared at their brother. "I mean, Dad and us made you a snack."

"I have a 7-Up for you, too," announced another.

"But you have to tell us stories about riding your bike," said the boy with glasses.

"Yeah. We want stories."

"Yeah. And you gotta promise to send us postcards."

"Yeah. Ya gotta," said the smallest boy.

With my lopsided grin, the bargain was sealed and the plate passed. I peeled the foil back. Perched atop a mountain of potato chips rested two magnificent hamburgers. My stomach rumbled.

"They look tasty. Thank you."

The boys gathered around, clearly expecting something miraculous to occur while I wrapped my mouth around the best burger ever. Thick and juicy, tasting wild and delicious, these patties were like no beef I had eaten before. If life were a spice like garlic and cumin from which a rich marinade could be made, then this burger had been soaking for hours in it. All beef should taste so.

"This is great," I said. "I've never tasted hamburger so good."

The youngest started giggling.

"That's because it isn't hamburger," mumbled the boy with glasses. "It's ost—" The tallest boy tackled his brother and yanked his glasses from his face.

"Told you he'd eat it," said another.

"Shut-up, Ryan. He isn't done yet."

I put down the burger and glanced at the boys. "What are you all up to?"

A few more giggles escaped Ryan.

"Nuttin'."

"We're just watching is all," said the tallest, still pinning his brother to the ground. His brother squinted in my direction.

"We don't like that bird—" The smallest boy started jabbing Ryan quiet.

And then it registered. I smiled and took a gigantic bite. "I don't see why you don't like these burgers. Ostrich is delicious. You sure you don't want some?"

"Gross!" Shouted the boys in unison.

"You're going to grow feathers," the smallest boy said.

"I hope so. I've got a long way to ride."

"No, he isn't," said the tallest as he climbed from his brother and returned the swiped glasses. "That's crazy."

I finished off the second burger.

"See." Ryan crossed his arms and nodded. "Told you he'd do it."

The youngest climbed on the rail behind me, trying to peek down my shirt.

"I don't see any feathers. You guys are liars. I'm telling Mom on you."

At that, I fell from the bench and curled into a ball, groaning and writhing. "Oh. It hurts. It hurts so much!"

The boys circled, worry rippling their faces.

"Are you all right, mister?"

"I'm never eating ostrich."

"Me neither."

"I'm getting Mom."

"He's dying."

Leaping to my feet, I began flapping my arms as if wings. I grabbed Ryan and began twirling him around.

"Look, guys, I'm flying." He spread his arms wide.

"Do me, too."

"And me."

Soon all of us were on our backs watching the sky swirl in one direction while feeling our stomachs spin in the other. The grass cooled my flushed cheeks, and I couldn't help but wonder if this happens every time you go off and eat a couple bird burgers.

Love,
David

DAY 37, PART III

....

A NUDIST ENCLAVE...
OF ONE

June 20
Texas Falls Campground
Shaded by Bread Loaf Mountain, Vermont

Dear Mary,

I am naked and alone.

A nearby creek sings with my heart as I rest on a log three miles from the road. Splinters tickle my rear. A breeze dries my skin. The moon rises, and I'm butt naked.

This is the first time in my life I have ever stripped to nothing and spent a prolonged period outside with Nature as my only companion. Some will say that I am not a true nudist, that nudity is meant to be shared with others, that such stripping of inhibitions requires an audience. Otherwise you are just bathing, and there is nothing special about that.

These people are wrong.

I'm more exposed now than I have ever been.

I am free.

I pray now, atop this log, that I'm able to hold this nakedness even when my journey is done. Although I feel the changes, I must wonder: are they sticking? Or when the adventure ceases, will old habits return?

My slow movement across the country has become a window through which my heart leaps toward something wonderful. There's still a tremendous pilgrimage ahead, but where once fear lulled, courage wakes; where once weakness lurked, strength grows.

The past holds nothing but memories. It no longer squeezes my gut and freezes my mouth when meeting new people. The shyness is gone, replaced by a more playful me who can flirt with a pretty cashier, who can feel comfortable surrounded by tattooed gangs, who can swill bad beer to the wee hours swapping stories with strangers. My past has no hold.

On a mossy bed will I sleep tonight, washed in starlight, nudist to the world, naked and far from alone.

Love,
David

DAY 38

....

FIGHT OR FLIGHT

June 21
Yogi Bear Jellystone Paradise Pines
North Hudson, New York

Dear Mary,

My animal nature is strong. It growls even now, some six hours later. Reflecting my mood, the sky alights with electricity and quivers with thunder. A storm comes. I lick my chops.

This world is such a strange place for bicycle tourists. One day, a glorious and wondrous universe pays homage to every hill climbed and mile conquered with birdsong and blue sky. On another, the life of man is solitary, poor, nasty, brutish, and short.

We are animals all, survival the only instinct.

It occurred after zipping down Bread Loaf toward the valley surrounding Lake Champlain. The day had been spectacular. Imagining how the wind would feel as I crossed the lake on a ferry into New York had buoyed my spirits all morning. I rode light-pedaled. When I feel as such, I get a bit chatty and have found myself in the habit of communicating with the roadside creatures who watch me pass, sometimes horses, occasionally pigs; but on this day, the animal of choice happened to be the cow. Fluency in cowish has remained elusive to my human mouth, but still, I mooed. Never would I be mistaken for a bull; this is true. Yet diversion is good on even the best rides, and so the cattle became my confidantes. I translated the joys of riding to my bovine pals.

Three deep barks from a car horn broke my narrative. Being in a good mood, I decided to interpret the slightly aggressive horn as a very enthusiastic "you-the-man-keep-it-up" rather than the dreaded "I'm-gonna-run-over-your-sorry-self-and-drag-your-spandex-wearing-butt-thirty-feet-so-you-remember-never-to-trespass-into-the-Northern-Kingdom-of-Vermont-ever-again" blast. There was no reason to have an otherwise wonderful day of riding ruined by an irate driver, so I intentionally chose the positive interpretation.

Despite my wishful translation, the driver had other intentions. He pulled ahead of me and slowed so that his bumper was aligned with my front tire. I looked through the windshield to see two birds raised in salute. I expanded my lungs. He slammed hard on the gas, trying to blast me from my saddle with a noxious cloud of carbon monoxide.

His plan failed, and I remained perched on leather.

Realizing the futility of his act, again the birds took flight. At this point, I had a choice. On any other day, I would have just kept pedaling, perhaps explaining the finer points of human interaction to the confused cows watching from their pasture. But my mind filled with memories of being buzzed by crazy New England drivers, being cursed at by impatient commuters, being forced off the shoulders by pickups. I couldn't shake the images. I was tired of being abused. I wanted to be a bull.

The largest shit-eating grin imaginable split my face, and I waved. It was a wave of arrogance and confidence. No three-thousand-pound car could beat me, it said. No fat, red-necked, ignorant road hog could keep me down, it shouted. I am a cross-country adventurer, my wave bellowed, and I will see and suffer more in one day than you will experience in your entire life, you diseased rhinoceros pizzle!

All that my wave roared, and I knew not a single word would be lost in translation.

The car came to a shrieking halt.

It looked like I had gotten myself in a wee bit of a pickle.

The door shot open and out leapt a shortish, roundish, mullet-sporting Neanderthal hefting an axe handle or blackjack or some equally menacing cudgeling device. Frankly, my mind was not focused on the exact nature of the tool that was soon to be pounding my skull but rather on the looming truth that in a few moments I would lay dead in a ditch, beaten by one ugly mother.

"What the fuck ya doin' givin' me the finger, boy? I'm gonna knock ya ass right off that fuckin' bike, ya piece a shit! Givin' me the finger! Ya bastard! Slow down, ya fucka! I'm gonna kick ya ass!"

At this point, I had two options. I could stop, grab my aluminum frame pump, and we could duel. Perhaps I would get the better of him with my Jackie Chan-like reflexes, or maybe he would be charmed by my incredible looks and persuasive words, deciding then and there that bicycles are the only way to travel. We would become fast friends, making peace, breaking bread, and sharing stories. More likely, this club-hefting nut-job would pulverize me neck-deep into asphalt.

My bullish courage fled, and I drifted to the far side of the road so that if this gentleman did indeed wish to knock me senseless, he would have to give chase, with any luck looking mighty foolish in the process.

"Git back here fucka. Take it like a man! Git back here!"

He started pounding the hood of his car.

I continued to pedal until the last vision I had was of the man kicking his tires and beating his Chevy, head wrenched and twisted in a rage so powerful that the cows had fled.

This is when I had to be careful.

To get doored at this moment was quite probable. Dooring is the revenge of all men of this type. Approaching as silently as possible, a passenger door would fling open and knock me senseless, possibly even breaking my leg or cracking my skull. If the chap didn't have the dexterity to operate the car and open the door simultaneously, I could expect a thrown beer bottle. I waited for the inevitable.

He pulled along side of me and reached across the car. Adrenaline saturated my blood. His arms were too short. I met his eyes and sneered. He pounded his steering wheel.

My legs were both weak and strong as I tried to push ahead.

For a full minute, he matched my pace and leaned on his horn. A truck passed traveling in the opposite direction. We both saw its brake lights flare. I turned to my tormentor, my little birdie exchanging song with his. As the truck came to a stop, the car furiously accelerated to disappear in the distance. I was saved. Yet the animal wanted to strike, to maim, to devour.

Despite the calming effect of the ferry into Ticonderoga, my animal remained, wishing release, craving attack. I fled to the foothills, hoping to exhaust the beast in the Adirondacks. I was stalked by thunderheads throughout the afternoon, and now, the storm approaches, a ping-pong ball between the paddles of peaks. Maybe it will cool my anger. But probably not. Still, I regret not stopping to defend myself.

Still, the animal growls.

David

PART VII

....

AN INTERLUDE

Raquette Lake, New York

DAY 40

....

ANSWERING MACHINE

June 23
Eighth Lake State Park
4.6 mi. W. of Raquette Lake, New York

Dear Oma,

I STILL HEAR THE ECHO of the message left in that soft, strange voice on your old analog answering machine when I called:

> Hi. You have reached the Spalding residence. We are unable to come the phone right now. Please leave a message, and we will get back to you. If this is Dave, please call your father as soon as possible. He needs to talk to you. It's important.

Whose voice was that, I had wondered, and what could my dad possibly want? What was so important that your recorded voice, imprinted on tape well over ten years ago and lasting through various storms and power outages, needed to be replaced?

I just talked to him the other day. What could he possibly have done now? Cut his finger on the hedge clippers again? Won big at the poker table? Gotten back together with Mom? What'd he do? What joke was he playing?

"What's up, Dad?"

There had been an accident he said.

An accident?

Was he all right? He had to be. I was talking to him.

How 'bout Mom, Rachael, Ben, Zack, Sara? What kind of accident?

A car accident. Mary and Oma. Serious. She didn't make it.

An accident.

She didn't make it.

An accident.

Here's the number at Shock Trauma. Call.

An accident. An accident…

So, Oma, I write you now knowing that this letter will never be mailed. Dead. How is this possible? What do I do? How did this happen? Why?

I remember before I left we all had discussed what it would take to force me to stop. I said pregnancy, and Mary had said hell no. If she were pregnant, which she wasn't, but if she were, she could manage just fine by herself for the first few months. I needed to finish my adventure she said. Although it would be nice to have someone to hold back her hair when the morning sickness came, she reminded us that she had managed through far worse. Pregnancy would not be an obstacle so long as the ride didn't take nine months.

And I remember at this moment, just as Mary said that—or maybe I'm simply inventing this moment, but it doesn't matter because I remember it now strongly—I remember you looking at me with those amber eyes as they filled with knowledge and sadness and something else. Something I couldn't understand. Something I still can't understand.

An accident.

How was this possible? You were just taking her to DC for a job interview. A Goddamn interview. If I had been home, she wouldn't have been looking for a job in the first place. She would have been relaxing and preparing for grad school. How did this happen? You had driven that route 100,000 times in your life. Why the hell now?

Oma, why did you have to die?

All you wanted was to see the new millennium. What sort of bastard world do I live in? All Mary and I wanted was for you to someday see us married at your house. Aren't Subarus supposed to be safe? All we wanted was for you to kiss our newly born child's head and whisper her name. Why are you gone?

You were supposed to die in sleep, in bed, with a smile.

Now there will be none of that.

An accident. A freakin' car accident.

Why did it have to be in a car? Why that? Why with Mary beside you? Why now? Why when I'm in who-the-hell-knows-where, New York? Why during the adventure of my life?

What am I going to do?

I hear you. Go back. Be with Mary. She needs you now.

But I screwed up, Oma. I ruined everything. Everything. I called the hospital. And Mary seemed okay. Well, not okay, but able at least to function, and I thought back to that conversation and your eyes and asked Mary:

Do you need me to come home?

I could hear the intake of breath. The long silence. The gathering anger then its release as machinery clicked and beeped and buzzed in the background.

"You need to do what you think is right," she said. "You need to make your own decisions."

Do I need to come back? What kind of question is that? I didn't say I'm on my way. Not I'll be there in a day. Not I'm here for you. Not even I love you.

Do I need to come back?

What kind of stupid, dumb, insensitive, selfish creature am I? Mary has a lacerated spleen, a severe concussion, broken ribs, and that is not the worst. I know that. Physical ailments heal quickly. It's the deeper wounds. The horror of it all. The sheer horror, and I ask do you need me to come back.

It should be obvious, right?

But Oma, it's not. I don't know what to do. My heart is torn in three, weeping for my love, my loss, my trip. My bike adventure has become organic, changing me, moving me, and those changes are yet unfinished. I don't want to go back. It's as if I'm giving birth and the head is in the birth canal. How do you stop? Can you even stop?

But I need to go back to Annapolis. I need to support Mary. She needs me. But I need me too. Either way I lose. I can't continue the trip because I will forsake the love inspiring the damn journey in the first place. Yet if the pilgrimage stops, so too will the growth; I will be a stunted man. I am a stunted man. How could Mary love that?

How can I even think these thoughts?

I need to return. But my gut wants me to continue.

Yes, I know. In the movies this is easy. Shoot, if it is someone else's life, this choice is no choice at all. You return home. No thought. There's no reason to even be tormented by such a decision. It's so obvious. But it is me who has to make the decisions. Not someone who has no idea what I've been going through, what I am going through.

Deep in my heart, I know Mary will recover. She is strong, far stronger than I, and far stronger than any support I can give. She would want me to continue. You would want me to continue. I need to finish what I start.

That's crap. I need to be the rock beneath her, supporting and healing. How could I continue west and expect to meet her in San Francisco with anything remotely resembling the relationship we had? We had love. Strong love. Continuing is a betrayal. Sleeping with ten thousand Sallies for ten thousand nights would be the act of a far less unfaithful lover. Pushing west ends our relationship. I might as well stay on the bike and continue to ride like Forrest Gump ran, never to know love again. I wouldn't be worthy.

I need to return. There is no question. But damn it. How can I? Your death just doesn't seem real from here in New York. But my adventure—it's dying right before my eyes. Its lifeblood pools around my feet, and if I give up everything, I can still save it.

How could God let this happen?

I was becoming His creature. The love Mary and I felt would be His reflection. Forty days on a bike to end like this—it's not right. There was so much beauty, so much happiness. I feel like Abraham guiding Isaac up a mountain. But is it my adventure or my love to be sacrificed? Or is it hopeless, and both are lost for good?

No one is answering. I tried to find answers. I did. I called my mom. I called Mary's mom. I spoke with my father. I think they all feel I should go back, but they won't come out and say it.

That's what I need—someone to just tell me what to do. At one point, I grabbed the Bible that had been buried in the bottom my left pannier and randomly flipped through the pages to find an answer. You know what it said?

> *I will cause them to fall by the sword before their enemies, and by the hands of them that seek their lives: and their carcass will I give to be meat for the fowls of the heaven, and for the beasts of the earth.*
> (JEREMIAH 19:7)

Uplifting, isn't it? What the hell does that even mean? What kind of answer is that? Where are the Bible's answers now? Where is the grace? The hope? The love? Where is He? Here I am, but where the hell is He? Explain this! Tell me what to do! I need answers!

It doesn't matter. The journey's over—the adventure is finished—the pilgrimage incomplete. I am done.

David

PART VIII

ALTERNATE ROUTES

Inlet, New York,
to Inlet, New York

DAY 41

....

WU WEI AND THE CORK

June 24
Beneath a Tree
Inlet, New York

Dear Mary,

The conversation might never have happened if I had left the counter upon finishing my breakfast. Knowing my mom would be another three hours before she picked me up, I remained slouched on a swiveling stool, with nothing more pressing than the wait. I needed to be alone, and yet I also craved the company of background conversation—something to distract me from the beautiful day outside—anything to keep my mind away from the emptiness just below the surface. So I sat, pushing caramelized onions and charred potatoes from one side of my plate to the other while nursing a mug of cold coffee thick with sugar and cream.

Caffeine didn't help. Neither did the overheard discussions of small town life. How could Barbara worry about her son's coming birthday party? It would be fine. They always are. How could Herb moan and groan about the drive to the airport? He would get there and make his flight with hours to spare. How could Susan complain so vehemently about the potluck dinner for which she must make dessert? She loves to cook and knows that no one for miles makes apple tart quite as tasty. And how could a man named Cork plop himself down next to me and ask, as if it were any other day, how far I planned on riding, without even realizing that Oma is gone?

Without looking up, I said today was the end. I was riding no farther. I had started in Annapolis forty days ago yesterday, and here in Inlet, I was heading back.

This town's an interesting choice to end a bike trip, he mused. He didn't suppose I had planned it that way. Sensing my agitation as I swirled my coffee and pushed my hash browns, he ordered breakfast and remained silent, reading the *Utica Observer-Dispatch* while waiting. Then, from that unbearable silence, broken by the occasional dropped fork or shaken newspaper, rose a story…

"You know, when my son turned twenty-nine, he wanted to hike the Appalachian Trail." Cork carefully folded his paper and placed it on an empty stool. I could feel his eyes watching me, but I refused to look up from my plate. "If I remember correctly, he was about six months from being married. He was working down in the City at some law firm. A huge place like Gaston, Tolzman, and Saperstein or some such. The place was gigantic. Must have been over two hundred lawyers in the firm. He seemed to like it, though. He had his own office on the sixth floor, a pert young secretary, and a closet full of fancy suits."

The waitress refilled my coffee cup and plopped a plate in front of Cork. "Thanks, Sheryl. The jelly fresh today?"

"What do you think, you old rascal? And how many times do I have to tell you, it's not jelly. You buy that stuff in stores. We've got fruit preserves here."

"Jelly. Jam. Fruit preserves. Whatever." Sheryl whipped the hand towel from her shoulder and flicked it at Cork. "Don't get all feisty on me now, Sheryl. I'm not saying your jam isn't tasty. In fact, why don't you get my friend here another piece of toast and scoot some of that jelly down this way?"

Sheryl painted a playful grimace across her face, tried to make eye contact with me, and went back to the kitchen.

"I love messing with her like that. Do it every day. Just like when we were in sixth grade. Miss Tonberger was constantly separating us. But you can't stop young love, now can you? You want cream in that coffee of yours?"

Just as a rocky shore is gradually pounded into sand by the ocean, I found myself giving way. His voice had broken through. I turned to Cork and tried to smile, studying his face for the first time. His head was almost a perfect square bouncing on the thin spring of his neck. His eyes were small and crowded the bridge of his nose as if they wanted to merge. His nose was a red ball and his drooping ears catcher's mitts. He yawned. "I think you'll really like the jelly. So you want cream?" He started pouring milk into my coffee.

I cleared my throat. "Sure, I guess."

"Tastes better that way, if you ask me." He stabbed a potato with his fork. "So, as I was saying, my son wanted to hike the AT, and everybody he knew told him that it was stupid…leaving his job, selling his condo, getting rid of all those suits. Even his fiancée. I never liked her much anyway. She was always scowling."

Sheryl returned with a pot of raspberry preserves and a plate of toast. "Eat up now."

"You don't have to worry about us. We've got it covered. Hope you have more jelly in the back, though. This might not be enough."

"Just eat your breakfast, Cork." She turned toward me. "Don't listen to a word that old codger says. He makes stuff up better than a big city politician."

"I'll try not to," I reassured her.

"Come on, Sheryl," he said between bites of jam-smeared toast. "I may tell a good story, but I don't just invent things. Too often." His rounded shoulders shook with silent laughter. He wiped his mouth and turned back toward me. "So, my young adventurer, this crazy son of mine decided to hike from Georgia to Maine. Of course, I was all for it, even if his fiancée hated the idea. I'm sure you know what that's like."

"Yeah. A bit."

"Well, with so little support from his friends, he just became more frustrated. One day in court, he even told the judge to shut up when she denied an objection. He was having a rough time with it all, that's for sure. Then, a few days after the whole judge fiasco, he just snapped, quit his job, and sold everything...bought himself a pair of boots, a plane ticket to Georgia, and started hiking."

Cork tapped my leg with stubby fingers.

"Of course, that's not the best way to begin an adventure. But you got to take what you can get. No?" Cork sipped his coffee, starring at me above the rim. He placed the mug on the counter as if it might break.

"Two weeks into his hike, I got a phone call from the Atlanta airport. It was my son. He was crying. He said he'd failed. His knee had swollen to the size of a football. He had contracted some creepy crawly stomach parasite, and then, on top of it all, it snowed, trapping him in a trail shelter for a day. He hadn't even made it through Georgia. His voyage was a disaster. He was coming home, defeated."

I nodded. I knew that emotion. It was as strong as the coffee I chugged.

"A funny thing happened on the plane to New York..." Cork swiveled on his stool and began smearing another piece of toast with butter and preserves. Sheryl scurried past, grinning slyly at Cork.

"Well? What happened?"

"Well, what always happens when an obstacle is thrown across your path: life continues. See, Chip—that's my son—ended up on a plane sitting right beside Sheryl's daughter, Natalie. Go figure?"

Sheryl refilled my coffee. "Don't listen to him too hard, son. Next thing you'll know, he'll have you convinced he won the Boston Marathon in '86."

"Sheryl, I never said I won the race. I just ran in it."

"Ran or won…" She cleared Cork's plate. "You still tell too many stories. Which one is it today?"

"I'm just telling this young adventurer here, how Chip met Natalie. You approve of that, right?"

"Now that's a good story." She rested her elbows on the counter, cupping her chin in her hands. "Please continue."

Cork leaned back on his stool. "Well, there's not much more to tell. On the flight from Atlanta, Natalie and Chip hit it off like gangbusters. Within the year, they were married, and soon me and Sheryl here were expecting our first—"

"Oh, Cork," Sheryl interrupted. "Come on. That's not where the story ends. That's where it begins. We've got two grandkids now. We're all part of the same family. Chip's hike along the Appalachian Trail wasn't the adventure. That was just the door. It's all that happened after. The huge wedding up near Schroon Lake. The farm. Their life together now."

"That's true, Sheryl. And that's what I'm trying to tell our young friend here. See, son, life throws obstacles in your way. That's what it does. And to face those obstacles with courage is the true test. Son, I don't know why you're stopping here in Inlet. But I can tell that your plans didn't account for whatever happened. I see Chip in your posture. But son, you don't have to be on the back of a bike or on the tops of mountains to be an adventurer. In the detours is where a life is made."

My hands began to shake. I could feel myself breaking on the inside. I needed to be outside. I needed to see the sky, to hear sparrows, to be bitten by deer flies. I couldn't be near people any longer. I stumbled from my stool.

"Let me pay for your breakfast." His eyes melted with mine. "Godspeed to you, son."

Cork's words pierced my side like a spear and washed my tattered mind with compassion. Yes, Oma is gone. Yes, you are suffering. And yes, my bike trip is over.

But the adventure is not. It is far from over. When my mom arrives to pick me up, it is just a 1,600 mile detour, and as I am beginning to understand, it's in the detours that adventures can be found and life bounces back like a bobbing cork in heavy rapids.

Love,
David

DAY 42

HEADACHE

June 25
Southbound New Jersey Turnpike
Between Exit 8A and 8, New Jersey

Dear Mary,

Who knows when I will next see you? We have been parked along the highway for thirty minutes, and things appear to be improving not a wit. My head is pounding as I alternately roll the window up and down trying in vain to mimic the breeze of riding. The air conditioner has dried my eyes, and I have never been thirstier than in this car, stopped dead along the Turnpike.

Having not been in a car for about eight weeks, I must admit that the speeds are more than a bit shocking. Watching cattle pass without a hello, seeing a cyclist struggle up a hill without acknowledgement—gazing at the globe through glass—I feel cocooned and alone, separated from the world I had come to know on the one hand and the world of my past on the other. My mother and brother both try to make conversation, yet I can do nothing but add the occasional grunt of agreement.

They both sense my frustration. All I want is to be holding your hand. Shoot! If I hadn't left my bike in Poughkeepsie, I could ride to Baltimore faster than we are going now. Maybe I can only pedal at ten mph, but at least I would be moving toward you. This dichotomy is so strange, my aversion to speed when we were zooming along the country roads of New York and my burning desire for greater and greater haste now that we are stopped on this highway.

I must see you. I must be near you. There is much to discuss, much to explain, much to apologize for. If you never want to see me again, I can understand. The pain I caused you in that moment on the phone…

We need to talk in person. Such words, coming from me now, stopped in a car, I imagine seem empty to you. I had my chance and failed. But I am coming. I will be beside you, if you will have me still. Mary, I care for you more than I can say. Forget past words. Let action be my only argument.

Love,
David

David Haber

DAY 49

....

THE HOUSE ON EDEN LANE

July 2
Eden Lane
Annapolis, Maryland

D<small>EAR</small> M<small>ARY</small>,
    O<small>MA WAS OUR HOME</small>. Her heart and her laughter…
But now the house is empty.
…Oma is gone.
The house stands, but our home is gone.

                                      David

DAY 56

....

THERE AND BACK AGAIN

July 9
The Maple Leaf, Unreserved Coach
Northbound, Amtrak

D<small>EAR</small> M<small>ARY</small>,
   W<small>E KIN</small>, <small>DO WE NOT</small>? I kin ye, as ye me, despite what I perceive in the looks of some of our friends, filled with their scorn and complete lack of comprehension. How can you leave her now, I read in their gaze. How can you love her if you leave?

What these people don't realize is that you have given your blessing. You saw the incompleteness of it all. You sensed the need to finish even as I tried to conceal it. For both of us, I must reach San Francisco.

We have an understanding, and without such, there can be no love. People think what they must, but their thoughts can in no way comprehend what has been forged between us during the past fifteen days. For two years, our relationship coasted down a hill, waiting for a moment that would define the rest. What sort of moment even we did not know—would it be a gravelly, slippery wipeout of bruised knees and scratched elbows or a humming, zooming ride of speed unmatched? Whichever, such a moment would shape our lives, together or apart. So close were we to being apart that I didn't even realize it until we were locked with a mutual understanding.

The hurt of my phone call I can never repair. I know that it will always snare you with doubts about my reliability. Will I be there for you in need? Will I be there for our children? If there's a crisis, can you depend on me or will I again ask, "Do you need me?"

There is no bandage for this hurt, just as there will never be surcease for the horror you have felt and are still feeling since the accident. Your loss is far greater than mine. The accident stole more than Oma. I understand. I can see it in your wounded eyes. I feel it every time I hear a car brake to a noisy stop. I saw the slump-shouldered back of your spirit fleeing to curl in some dark corner of your brain.

You will never be the same. That Mary is past, and this new recovering Mary is present. We have both changed—are still changing and recognizing ourselves—yet we have, at the core, an understanding. One moment together—you on the couch, me on my knees, your hands tangled with my hair, our eyes watering loss with hope—announces our understanding.

Life moves us forward, Mary. It has pushed us closer than we have ever been.

Love is strange—and demanding, too, as we have discovered time and again. For us, love and suffering will always be married; we cannot escape one and have the other. Suffering colors our love just as love tints the pain, making both bearable. For love unchecked leads to madness. Look at poor Don Quixote. And suffering without the touch of love…that too brings insanity, as Job can attest. It's only when the two are tied together, as they are so deeply in us, that life can be felt, real with all her dark mud and alive pumping her rich blood.

The world, with its muck and slime, may not be the pretty place we were told of as children. But I recall that as a child I would lift rocks to find salamanders and crickets and potato bugs and slugs and worms and ants—all so wonderfully alive. That is our love—despite the suffering—no, because of the suffering—wonderfully alive.

Someday you will be my wife.

Maybe not today or tomorrow or two years from now. But someday.

We kin.

We have an understanding.

That is why I ride west and finish. I must.

Our love demands it.

David

PART IX

SECOND WIND HYMNS

From Inlet, New York,
to Brook, Indiana

DAY 57

....

CHEAP TUBE BLUES IN B♭

July 10
Arrowhead Park
Inlet, New York

Dear Mary,

Sing along with me:

Da...na-na-na-na...na-na...na-na...
Da...na-na-na-na...na-na...na-na...

Gypsy Woman done told me, b'ware the noon
The Mojo be strong from the Johnny Cockeroo
Done gone cursed my pump, Lord, he done cursed me strong
Stuck in this here dump, Baby, it's just all wrong.
Hard luck and trouble, putting me in a mood
Handlin' my limp, flat cheap tire tube.
Oh...ohhhh! That damn flat cheap tire tube!

Love,
David

David Haber

DAY 57, REPRISE

....

SPEAKING UP

July 10
50 ft. S. of Railroad Tracks
Nelson Lake, New York

Dear Mary,

After fixing my first flat—which came not from a nail or tack, but rather when my pump's nozzle came away with the tube's valve—I left Inlet. For the second time. Despite my groaning joints and screaming muscles, it felt wonderful being back on the bike. My form was not as it had been a month ago, but the Professor's lessons were unforgotten. I didn't try to fight up hills; I kept my cadence high. And most importantly, I stopped when my energy waned, which happened very quickly.

By three o'clock, I was exhausted and craved a warm shower. Finding a campground, I stumbled into the manager's office and asked how much it would be for a night.

"Thirty dollars," he said, peering above the half-moons of his glasses.

Considering I anticipated using about twenty-three dollars worth of his hot water in the shower, thirty bucks didn't seem completely outrageous. Still, I am cycling. I don't have a car. I'm not pulling a trailer. It was just me, my bike, and the voices in my head.

"How about ten bucks?" I offered smiling.

I was shocked. You're the haggler, Mary. Not me. Never done it before in my life. I don't even know how. I'm the one who won't complain about bad food or service in a restaurant. I'm the one who is reluctant to speak up when someone cuts in line. I'm the quiet accepting one, willing to overpay for most anything so long as there was no fuss.

At this point, the man took off his glasses and creased his wrinkled face with a grin.

"If we were to do this proper, I'd say twenty bucks, and I'm sure you'd say twelve, then I'd say eighteen, and we'd settle on fifteen. Haggling's great. Lost art. But see, the problem is, I just work here, and the manager would skin me alive if I gave a site to someone for as cheap as fifteen dollars. So I hate to say it, but…it's still thirty bucks."

I sighed and yanked myself upright, digging in my pocket for some cash.

"Course, if I were you and wanted to keep my thirty bucks, I might turn myself about a bit and travel—oh maybe 'round half mile or so back down Rt. 28 toward Old Forge. On the right, just past the old Wilbur Mill, there's a boat access point. If you go down that a-way, you'll cross some rail tracks and be right near Nelson

Lake. She's a beaut this time of year. Don't tell anybody I told you so, but it beats paying cash."

Maybe I'm making more of this than I should. Maybe I'm trying to create an adventure rather than simply experiencing it. I so wish to capture something of the feelings I had pre-accident, and maybe I'm forcing myself into things I normally wouldn't try.

I can't say for sure. What I can say is that—flanked by train tracks to the north and Nelson Lake to the south, encircled by a copse of pines and cushioned by their needled floor—I am not simply thirty dollars the richer for having spoken up.

Love,
David

Letters to Eden

DAY 60

....

WATERMELON WITH MORMONS

July 13
Lunchtime
Palmyra, New York

Dear Mary,

I NEED A SHOWER, and it isn't even past noon. My body is coated with layers of crud bound together by my own sweat. There is an odor following me, and I can't quite out pedal it. Free camping at boat launches and along snowmobile trails for the past few days—and therefore not paying for campsites or showers—has taught me new lessons about cleanliness as I try to scrub off in the filthy bathrooms of gas stations. After leaving new grime stains in the rusty sinks of those toilet paper-coated Petri dishes, I delude myself into thinking that I am clean enough for social interaction. When I walk past the cashier and she glances at me crosswise with a twitching nose, I know I failed. What I really need is a good, long summer rain.

This morning I awoke with the hope of a steaming shower to cap my ride along the Eerie Canal Towpath. During breakfast, I studied my maps and fantasized about the steady whir of my dusty tires buzzing over that crushed limestone path, dreamt of the gentle flow of the Erie Canal beside me, and imagined the plop of baited hooks as dads taught sons the peace of fishing. With luck, I hoped to reach the trail by midmorning and then continue on through Rochester and beyond. I rode with a bounce long forgotten and presumed lost in the Adirondacks. I was finally free of the mountains. I had regained my legs, and as I pulled into the city park at Palmyra, my shoulders were already anticipating the exquisite pelting of a forty-five minute shower at the end of day.

Now, some two hours later, I have yet to begin the ride along the Eerie Canal and that imagined shower seems but the hallucination of a deranged man. I'm still at the city park, and the sun climbs well past noon. I can't move. I'm digesting; I ate quite a bit of watermelon. I think the Mormons were trying to ripen me for conversion.

Distracted by my third peanut butter and jelly sandwich of the day, I had hardly noticed when a bus—*LDS Tours* painted across its side—rolled into the parking lot. An entire ward of Mormons—all blonde and smiley—disembarked carrying large coolers filled with who knew what kind of goodies to tempt a sinning cyclist. They spread out beneath the pavilion, and very quickly, their chatter engulfed me.

"Riding along the Towpath, are you?" Asked the clean-shaven man who sat across from me. His jowls, heavy with age, hung loosely from his cheeks. A crooked name tag stuck to his tan button-down shirt announced that I was in the presence of CharLee Young.

"Yeah. I'm actually about to leave, so…" I rose and began walking toward my bike.

"No need to scurry off on our account." CharLee waved about the now crowded pavilion. "Fact is, we've got plenty of extra watermelon. Come on. Have a seat. On a hot day like today, you need all the fruit you can get." He gestured to a paper plate piled high with slices of crisp melon. "Don't be shy. Dig in."

I sat down. A blonde woman—eyelids slathered with purple make-up, lips coated with crimson, and plump body draped in a garish yellow dress—sidled up next to me. "Hi. My name's Olene Olsen. Nice to meet you." With this woman pinning me uncomfortably against the pavilion's support beam, I had no choice but to tackle the pile of melon.

"My grandfather used to take me along the canal when I was a kid," mused CharLee. "The locks always fascinated me."

"You never told me you lived around here," Olene said. With her pudgy fingers, she reached across my chest and grabbed a slice of melon. "I always thought you were from Park City."

"Nah. I moved there when I was about twelve." He turned toward me. "I grew up right here in Palmyra. Best town there is, if you ask me." He took a wet bite of melon. "You know, they used to call the canal Clinton's Big Folly. Can you believe that?"

"Figures. Bill Clinton is always ruining things."

"Oh, Orlene." CharLee shook his head and pulled at his ear. "Not Bill. DeWitt Clinton. The governor of New York in eighteen-something or another. Don't you listen to the tour guides?"

"Of course not." She smiled. Red lipstick stained her front teeth. "I'm sitting next to Anne. You know how much of a talker she is."

"Sure. Sure. She puts you to shame." CharLee winked at me. I grabbed a slice of melon. "I think you'll like the locks. They're amazing. There're these two gigantic steel and concrete doors, right? I guess they're about 150 feet apart or something. When a boat is heading upstream, she enters the lock—you know, the space between the doors—the southern one slams shut while the northern door opens, and presto. The chamber floods, the boat rises, and continues toward Buffalo."

I tried spitting a few seeds toward the trash barrel. They dribbled from my mouth.

"Why do they need all that?" Olene asked as she caught her own seeds within a paper napkin. "It seems like a waste to me. Regular rivers don't need locks. It just doesn't seem natural."

"Some rivers, like the Saint Lawrence, have locks to get over rough rapids. And anyway, the canal goes uphill. A boat going north has to climb about five hundred feet in elevation to reach Buffalo."

"That doesn't seem like that much. Utah has higher mountains than that." Olene patted my leg. "I'm sure he's even biked up taller hills."

"Utah's different. Boats aren't trying to go up the mountainside in a gondola pulled by tired mules." CharLee sucked on his rind and then tossed it with a ping into the garbage can. He leaned forward, practically folding himself in two, eyes glowing with excitement. "Imagine this: Buffalo is here on Lake Eerie. Okay?" He placed a piece of watermelon on top of his soda can. "And New York Harbor is down this away." He moved an empty plate across the table. "Now this," he said, plucking a seed from the melon, "is a barge carrying goods imported from France."

"What kind of goods?" Olene asked, picking up the seed and studying as if it would reveal the mysteries of the universe.

"Oh, I don't know. What does—"

"How about yellow parasols from Paris?" I interrupted.

"Yellow's my favorite color." Olene clapped and placed the seed back on the plate. "What happens next?"

"Well, from this plate, our parasols need to reach the fashionable ladies of Buffalo." CharLee steered the seed along a winding path across the table. "First, along the Hudson. Then, we hit Albany." The seed ran aground at our plate of watermelon. "This is where the Mohawk and Hudson meet; there're all kinds of waterfalls and swamps here. Before Governor Clinton decided to build the canal, it took three weeks to navigate the terrain from Albany to Buffalo." He looked at Olene. "Now, if you were a stylish lady in the city, would you want to wait all that time for the latest French fashions?"

She shook her head.

"I didn't think so. That's where the canal comes in. It's a work of genius. Some of the best engineers around came up with this lock system so that large barges could be pulled over the rapids by mules and such. You know the song: I've got a mule and her name is Sal, Fifteen miles along the Eerie Canal…"

CharLee's rich tenor voice broke in embarrassment. With a cough, he hopped the seed over the watermelon and to the top of the can. "I think there're over eighty locks, and the ones at Lockport are the most amazing. It's a double lock so that two boats can move at the same time, one up, one down, over the Niagara Escarpment, which is sixty feet straight up. That means that vessels carrying French parasols north wouldn't interfere with barges hauling beaver pelts back to New York. In 1825, Governor Clinton made the first voyage along the canal to marry, so to speak, the Great Lake's fresh waters to the salty harbor of New York City. The trip took eleven days. New York became the Queen of an Empire and the west opened."

"So how long did it take to build the canal?" I asked.

"About eight years, I think."

"Eight years?" Olene yawned and leaned heavily against me. "What took so long?"

"It's not like the workers had Bobcats and huge diesel-powered digging machines, Olene. Immigrants dug this Big Ditch using shovels and horses. Everyone contracted malaria. So many trees needed chopping that the immigrants resorted to cables and winches because there weren't enough axes. So of course it took a long time. I mean, the workers were jabbing at dirt with hoes and picks. Just think how long it took our ancestors to find a home in Utah. First, Joseph Smith moved us west from Palmyra to Illinois. Then the Prophet was murdered when we were driven from Nauvoo. It took Brigham Young to lead us to Utah. And he had God's help. Governor Clinton didn't even have the support of President Jefferson when he built the canal."

Olene jerked her head from my shoulder and grabbed my knee. "Are you going to see *America's Witness for Christ*?"

"What's that?" I asked.

"Oh. You must see it." Her eyes pleaded. Her bottom lip trembled. "It's fabulous. The play is the only reason why I come on these trips."

"It is quite a show." CharLee agreed. "You should stay the night and see it. You'll learn all about Prophet Smith's vision. It happened on the Hill Cumorah just outside town…"

On September 21, 1821, the angel Moroni materialized before the prophet Joseph Smith. This divine creature explained how he, Moroni—being the last of the great and glorious people residing on this continent, long before its discovery by Columbus and its conquest by Cortez—buried the history of the Nephites in 421 A.D. These tablets were written by his father, the prophet Mormon, and were buried a few miles away beneath the Hill Cumorah after the final battle during which the curséd Lamanites annihilated the blesséd children of Lehi.

According to CharLee and Olene, in 600 B.C., Lehi, a wealthy merchant born in Jerusalem, received a prophecy from the Lord about the coming destruction of his city and fled to the desert with his family and followers. Through eight years of trial and tribulation, progress constantly stalled by the rebelliousness of the elder brothers Laman and Lemuel, this clan eventually reached the sea and crossed to the New World in a boat crafted by Lehi's virtuous younger son Nephi.

After Lehi's death, the brothers, much like Esau and Jacob, had a falling out, which eventually led to the division of this clan into two tribes, one subscribing to the proper and true teaching of the Lord and the other succumbing to greed and sin. This tale had been etched onto the golden plates unearthed by the Prophet Smith, which eventually were translated into the *Book of Mormon*. To commemorate this record of Christ's resurrection in the New World, every summer for about a week, the Church of Latter Day Saints produces a huge pageant called *America's Witness for Christ*, which is performed on the Hill Cumorah and is completely free to the public.

As I munched on my melon and spat the seeds in the general direction of my bike, I listened to my new Mormon friends try to convert me in subtle and devious ways. Like the honeyed speech of a new-age guru, their words wrapped around the parts of me that so need to believe in something greater than the greatest thing I can conceive—something divine and glorious and magnificent—something that transforms my sometimes animal-seeming existence into a life worthy of the name. To that elemental nakedness deep in my breast, it doesn't matter where the divine is found, only that I, too, am touched and can share that touch.

Yet there is another part of me. This part is tired of kind-hearted attempts at conversion. My raw soul may attract the religious like the Statue of Liberty draws immigrants, but being converted won't change that we all will die, and before we die, we will suffer. I know these folks just want to help, to soothe, to save. But can't they see that I have all I need? I have a quest. I have love. And I have a mouthful of watermelon seeds to spit west.

Love,
David

David Haber

NIGHT 60

....

A HUNDRED MILES

July 13
Stranded along the Erie Canal
A few miles east of Medina, New York

D<small>EAR</small> M<small>ARY</small>,
M<small>Y LETTERS HAVE BECOME</small> more than a simple recording of events. They are my balm to you, Mary. My only wish is to massage your wounds with my adventure. I'm not going to edit the pain and loneliness I feel. But I will use a careful pen to apply this medicine. You're in a fragile state, I know, and too much salve on any wound may hinder more than help in healing.

So, instead of complaining about getting lost on a bike trail, being unable to find a shower, and being forced to camp along the limestone of the Eerie Canal Towpath, I will rather sing a song of triumph, of joy, and of companionship…

I've got a bike and her name is Sal,
Hun-dred miles on the Er-ie Canal,
She's a good ol' worker and a good ol' pal,
Hun-dred miles on the Er-ie Canal,

We've hauled some panniers in our day,
Filled with trinkets gathered along the way,
Quite an adventure it is we know,
From Maryland to Buff-a-lo!

Low bridge ev'ry body down,
Low bridge for we're comin' to a town,
And you always know your neighbor,
You'll always know your pal,
If you've ever nav-I-gated on the Er-ie Canal.

We'd better look for a campsite old gal,
Hun-dred miles on the Er-ie Can-al,
You bet your life I wouldn't part with Sal,
Hun-dred miles on the Er-ie Canal,
Giddap 'there gal we've passed that lock,
We won't find showers, it's nine o'clock,
So, beneath the stars to let sleep grow,
We won't make it to Buff-a-lo!

Low bridge ev'ry body down,
Low bridge for we're comin' to a town,
And you always know your neighbor,
You'll always know your pal,
If you've ever nav-I-gated on the Er-ie Canal.

Oh, where would I be if I lost my pal?
Hun-dred miles on the Erie Canal.
I'd like to see a bike as good as Sal,
Hun-dred miles on the Erie Canal,
Although I am a little sore,
We'll still reach those western shores,
'Cause she flies on rubber toes,
Only to zoom through Buff-a-lo!

David Haber

Low bridge ev'ry body down,
Low bridge for we're comin' to a town,
And you always know your neighbor,
You'll always know your pal,
If you've ever nav-I-gated on the Er-ie Canal.

Don't have to call when I want my Sal,
Hun-dred miles on the Er-ie Canal,
She rolls along like a good old gal,
Hun-dred miles on the Er-ie Canal,
I eat my meals with Sal each day,
I eat peanut butter and jelly, she leads the way,
And she ain't so slow if you want to know,
She put the "Buff" in Buff-a-lo!

Low bridge ev'ry body down,
Low bridge, we passed another town,
Tonight I won't know my neighbor,
But I'll always know my pal,
Because she guided me along the Er-ie Canal!

Love,
David

DAY 61

WHAT WOULD MACGYVER DO?

July 14
Canadian Immigration Office
U.S./Canada Border

Dear Mary,

Perhaps I was a tad jittery in the long queue stopped at the Canadian border. Perhaps I had inhaled far too much carbon monoxide while waiting behind the cars for my turn at the booth, adding further to any suspicious-seeming ticks I might already have. Perhaps, Interpol had warned Canadian Customs about the deadly Spoke Cartel, composed completely of sinister drug-smuggling bicycle banditos. I don't know what exactly I may have done, but I'm being held—told to wait for my turn—in a room packed with Kenyans pleading with official-looking agents of the Man, in a chamber filled with frustrated Germans frothing at overly happy Canadian officials, in a cinder block lobby crammed with a huge Vietnamese family begging clipboard-carrying administrators for a moment, a tissue, a diaper, anything to stop their baby's wails.

Why I ended up in the immigration office, I can't quite figure. When I initially rolled up to the custom agent's booth, I aped my most charming smile, assuming the border crossing was a simple formality.

"Name?" A severe woman scribbled on a clipboard without glancing up.

"Uh. David Haber."

"I.D. and plate number?"

"Um. Here's my driver's license and passport. But I'm riding a bike…"

The agent finally looked up as she took my license.

"Why, yes. You are indeed." She stepped from her booth and whistled. "That's quite a setup you've got there. Where you off to?"

"San Francisco. But first I want to see Niagara Falls."

"Amazing! Where'd you start?"

"Maryland. But I went to Bar Harbor first."

"Must be quite fun…seeing the country—"

"Yeah—"

"My husband bought bikes for the two of us last Christmas so we could spend more time together. But we haven't ridden that much. Maybe we should try a bike trip." She glanced back at her clipboard.

"Totally. I can't tell you how great—"

"What was your name again?" She interrupted. Her voice broke in staccato bursts like the soundtrack to a Hitchcockian thriller.

"Um. David. David Haber."

"And you're traveling to the Falls?"

"Yes."
"How long do you plan on being in Canada?"
"I'm not really sure. Maybe a day or two. It depends how tired I feel, I suppose."
"So you started in Maryland?"
"Yeah. Annapolis."
"Where were you born?"
"Poughkeepsie."
"And Poughkeepsie is in Maryland?"
"No, it's in New York. I went to school in Annapolis."
"Annapolis, Maryland?"
"Yes."
"When were you born?"
"December twenty-six."
"In Annapolis right?"
"No. In New York. In Poughkeepsie."
"But you live in Annapolis now?"
"That is where I last lived. Yes."
"In New York?"
"No Maryland."
"Are you transporting any drugs?"
"I've got a bottle of Advil."
"How about weapons—brass knuckles, guns, clubs, knives?"
"I don't think so. I have this frame pump though."
"No knives?"
"Well, I do have a Swiss Army knife that I use for opening cans and chopping up food."
"May I see it?"

I reached into my handle bar bag and handed over my knife.

"Hmmmmm."

"Is everything okay?"

"Well...you said you were born in Annapolis right?"

"Yeah—Wait. I mean no. Poughkeepsie."

"Okay, Mr. Haber. About this knife...you're going to have to register it at the immigration office."

"But it's just a pocket knife."

"Nevertheless, there are laws in Canada. I don't think it'll be confiscated. But still the government needs a record of all bladed weapons entering the country. Don't worry. It shouldn't take that long. Fifteen minutes max. You'll still see the Falls today."

Sure I will, which explains why I've been sitting on this molded plastic torture device the Canadians call a chair for the last hour, watching disgruntled people pace the room in one direction only to be stopped by irritated individuals stomping in the other—just like Dr. Seuss' North-Going Zax and South-Going Zax banging heads on the prairie of Prax. Exasperation hangs so thick in the air that even my Swiss Army knife, newly sharpened, couldn't slice it. I can't believe I'm stuck in this room. How is this possible?

MacGyver never seemed to have any difficulty crossing foreign borders with his Swiss Army knife. He carried it everywhere while on top-secret missions for the Phoenix Foundation—into the wilds of Mexico, atop the tallest mountains, through lush rainforests. The knife, like my bike, was his companion. It untangled him from all sorts of sticky situations: from being captured by smugglers to dismantling nefarious terrorist organizations bent on world domination. Once his trusty knife even helped him outmaneuver Russian oil bootleggers who had disguised themselves as Sasquatch to frighten the locals. His Swiss Army knife was the key to his improvisation.

I should have realized that the Canadian government would recognize that, just like MacGyver, I'm a covert operative. I should have anticipated that my knife would reveal my mission: to be the first man ever to plunge over Niagara Falls in a barrel woven together from spare Advil containers, duct tape, and old fence posts carved with my Swiss Army knife.

Mac would never find himself in this predicament. He was too smooth, too cool, too savvy; give him his Swiss Army knife and a few locks of hair from his mullet, and MacGyver would fashion an escape for the visa-less Kenyans, a solution for the angry Germans, and a diaper for that wailing Vietnamese infant. But I somehow blundered, and my knife is probably going to be confiscated. There is no escape but to wait

With patience,
David

David Haber

ENDLESS DAY 61

....

BEFORE THE FALLS

July 14
Frenchman's Creek Park
Fort Erie, Ontario, Canada

DEAR MARY,
THIS IS BECOMING INCREASINGLY RIDICULOUS. All I had wanted was to enjoy my snow cone. To feel the cool touch of the maid of the mist tickle my eyebrows as 600,000 gallons of water per second tumbled 167 feet over the Horseshoe Falls. To finally cool my frustration after being informed by a confused Canadian official that the knife-registering regulation applies only to bladed weapons of six inches or more. But two fervent teenagers had other plans. They wanted to teach, but unlike the Mormons, they didn't have any watermelon.

Before the Falls, I learned that God loves us, which is why He sent His only begotten Son to this sin-riddled planet to live as a man and die ridiculed and forsaken. Was I willing to acknowledge that sacrifice, they asked, and accept Christ in my heart as my Lord and Savior?

See, I sin something powerful. It isn't my fault, of course. Eve with her curiosity and easily persuaded mind corrupted man with a forked tongue, thereby punishing all their ancestors—including me and you—with death and sorrow. Sure we have this great and constantly growing knowledge of all things, good and evil both, but we are destined to a short and bestial life scraping away at the dusty earth. We just had to go and eat that apple.

In so satiating our hunger for the shiny and sweet, our relatives brought sin and death to an otherwise perfect and very good creation, condemning it all to Hell. The only path to salvation is in recognizing God's wondrous sacrifice of his only Son. For us. The weak and damned.

Will you accept Christ's sacrifice?

Whoa! Big fella! Slow it down a little bit.

Let me try to explain how incongruous this all seemed to me. Two teenagers—one blonde and perfectly groomed, looking like an All-American High School quarterback, the other a short Korean boy with the fervor of the divine in his eyes—had cornered me along an iron rail as hundreds of people swarmed around, soaking in the magnificence of Niagara Falls. What it was that attracted them to me, I can't say for sure. But just like the Mormons, these two wanted to be midwife to a born-again soul.

While we verbally wrestled, the water pounded over the brink, swallowing our words in nature's melody. The spray, reaching heavenward with vaporous fingers, cooled my forehead. The snow cone, melting in the hot sun, trickled down my arm. To me, the Falls destroyed all thoughts of sin because of its power and beauty and sheer elemental nature; yet these two evangelicals poked and prodded, forsaking the world right before them for their own of sin and guilt, shouting descriptions of our own culpability through Christ's mouthpiece.

I respect their belief. Perhaps they're right, perhaps they're not. It doesn't much matter one way or the other because faith has little to do with truth or falsehood. There is no proof and never will be (although my missionaries-in-training would disagree). That's fine. Faith in such things is wonderful, and those lucky ones are blessed. But any sort of faith, whether in science, in God, or simply in life, is in itself wonderful; such belief is so important because of how it manifests itself on the inside of people and how that internal ghost moves one externally toward action in this world. I'm far from faithless; it's just a faith of a slightly different sort from that of these young preacher men.

I believe in symbols, and those symbols move me closer to my deep-inside-hidden places that are hard to see in the light of day because they provide the light to my life. I believe in the image of Abraham sacrificing Isaac, the idea of Jacob wrestling an angel, the picture of Don Quixote challenging windmills to battle, the story of Odysseus returning home, not because I think these events happened, but rather because these symbols deepen my life and color my own experience. In my mind, the unsymbolic life is simply not worth living.

I admit that the symbol of Jesus is fascinating. I see his sacrifice. But actual belief in and acceptance of biblical events? No. I recognize Christ as a teacher with some very important parables to tell. The Son of God? I can't say. I do, however, respect the image of a God–Man, something divine and wonderful in us all.

I tried explaining how I felt, how being an image of God makes me appreciate the symbolic nature of things—life as a symbol guiding me through and around obstacles. This world is too good to be called corrupt, I explained. Good doesn't mean without suffering. Good doesn't mean without tears or mistakes. What it means is what we have. Nothing more and nothing less. It is very good indeed. Just look at Niagara Falls.

All my would-be converters could focus on was the sin of Adam and Eve and our own forsaken state. Well, if they wanted to argue scripture, I could handle that. Back and forth we went about the Fall before the Falls—they denouncing Adam and Eve for accepting the fruit, I affirming that choice because of the curiosity that has frequently put me in bit of a bind; they blaming God's wrath on Satan's influence now tainting His once-perfect creation, I acknowledging the anger but finding its cause—not in some serpent—but rather in humanity's inability to accept personal responsibility; they citing countless examples of God's continued wrath, I reminding how the Creator clothed Adam and Eve with a tender hand, despite His disappointments, as a father would his children.

During this rather rambunctious discussion shouted over the booming water, I wondered if these two fishers of men actually thought you could convert someone through argument alone. Didn't they realize that reason has little to do with faith?

I simply can't reason myself to Jesus anymore than I can think myself across America. No one can. We just have to go and live and see. What happens will move us as it does. Thus, I left these two teenagers pointed toward Palmyra to duel with the waiting Mormons, while my wheels spun me west, away from all Falls.

Love,
David

DAY 62

....

ASTRONAUT FUEL

July 15
Lackawanna Post Office
Lackawanna, New York

Dear Mary,

Breakfast was hard to come by this morning. Nothing seemed open except a hotdog stand, and because a heavy dose of nitrates is not recommended for consumption at 7:15 in the morning, I passed on the boiled frankfurters despite my growing hunger. I couldn't even find a McDonalds, the default breakfast choice of the desperate.

Then I saw the small battered chalkboard reading:

All-U-Can-Eat Breakfast Buffet...$3.67.

Now that's what I'm talking about! Fortune, she's a-smilin'!

When I parked my bike, I realized that Fortune wasn't smiling as much as she was laughing. The buffet, wedged between a dilapidated thrift shop and seedy-looking strip club, was called Shanghai Palace. I'm sure people from China eat in the mornings, but I had never heard of a

Chinese restaurant serving breakfast on this continent. Then again, there aren't too many hotdog stands open at 7:00 a.m. either. Given the choice between franks with ketchup or Kung Pao chicken in the morning, I'll take the Chinese food every time. I have always found that a touch of MSG as the sun rises really gets the heart pumping.

I didn't know quite what to expect when I pushed through the door and was seated in the middle of the empty room, a red dragon twisting below the protective glass covering the tablecloth.

"You want buffet? Yes? Buffet very good. You like buffet. Very good. Promise. And orange juice, too? It just made. It very very good. Yes. Juice and buffet. You like."

I grabbed a plate and piled it high with corned beef hash that appeared to come from a can, a few dumpling-looking things stuffed with some sort of mystery filling, three plump Jimmy Dean sausages, a spoonful of beef with broccoli, a dab of white rice, and a mountain of eggs smelling strongly of chili oil.

"You like? Yes? Here's juice. Very very good. You like."

Fluorescent orange liquid filled the chipped pilsner glass placed beside my plate.

"Try it. You like. It very good."

Without touching the glass for fear of spilling juice all over my beef with broccoli, I leaned over and noisily slurped.

Yes! Of all the unlikely places to have discovered the favored beverage of astronauts. Tang…oh glorious Tang!

I gulped the juice down in four swallows. Another glass took its place. And another and another and another.

I guess I hadn't been drinking enough because, before I knew it, my $3.67 buffet bill climbed to $13.67. At two bucks per half liter glass, I drank more Tang than I had my entire life. I'm confident that my blood is still orange.

And so, with a Tang-flooded gut sloshing as I rode, I was finally prepared to cross the Peace Bridge back into the States. I would be respectful and courteous and answer all of the Man's questions with a smile, but under no circumstances would I mention my knife. Approaching the long line of cars gurgling in wait, I noticed a sign instructing cyclists:

This way ↪

I followed the instruction dutifully.

Then that way ⤵

I turned.

Then back around this way ↺

Blazoned across red brick and blue glass was a sign stating:

UNITED STATES IMMIGRATION OFFICE

Oh no. Not again.

I confirmed that my knife was still hidden in a dirty sock at the bottom of my right pannier and stepped into the building. The sheer volume of voices curled the hairs on my arms. I took one look around the room—seeing what had to be the same two Kenyans from Canada on the brink of tears, the same angry Germans spitting phlegm, the same Vietnamese family now needing diapers more than ever—and immediately turned and departed.

That's right. I left. And snuck across the border.

Which I suppose makes me a legal illegal alien or something.

I've been on the run since, dodging the Man and his many operatives. It's rather exhausting on such a hot day. Thankfully, along with my hearty breakfast, I drank those five glasses of Tang. Rocket fuel, baby, and this astronaut's ready to fly!

Love,
David

DAY 64

....

SHADOWS ACROSS THE SKY

July 17
Geneva State Park
Geneva-on-the-Lake, Ohio

Dear Mary,

Mostly flat. Mostly straight. Mostly brain-fryin' hot.

That's what riding has been like for the past few days, and today was no different. Little breeze, little shade, buckets of sweat. During the afternoons, it has been so hazy that the air seems filled with mist—a mist that neither cools nor relieves but rather burns and chokes and suffocates.

I keep telling myself that the heat will soon break—that the smudge on the horizon is an approaching storm—but so far, my hopes remain unfulfilled, and the distant blotch has been nothing more than a hallucination. Hallucinating has become my favorite activity these last couple of days. It seems that the only things keeping me sane are my noon naps beneath the shaded umbrella of picnic tables, frequent and large scoops of cantaloupe ice cream, and the letters from you I collected in Lackawanna. The echo of your words as I ride comfort a lonely brain frazzled by heat. And that is good. Otherwise, there would be many more moments of darkness as I ride…

The cloudless morning had taunted me to the point of shouting, and I realized I was finally losing it when a black ray, laser-like, sliced across the sky. This absence of blue in an otherwise perfect sky puzzled me. Was it the underside of a rainbow? Or could it be a tractor beam shot from a UFO? Naturally, I prepared myself to be sucked into the underbelly of a spaceship—at least until I saw the silvery glint of a fighter jet and realized that the beam was but its own shadow cutting across the sky.

That shadow got me to thinking—not about cool relief—but about Oma.

The blue heavens seemed to be my cross-country ride in all its potential…and that shadow, the accident. It cut across my ride just as the line of darkness split the sky overhead. As I move westward like the plane above, the shadow shifts, sometimes lengthening other times shrinking, controlled by angles and the sun. But the plane cannot outpace its shade any more than I can run from loss. So long as there is sun in the sky, there is Oma and memory.

Your written words, colored with troubles and grief, remind me that all is not blue and bright as the sky. For you, perhaps the heavens are death and the shadow a fleeting glimpse of escape, which narrows as the sun works across the sky until there is only night...and loneliness.

You feel alone, I know, and my letters from the road probably don't diminish the emptiness. I can't imagine the magnitude of what you feel. Being on a bike in the heat is my distraction; you have none, and I can only offer my scribbled secondhand stories. To me, every inch farther west is an inch closer to you.

Yet I understand how it seems to you—that every day carries death that much closer—that there's no reason, no purpose, no goal. It has all been lost in the mad chaos of life.

The more I think about it perhaps the sky is just sky, shadow is simply shadow, and all this talk of symbols and images to get at the truth is as fruitless as drinking pond water at midnight in an effort to taste the stars. My pretty pictures cannot conceal the truth. Life is pain, and it's by that suffering we live.

Despite your broken ribs, I just wish we could laugh—together—right now. Such tonic would surely grant a momentary respite from the pain and the loneliness and the heat, cooling as shadows should.

Love,
David

David Haber

DAY 65

....

HEY BABY, WHAT'S YOUR SIGN?

July 18
Camp Wahoo Camping Grounds
Avon Lake, Ohio

DEAR MARY,
　　AFTER RIDING SO MANY MILES, my balance has improved enough that I can completely stop for short periods without having to unclip from my pedals. I wobble about but don't fall. I may not be the most graceful sight around, but this trapeze act gives me something to do while waiting for traffic lights to change. So, imagine me practicing my little Red Light Dance at a Cleveland intersection, shifting my weight from pedal to pedal when, as a minivan pulled up, the wolf whistles started.

"Shake those hips, baby! Look at you move!"

With concentration wavering, my feet clicked from the pedals to rest on the asphalt. I turned and was raked across the coals of a teenager's heavily eye-shadowed blue eyes. "Damn you're fine. Tiff, check him out!"

The driver leaned across her passenger and whistled.

"Look what we have here! Damn, he's hot."

"Maybe we should take him home."
"Do you think he could handle it?"
"Well, let's ask him."

The light turned green. The girl locked my eyes within her own and refused to blink. She licked her lips.

"Hey, Sexy! You need to call us. My number is 216-78…"

A car started honking. The minivan began pulling away. She leaned out the window and shouted.

"Hey baby, what's your sign?"

Dumbfounded, I stood straddling my bike at the light as it flashed back to red.

My own whisper broke the spell. "I'm a Capricorn."

Your sexy lover,
David

David Haber

DAY 68

....

DONA NOBIS PACHEM

July 21
Kil-So-Quath Recreation Area
0.5 mi. S. of U.S. 224, Indiana

D<small>EAR</small> M<small>ARY</small>,
 A<small>S</small> I <small>SNAKE</small> along the Bible Belt's peaceful roads, I sometimes imagine a Benedictine choir rustling the crops with song. Bees keep time. The wind conducts. The monks chant in the fields. And farmers, straw hats pulled low over sweaty brows, rest atop their idling tractors and listen.

 The song is simple—a few words repeated in a choral round—tenors rising high with the corn and bases carrying the melody low with the soy. It's a green song, and this chorale goes something like this:

> *Soybeans corncobs ev'rywhere, everywhere*
> *soybeans, corn-cobs ev-ery-where.*

> *Soybeans, corncobs ev'rywhere*
> *soybeans, corncobs ev'rywhere*

> *Soybeans, corncobs ev'rywhere*
> *soybeans, corncobs ev'rywhere.*

In peace, I, too, am but a monk wandering the fields singing

With love,
David

David Haber

DAY 69

....

THE OCTOPUS

July 22
Fletcher Lake Campground
Fletcher, Indiana

Dear Mary,

I was riding west through the high halls of corn, minding my own business and sweating beyond belief, when the sunlight disappeared. I was completely blinded.

In that instant, my brain drew fantastic pictures…an octopus fastened to my face…gray slimy tentacles tightening…my brain being drained from my nostrils…a loud sucking noise as the surgeons removed the oily beast…

With the slight tickling of fuzzy somethings around my nose and the sudden loss of balance that followed, I realized that I had suffered my very first accident—a head-on collision in fact—with an enormous azure butterfly splayed across the windshield of my sunglasses. As it peeled itself from my face and took flight, I forgot everything.

If only all accidents could be so delicate.

Love,
David

DAY 70

....

WELCOME TO BROOK

July 23
107 West Main Street
Brook, Indiana

Dear Mary,

By noon, my thermometer read 118 degrees. I know it wasn't quite that hot. It couldn't have been. Surely the lack of shade and constant pounding that the mercury withstood contributed to such a ludicrous reading. To my crisped skin, however, there isn't much difference between 118 and 98 degrees. How much more of this heat I will be able to endure I can't say with any certainty, but it's definitely becoming a problem.

For almost a week, I have embraced mornings like never before; yet still, the heat burns the oxygen from my lungs. Lately, I have been soaking a bandana and tying it around my neck. I only exist to feel the slow drip of lukewarm water along the canal of my spine. In such moments, I find the drive to continue west. Barely.

Why am I doing this? I have ridden more than two thousand miles. Isn't that enough? What am I trying to prove? Why am I still cycling farther and farther from you when all I really want is to cool my skin against yours?

But then I'll ride into a town like Brook...and feel the quest of Don Quixote, the voyage of Odysseus, the sheer joy of wandering as my belly swirls with adventure and its love for it. This feeling makes me jitter as if I had just guzzled a pot of coffee. I am captured by the same feelings when the sun melts the mist from the soybean fields in the early morning. That same emotion tickles goose bumps along my arms while listening to Beethoven's *Ninth Symphony* or lines read from Shakespeare. It even fills my pen as I prepare to write you everyday. Such is the feeling of life.

It amazes me how this emotion bursts inside to grow and burn at the oddest moments, particularly when all life appears charred and blasted upon that cherished landscape hidden deep. A thirsty man—dying on a desert of asphalt, seared and blistered by the cumulative effect of relentless heat—is how I entered Brook.

A dented and rusting green pickup didn't even register until it swerved wildly to avoid me. Two teenagers riding in the back, legs dangling dangerously close to the road from the lowered tailgate, shouted incomprehensible curses in my general direction. I climbed from my heat-induced stupor long enough to look for the public park where my map suggested I camp. When I passed the park, I realized that my plans needed amending. Broken bottles reflected the late afternoon sun. Beer cans and condoms signaled the presence of an idle youth. Graffiti swirled a story of teen angst across the weather-beaten boards of the park's gazebo.

Welcome to Brook.

I checked my map to see where the next closest town was—far too many miles in this heat. What I needed was some water and pizza. Then a plan would come.

The pizza joint turned out to be the local teen hangout, which only increased my desire to flee Brook in all possible haste. All I had wanted was silence enough to enjoy a slice, but the constant prattle turned the pizza to tar in my mouth. I stood up to leave, heading toward the park to see if I could find a clear spot to roll out my sleeping bag for the night.

"Cool shoes you got there, dude. They for tap dancing or something?"

A pimply faced kid pointed toward my feet and smirked. His friends huddled around a pinball machine and elbowed each other, clearly envious at the daring it took to actually speak to such a Mysterious Stranger.

I did a little dance, slapping the metal cleats on the bottom of my shoes hard against the linoleum.

"No. They're for bike riding. They hurt like heck though."

"Then that was you we passed riding into town?" Called a voice from among the huddle.

"I guess s—"

"Hey, are you riding around the world?" Interrupted Pimples.

"How's he going to do that you idiot?" The same voice called from the group. "There's like five oceans in the way."

"I was just wondering is all."

"Actually I may do that another trip. Right now, I'm just pedaling to San Francisco."

"Told you so, idiot."

"Well, San Francisco is across the world to me." Pimples turned toward his friends. "And it is for you, too, Tom. You haven't even been to Chicago. If you ask me, I think your mom is afraid of leaving her beloved hogs! That's probably why your dad ran off with old widow Humphrey." There were a chorus of gasps and giggles as the huddle moved away from Tom and closer to Pimples. Pimples turned back toward me and shrugged his shoulders.

"So where are you headed tonight?"

"I was actually thinking of camping in the park across the way."

I might have imagined it, but everyone's glance was unified for a brief moment toward Tom.

"You don't want to do that. There's a lot of vandalism 'round here. Someone's liable to spray-paint your tent. You should try Watseka. They got a nice motel."

"That's a bit far. I'll just have to risk the park, I guess."

"Well, go to the Marathon Station down the road," suggested Pimples. "Let them know. They'll watch out for you."

The next fifteen minutes were the most surreal of my trip. When I explained to the gas station cashier that I was planning on camping in the park, phones were dialed, people were called, and soon, I was surrounded by the Elder Council of Brook. Amid a cloud of Marlboro smoke rumbling with a thunder of wet coughs from toothless mouths, this group debated the flaws of my Grand Park Plan with a vehemence I have seldom witnessed.

"Can't be done, I say. That last feller who biked through lost all his money when he stayed at the park—"

"I say he was robbed. Damned teenagers!" A few silver heads bobbed in agreement.

"Robbed my arse! He just ran out of money. I lent him five hundred bucks from my own pocket. He was such a nice boy…a few months later he even sent me a check—with interest!"

Voices were raised as the past was shaped and re-shaped in a tug-a-war between the cynics and the Pollyannas. I tried interrupting this growing argument, explaining that the park seemed fine enough for me, that no one would even notice me, that they needn't worry because I didn't travel with much cash. I'd be fine.

Just as I thought progress was being made, another horror story riled the group with a shocking tale of someone's wandering cousin—no brother—no mother!—who had been mugged—no beaten—no killed!—in a town very similar to Brook…was in fact even rumored to be Brook.

This was hopeless.

"Calm down, everybody," said a man, chewing on the stub of a cigar. "What happened or didn't happen five years ago doesn't help us with this young gentlemen's dilemma today. Brook shouldn't be remembered as the place where the young are left to fend for themselves. We aren't a big city. We're Brook."

"George is right. I guess that's why he's mayor."

"No it ain't. He's mayor 'cause he owns the only gas station in town."

"Oh, shut up, Wendel." A woman mumbled.

"Anyway," George continued. "Back to the problem at hand. It seems to me this chap needs a place to stay."

There was a collective nod.

"And I think we can all agree that the park is no place for a guest of Brook. Stories notwithstanding, Carol."

There was a mummer of agreement.

"So, I think that this young bicyclist—what's your name again?"

"David."

"I think young David here should follow me on that bike of his to Frank Witherspoon's place—"

"That's perfect, George."

George smiled. "See, David, Frank is a bicycle enthusiast. He has about seven bikes. And since '94 when he hurt his back, he's been riding around town on one of those sit-down contraptions. What are they called again? Recombinants or something, I think."

"Do you mean a recumbent? That's really cool."

"Yeah, well if you follow me in my Suburban, I'll take you there. Frank may even let you ride it. I'm sure he'd love to meet you, and if between the two of us we can't think of somewhere for you to stay, then I guess you can always camp out at my farm."

Following George's beat up truck through town made me feel as if I was riding, not on a bike, but rather on a float—the main attraction of some little-known holiday parade. Although there were no marching bands or beauty queens or massed throngs of watching children, this parade of two did indeed have a mayor waving me onward and the broken beat of country music blaring from the Suburban's AM radio.

Brook is not a large town, but it seemed George greatly desired to show me every house, every tree, every blade of grass that made up the town he called home. I didn't have a clue where he was going, but we circled and then circled back again until my legs began to tire; we crossed and re-crossed until my shoulders began to ache; we traveled up and then back down the streets until the pizza began to cramp my sides with knots. He finally stopped in front a small house not two blocks from the gas station.

"Hey! Anybody home? I've got someone you might like to meet. Frank? Marge? Anybody?"

"Marge is looking in on her sister," called a woman from behind a low, white-washed fence across the road. "She won't be back 'til late. And Frank got called into the factory. Something about some rush order or some such thing."

The mayor and I turned as the woman approached.

"Hi, Susan. This is David, and he's riding his bike across the country—"

"For real?"

I nodded.

"That's pretty great."

"—And I brought him here figuring Frank would like to meet him, and we—"

"That makes sense." She turned to me. "Frank loves meeting cyclists. He will be quite upset that he missed you. So where are you staying for the night?"

"Well, actually—" I started.

"See, Susan, that's why I brought him over to Frank's. You know how he loves talkin' shop, and I figured he might like to chat all night."

"Jiminy crickets! Frank's going to be mad."

"I guess I'll just camp out at the park, George. There's no sense—"

"Oh, no you can't do that," Susan interrupted. "There's tornado warnings all across the state, and besides, we have an extra apartment above our shop on Main Street. You know, George, next to that hippie lady we're renting to. It's empty except for a washing machine, an old air conditioner, and a bed, but you're free to use it."

"A bed? I haven't slept in a bed in I don't know how long."

"Well, then it's settled. Come on over. I hope you like chicken. We got a few extra pieces on the grill, and there's corn and potatoes, of course."

I hesitated for a moment. "Are you sure?"

"Don't be silly. Come on. My kids will love to meet you. Maybe we'll even be able to convince my husband to play a few tunes on his banjo after dinner. Then I'll take you over to the apartment."

An apartment. Air conditioning. A bed.

Can you believe it?

An actual bed with clean sheets.

Welcome to Brook indeed!

Love,
David

PART X

AN INTERLUDE

Streator, Illinois

DAY 72

....

CURSES

July 25
Carriage Lane Estates
2 mi. S. of Streator, Illinois

C OVER YOUR EARS AND CLOSE YOUR EYES FOR A MINUTE. Motherfuckingpieceofshitbastards!cocksuckingsonbitches!GoddamnfuckersIcan'tbelievethisfuckingshitfuck!fuckfuckshittymother!fuckingshittymotherfuchingtarandsun!andgravelandbike!fuckfuckfuck...
...aaaaaaaaaaahhhhhhhhhhhhhhhhhh...

David Haber

DAY 72, PART II

....

THE HOMEMADE HACKSAW

> *July 25*
> *Carriage Lane Estates*
> *Not one inch farther, Illinois*

Dear Mary,
    In the beginning was fire, and the fire was with the Sun, and the fire was the Sun. This Heat was in the beginning with the Sun. All things were made through Heat, and without Heat was not anything made that was ever made, including hacksaws. To make this hacksaw, there also had to be a flaw in creation; not a major flaw, mind you, just a small little mistake, a miscalculation of a gravel order perhaps.

    To comprehend this error, Mary, you must first understand the nature of tar-and-chip road construction. When a road in these parts is in need of resurfacing, a layer of hot tar is sprayed and then completely covered with gravel, sometimes called chip. Eventually the tar hardens, holding the gravel in place. When the proper amount of chip is spread, this is an effective way for creating a road surface that will neither wash away with every storm nor bankrupt the coffers of an agricultural community's Department of Transportation.

When I turned onto CR 900E and heard that familiar pop and ping of tar and chip—breaking a very wonderful musing on the mathematical pattern of swaying corn—I paid little attention and instead tried to reconstruct the formula I had been so close to realizing. I imagined making a speech before the International Congress of Mathematicians as I accepted the Fields Medal for the Haberian Corn Formulation, which miraculously proved Fermat's Last Theorem. My mind was far from the road.

About a mile later, I began to notice a substantial layer of gravel collecting on my front wheel. Reaching down to flick away the offending particles blackened my fingers with tar.

I stopped and hopped off my bike.

My shoes stuck to the road.

With no breeze created by forward progress, sweat sprang from my skin and dripped down my nose. Rooted in place, I bent to examine my tires. The front tire was easy enough to clean with my Swiss Army knife. The gravel sticking to the rear wheel, however, had been shaped by the fender into a solid sheet of what looked like toffee and nuts encasing the tread. Almost an inch thick, the coating refused to peel away.

I shuffled around for a better angle, wielding my knife and frame pump like a hammer and chisel. I stumbled to my knees. The tar crept higher up my body. For fifteen minutes, I worked on that tire, peeling, chipping, and sweating. Finally the rubber was revealed. Mostly.

My brain, beating against my skull, passed the point of all coherent thought. Otherwise, I would have done the intelligent thing and backtracked. For the life of me, though, I couldn't remember how far back I would actually have to track. The temperature continued to rise; my only concern was movement…any movement…forward.

Feet sucking to the road with each step, I guided my bike to the browning grass next to the shoulder—figuring that my tires would remain free of gunk. After failing to clip into the pedals because of a thick layer of now-hardening tar on the bottom of my shoes, I wobbled forward ten feet and soon realized what you probably have surmised already: when hot tar coats your tires, the best idea is to avoid debris that can be collected easily, like twigs, grass, and feathers—all things found in abundance beside the road.

Soon, my bike's rubber tires transformed into two spinning bird's nests. A rather large stick wedged itself between tire and fork. I fell to the coarse grass. Bits of straw clung to my neck and arms. I had no other alternative but to return to the melting highway of tar and chip.

Again I chiseled at my tires.

Again my legs were coated.

Again sweat mixed with the La Brea pit that had become my body.

I thought about waiting for a car to pass so that I could finagle a ride to blacktop. The unbearable heat and that a vehicle hadn't passed in over an hour soon convinced me otherwise. I needed the breeze of forward movement or surely I would fry.

Three more times I stopped in that half-mile journey to solid asphalt. Three more times I chipped my wheels clean. Three more times the still air pelted me with heat.

When I hit the smooth surface of SR 17, my bike groaned and creaked and lurched. I felt like a passenger in a car with a stiff clutch driven by a ten-year-old. Where tar didn't completely cover the green paint of my bike, it speckled and dotted the frame as if dripped from Jackson Pollack. As the wheels strained forward, metal whined. It appeared I would have to buy some touch-up paint.

Two hours later, after I had reached the campground and finished prying the majority of tar from both wheels and myself, I spit out my last letter in utter frustration...

...Realizing that this trip is over.

I am such a colossal idiot. Who else but me could make a hacksaw of tar and chip and slice a quarter of the way through my rear chainstay? The crevice is four-millimeters wide, and although it doesn't appear to flex with pressure, I don't really trust it carrying sixty pounds of crap during a six-thousand-foot descent from the Rockies. My frame is shot. Old Sal has torn her Achilles tendon and needs to be put down.

Even though I plan to go to a bike shop tomorrow for a second opinion, I know what they'll say. I don't need to be a frame builder to understand that a conspiracy between two weeks of heat, a melting road stolen from a Dali canvas, and my own sun-raddled brain have left me stranded in Streator, Illinois.

I never imagined an end like this. Since the accident, I always thought we would meet in San Francisco and ride off in the sunset. But how can I ride without a bike? And more importantly, how can I continue without *my* bike? She is far more than a thing I own, more than just stuff. She has carried me some 2,750 miles. She has listened stoically as I bitch about the heat, rant about the rain, and pine daily for you. Without resentment, she has been passed by unencumbered racers even as I add more to her already heavy load. She has become more than Don Quixote's Rozinante. She has been transformed into his loyal companion, Sancho Panza, and now Sancho is dead.

    I am past regret and anger, beyond sorrow and frustration. There's just this hole cut by my homemade hacksaw.

David

PART XI

....

REPAIRS AND ROADBLOCKS

From Streator, Illinois,
to Bemidji, Minnesota

DAY 73

....

MRS. FRANKENSTEIN

July 26
Super 8 Motel
Streator, Illinois

Dear Mary,

She's alive! She's alive!

For the past two days, in the cluttered laboratory of Bellap Bicycles, I played Igor to the shop owner's Dr. Frankenstein. Initially, the prognosis was poor. Grant, the owner and hero of this story, recognized the smudged tar still clinging to my various body parts and knew instantly we had a situation.

"Rough day, eh?" Grant peered at my once blue, now black, gloves as I pulled them from my hands. His eyes then darted to my tar-encased shoes, dashed to the stains crusting my shirt, and then settled on my bike. He grunted and pursed his lips.

"You can say that."

"I see you've been introduced to the Illinois highway system." He crossed his arms and spat. "We send letters over there to the capital about the roads, but the politicians don't seem to care about bike riders." His voice dropped, resigned to the worst. "What seems to be the problem today?"

"Well, I somehow managed to cut through my frame." I pointed to my chainstay. Grant squatted and studied the rear triangle of my bike.

"Now, what do we—" He interrupted himself with a whistle. He fingered the gash and pursed his lips "This is a first. You should sue the state of Illinois."

"Maybe. It won't do me much good now, though. So, I take it I shouldn't continue riding?"

Grant stood, wiping his hands on his knees. He gazed down the street. "It certainly doesn't look good." Grant turned back to me and took a deep breath. "Me? I wouldn't ride that bike anymore. But I can't really tell you what to do. I mean, it may not bust on you. Then again, it may. If you weren't carrying so much weight, I'm sure it'd be fine. With all that equipment, though…there's a all kinds of forces pulling this way and that when you ride. Who knows what might happen?"

I frowned.

"If the bike had been made of steel, I could easily fix it. We could just weld on a new chainstay. Take maybe a day or so. The paint wouldn't match, but it'd be easy." He pulled his fingers through his hair. "The problem is that your bike's made of aluminum. Steel's simple to work with…aluminum is a whole other issue. Although I do have a buddy who could do it…"

Even before he finished speaking, Grant's head was shaking.

"No that wouldn't work. It would void the frame's warranty. And God forbid if the blasted thing broke. No, that wouldn't do at all."

"Well, could I make a claim on the warranty? Maybe, the manufacturer would send me a new bike."

Grant laughed.

"I doubt it. Usually warranties are specifically for manufacturing defects, not moronic highway workers. Back in the day, aluminum frames failed all the time. But now it almost never happens. I suppose, it wouldn't hurt to check it out though. Come on inside."

We brought the bike in and hung it from a stand.

"Let's see now." Grant circled my crippled bike. He tapped his nose and hummed *Amazing Grace*. "Check this out." Spinning the wheel, he pointed at the crevice. "See how your wheel's only cut one side? The right chainstay isn't damaged at all. Just a few scratches in the paint. Let's take a look at that rim." He pulled the rear wheel from the dropouts, removed the tire, grabbed a curved something or another, and began fiddling with it. "You haven't had your tire re-dished since you bought the bike have you?"

"What do you mean?"

"This tool determines if the dish of your wheel is correct, meaning that the rim is centered between the flanges on the hub. See how it rubs on one side of the rim and when I flip it to the other side there is a good two-millimeter gap? Well, because your wheel still seems relatively true, that means your rim has been incorrectly dished—more than likely from the factory—which explains *why* there is that gash on one side of your frame and which also means we should probably give a call to manufacturer."

Woo-hoo! My heart sung. Back in business.

Ten minutes turned to twenty as a switchboard operator maneuvered Grant from sales rep to technician and then back again to customer service. Moments of quick conversation were punctuated by bored looks while Grant attempted to ignore the overly soothing versions of pop classics that surely assaulted him.

Meanwhile, I wandered about the shop, not quite pacing, trying to distract my rising excitement by exploring the chaos of the store. Old parts lay scattered about the workbenches. Homemade frames hung from the walls. An ancient Firestone with whitewall tires, chrome detailing, and a miniature light generator stood proudly in the display window. Various BMX and skateboarding accessories were piled behind a counter stacked high with copies of last year's *Velo News*.

"They want to talk to you."

I scurried around a box of spare parts and grabbed the phone.

"Mr. Haber? We understand you have a situation."

"Yes. My frame is busted, and I hoped you might have some ideas how to fix it."

"Actually, there may be some issues."

"Issues? My wheel came from the manufacturer misdished or whatever, which caused this huge gash to be cut in my chainstay."

"Yes, the gentlemen I spoke to earlier, Gus I believe, explained—"

"Grant. His name is Grant."

"Either way though, Grant is not one of our authorized dealers, and our own mechanics need to verify the damage before anything can be—"

"You can't take his word for it?"

"Mr. Haber, our dealers go through exhaustive training and are rigorously tested to insure the highest quality product for customers."

"So what do you suggest?"

"That you go to your local dealer, preferably where you purchased the bike, and then—"

"Hold on a minute. I don't think you fully appreciate my circumstances. See, I'm riding across America—from Annapolis to San Francisco—and my local dealer is about three thousand miles away. I don't have a clue where the closest dealer is, and I'm pretty sure you are not seriously suggesting I ride back to Maryland to have my bike examined."

"Of course not, Mr. Haber. In fact, you should not be riding that bike at all. A bicycle damaged like you say has an incredible risk of failure. All I mean to suggest is that you go to an authorized dealer."

"But I don't know where one is."

"What's your zip code?"

"I'm not really sure. Hold on." I looked to Grant ready to spit acid. "What's the zip around here?"

"61364. Not going well?"

I shook my head and told the woman the number.

"It looks like the closest one is about forty miles away in a town called Washington. A few miles east of Peoria."

"Forty miles! How am I supposed to get there if I can't ride my bike? I don't even know where Peoria is."

"Do you have any family in the area? Maybe Gus could give you ride?"

"I can't ask him that. Even on a slow day I couldn't—his name is Grant, by the way, not Gus."

"Maybe you could take a bus. Or rent a car."

"Listen. I'm in Streator, Illinois, not New York City or Chicago. I can't just walk a couple of blocks and flag down a limo with a bike rack. Jesus."

"Well, there is another option."

"Which is?"

"You could have the bike shop send your frame directly to us, and we could determine the validity of any claim against the warranty."

"That's a possibility, I guess. If I overnight the frame, how long would it take? Two or three days?"

"If it's determined that the damage is covered, it should take six to eight weeks…if the frame is in stock."

"Are you nuts? Where am I going to stay during that time? And what happens when you determine that this whole situation was caused by my own stupidity, which I am sure you will?"

"In that case, you will have to purchase a new frame. Of course, we would be happy to move your existing parts to the new frame free of charge. As a courtesy, for being such a good customer."

"Of course you will...It would probably be cheaper to buy a new bike, and I wouldn't have to deal with all this mess."

"That's your prerogative, of course, Mr. Haber. We would be happy to assist you in anyway possible—"

"Yeah, if I can get the forty odd miles to your authorized dealer, I'm sure you'd be willing to take my money just like the next guy."

"Just remember that you don't have to decide today. It's a lifetime guarantee after all. For as long as you're the original owner of the frame, the manufacturer will cover all defects. So you can always ship the bike home and, after your trip is over, show the frame and wheel to an authorized dealer. Please feel free to contact us again if you have any more questions or concerns. My name is Lori. You have a real nice day now."

I screamed and began pacing.

To be honest, I didn't really expect a new frame free of charge because no matter how much the rear wheel was or was not dished correctly, I must be held accountable for my own part in creating the hacksaw that destroyed my frame and shortened my ride. I should have stopped when I first noticed the gravel collecting. I should have waited for a car to pass. I should not have forced the bike onward.

Yet the manufacturer could have helped in some way. A little understanding. Some realistic suggestions. Perhaps, even a guarantee for expedited service if I had shipped my bike to their technical gurus. I could have waited a week. God knows I need the rest. They could have offered to fix the frame. They could have offered me a deal on a new frame. They could have…

But they didn't. I'm loyal to a fault and would have praised the virtues of their company across the country. There's no more powerful advertising than personal endorsement, and what could be more endearing than the testimonial of a once-stranded cross-country adventurer who had been helped from a bind by a company that understood the fear of being marooned far from home? A corporation can spend millions on commercials, but if the customer service sucks, word will travel; even with the slickest product, a business cannot survive without happy customers. Companies shouldn't forget the principles on which they were founded. All companies were at one time small and because of that smallness attentive to their customers. Such a willingness to help each other is why we are human and not aardvark. A little help was all I needed.

"I've got an idea. It may not work, but hey, it's worth a shot, right?"

"Sure. What do you have in mind?"

"Well, when I was on hold, I got to thinking about your predicament." He again pulled his hands through his hair. His brow creased, and he began speaking in almost whispers. "Now, I don't want to get your hopes up because it probably won't work, but I may have a spare frame."

"Really?"

"Now don't get all excited." He pushed his hands against an invisible wall and took a deep breath. "I've got a small shop—business in Streator is difficult—so I've tailored the shop to kids and my interest in old bikes."

"Yeah, I saw the Firestone in the window. Pretty sweet."

"Thanks. But Pee Wee Herman you're not. You can't take that on your Big Adventure. You certainly can't ride across the country on a BMX, and those cheap mountain bikes wouldn't last the trip. But I do have a road frame I was planning on building for myself—you seem about my height."

"I couldn't take your—"

"Don't be silly. The frame has been sitting there for a year and half. Why shouldn't I sell it to you? It's just collecting dust."

"Are you sure about this? You bought it for yourself."

"Look, this may not even work. It's a racing frame, so the geometry is different. It's made of steel instead of aluminum and not designed for touring, so your bottom bracket may not make the switch. We'll also have to improvise something for your racks...the brakes will definitely be a problem...I say we give it a whirl. Come take a look."

He guided me to the back of the store where a seafoam green frame hung on the wall—a bit dusty but otherwise flawless.

"See how the wheel base is shorter than that tank you've been riding? Hopefully it will give your heels enough clearance with your bags loaded on the back. It's also a twenty-one-inch rather than a nineteen, but your seat post was raised quite high on the other bike, which seemed a tad small for you anyway. I think it will be perfect."

"Grant, it looks great. But I can't take your frame. It's yours. You must have plans for it. Besides, I don't think I could afford a new frame."

"Nonsense. It's not new anyway. It's been hanging up there for a long time. You have a far greater need than I ever could have." He reached up and took it from the wall. "I would be honored if you used it. And don't worry about the price. I'll give you a good deal. How's eighty bucks sound?"

I gaped. "Are you serious? That frame is worth ten times that."

"Nah. Not really. Besides, it may not work. We'll just have to move all your parts over to this puppy and see if she'll go."

Grant allowed me free reign in his shop. Because the store was unusually busy, he could only help me in his spare moments, but every so often he peeked in on me, making sure I didn't screw things up terribly. Not knowing exactly what I was doing, it took the morning and much of the afternoon to properly remove and clean the tar-coated parts for the big switch.

I learned how to pull cranks, install a headset, and properly set my rear derailleur. The chain had to be shortened. The seat post designed for the wide-tubed aluminum frame needed to be replaced, and buried in a pile of old banana seats was a post that miraculously fit the narrow-diameter steel tubing with only a thin shim. There were no braze-ons to attach the racks properly because the new frame had been designed for racing, but with a little ingenuity and a few U-clips, we found a way. Lady Fortune watched, matching my own grin the whole afternoon…

…Until the brakes were installed.

"We're going to have a slight problem with these."

"Didn't we know we would, though? You said that the V-brakes on my old frame couldn't be used. Isn't there anything lying around in the scrap bins?"

"Well, that's the problem. I only have standard-reach calipers. This frame is going to need long-reach brakes to work properly."

"What do you mean?"

"Look at the arms there."

With a grease-stained finger, Grant pointed to where the rim and brake met—or rather were supposed to meet. The pads fell a few millimeters short, aligning to cut into the tire instead of the rims every time the arms squeezed.

"If you try taking that set up through the Rockies, this frame will end up twisted around your dead body, and your family will have to blow fifteen grand on a coffin big enough for both you and your bike."

"Is there anything we can do? Maybe we could put different brake pads on. Like from the V-brakes? They're narrower so they may not hit the tires."

"You can do that temporarily, but I still wouldn't trust it. This bike's hauling quite a bit a weight. You want to be able to stop when you need to."

"What if we put narrower tires on also? My old tires look way too fat for the frame anyway. Would that give us the room?"

"I don't think so. Still, I think you're right. You definitely should replace the tires with a narrower tread. If your wheels lose their trueness, they'll be rubbing against the frame. And let's not even consider what would happen if you ran across another fine Illinois tar-and-chip highway."

"Do you have any cheap tires that would work?"

Grant sent me scurrying around to find something suitable in the many piles of mismatched tires scattered around the shop. I returned with one slick and one knobby.

"Those should do until you make it to a bigger shop. I don't have too many 700-cc tires around—mostly I stock twenty-six-inchers. Mountain bikes are what sell around these parts…"

"With the roads around here, I understand why. These will work great."

After switching the tires, the front brakes at least became serviceable, although the pads in the rear still hit more tire than rim.

"Now, back to these brakes…What I think I'll do is order you a pair of dual-pull, long-reach brakes and have them shipped overnight. They run about forty-five bucks at my cost. Don't worry about the shipping charges. I'll take care of it. Consider it a bon voyage gift."

"You don't really have to—"

"The package should get here around ten o'clock tomorrow. Just come in then, and I'll re-dish your wheel. Those Jerry-rigged brakes should make it to a motel for the night. Just leave your tent and other equipment here so you don't have to worry about the added weight. Unfortunately, I'm going camping with my kids for the week and can't stay much past one or they'll kill me."

"I can't tell you how much—"

"One other thing, just to let you know, re-dishing the wheel will get rid of all the evidence for any fight you pick with the manufacturer. You really ought to do it, though. Steel is easy to repair, of course, but there is no sense risking this mess again."

"Definitely. Grant, this is beyond—"

"Don't worry about it. Just send us a postcard. You are doing something important. Just don't stop. Finish whatever it is you've started. It may not take you to where you think you are going, but I am pretty sure Streator isn't your final destination. Just keep riding. And remember us."

In the motel room, my new bike rests propped against the bed. Mrs. Frankenstein captivates me. She holds within her metal bones both the excitement of tomorrow and the adventures of yesterday. Sal has been reincarnated. My leather saddle is ready. The journey continues, and I am

Overwhelmed with memories,
David

David Haber

DAY 75

SOMETHING OLD, SOMETHING NEW

July 28
Midland Varna Grade School
Varna, Illinois

DEAR MARY,
 I AM BRIMMING and had to stop momentarily. A hum, adding a tenor to the bass of the wind, has been running with my blood since I hopped on the sea-tinted skeleton of my new frame this morning. She dances, Mary. She moves with your heart, free and giving and joyous. Fred Astaire I'm not, but despite my awkward lead, she still spins like Ginger Rogers as we dance cheek to cheek across America.

I haven't felt this light and excited for months. The road had been wearing me down, and I didn't even notice—so insidious it was. With the scales of exhaustion yanked from my eyes by Ginger's light touch, this journey is reborn. I'm happy. I'm excited. I am ready to dance.

The rest of America waits to be asked.

Even as storm clouds gather in the distance threatening with rain, I know I will cross the grand Mississippi in but a few days, spinning my new partner with that old excitement, my helmet, gel-filled gloves, and padded shorts feeling more like a top hat, white tie, and tails.

Isn't this a lovely day to be caught in the rain?

Love,
David

David Haber

DAY 79

....

RAGBRAI AND THE STONER

August 1
Twin Bridges Park
5 mi. S. of Colesburg, Iowa

Dear Mary,

 After a cold can of soda had been placed beside me on the picnic table, a tiny glass pipe was waved in front of my face…and so ended my first attempt to write you a letter with words fueled by Sam Cooke crackling over my pocket radio.

 "Here's your pop, man. The name's Lance. Hey, ya wanna a hit? This is some real good puff. Hawaiian, I think—Dude, good tune…*You send me…*"

 With voice raised in a crackling attempt to meet Sam Cooke's sublime heights, Lance twirled his way around the picnic table, dancing with an invisible lover in one hand and a very visible one in the other.

 "It makes me wish I had a radio on my bike." He pointed to an ancient Triumph Bonneville motorcycle parked a few sites over. "Damn, I love that song…"

 Lance had rumbled into the empty campground about an hour earlier, parking far enough away to indicate that he would respect any desire I may have had for solitude yet close enough to welcome me with companionship if I so chose. As I went about setting up my tent and laying out my bed for the night, he tinkered with his bike. After a few metallic bangs swallowed a series of muffled curses, he climbed back atop his motorcycle and called, "Hey there, I'm making a run to the store to get some jerky and pop. You want some?"

I nodded, and with a kick and a cloud, away he went.

That was all the invitation he had needed.

"So you wanna a hit, man?"

Hmmmmmm...let me think for a moment...a case of the late night munchies, with all the jerky long since devoured, and the closest grocery a good five miles away, the only means of transport a burping and rattling motorcycle controlled by the unsteady hand of a mildly toasted pothead or an evening of cold sobriety entertained by the off-key falsetto of this slightly stoned chap.

"I think I'll pass tonight. Thanks for the soda though."

"Suit yourself, man. Your loss." He wrapped his lips around the end of his pipe and inhaled deeply. "You don't mind right? I mean, this is some righteous cheeba, bro. Shame to waste it."

"It's a free enough country."

Lance plopped himself down next to me, cracked leather jacket creaking as he settled in, and held a lighter above the pipe. A long toke followed. THC-rich smoke heated Lance's lungs and lightened his head.

"Sam Cooke. Shame he was shot in '64. Hell of a voice. Hell of a soul." With dilated eyes, he peered mole-like at my paper. "You a writer or something? Writing the great American novel?"

"Nah, just a letter."

"Love letter, eh? There is nothing like seeing familiar handwriting mixed in with bills and coupons. My lady loves it." A long satisfied sigh punctuated the hiss of his lighter. "You in Iowa because of RAGBRAI?" His words slurred together with the smoke.

"What's rag-eyes?"

"RAGBRAI, man. R-A-G-B-R-A-I. Stands for Register's Annual Great Bicycle Ride Across Iowa. It's only the best mass bike ride ever imagined. It's Sturgis for pedalers. They just passed through these parts this morning."

"Never heard of it. I guess I could have crossed their route and not seen the riders."

Lance started giggling.

"Ten thousand dudes in spandex? No way. You really missed out, man. Since that first year in '73, I try to make it down to Iowa in time for the festivities. I like tailing the riders on Bertha over there." He gestured vaguely to his Triumph. "Fun lovin' cats, those bikers. Really know how to party. And my lady, she volunteers giving massages. Sometimes she even gives me one."

"So you've ridden in it?"

"Are you nuts? I haven't been on a pedaling bike since I was twelve. I just like the company. And Iowa is beautiful. I grew up here, don't ya know? And my lady...she has nice hands..." He grinned. "Of course, she doesn't know she's my lady. I figure, I'll tell her I'm the one sending her all those letters one of these days."

"If you say so."

"She suspects it's me, of course. We've known each other for years, but I'm just waiting for the right moment. Ya know how it is. Hey, ya know what's so great about the ride?"

"Beside the massages?"

"Well, nothing beats them. But seriously man, what's so cool is, anybody can do it. You just have to sign up. My fat self could do it if I wanted. I don't, of course. But I could. Just like Clarence Pickard."

"Who's that?"

"You never heard of Mr. Pickard? Everybody's heard of him, especially if you ride a bike. He's what brought me out of Indianola in the first place. Great story, man. Maybe I'll tell it to you."

Lance leaned back and watched the clouds drift in front of the moon. "Beautiful night. Wish my lady was here." He started whistling softly.

"Um. What were you saying about Mr.—"

"Oh, sorry. Just got to thinking about when I first bought Bertha over there. She looks a bit worn now, but back in '73, she was a sight. All shiny and new. I had just turned eighteen and was ready to be out on my own and figured Bertha there was my ticket. Of course, there was a slight problem. See, I was a bit reluctant to—no wait—what do I care? It was a long time ago and you seem to be a nice enough fellow…" He leaned close to my ear. "I was scared, bro. I was real scared. I had been raised on a farm, a couple ten miles outside Indianola. What did I know of the real world?"

Lance leaned back.

"The only thing I knew for sure was that it was a scary place…wars over there in Asia, people killing each other in cities, the Russians sneaking into small towns and stealing kids to become secret agents. Most of it was hogwash, but being only eighteen, how was I to know?

"Like a good kid, I had saved all my money for college, even though I hated school. It was in that summer of '73, a few weeks after I fell in love with my bike Bertha—but was afraid to buy her—that I first learned about Mr. Pickard.

"For days, the stories were all over the *Des Moines Register*. Everybody was rooting for him, too, being from Indianola and all. Shoot, my Great-Aunt Harriet was real good friends with his wife. He was practically kin, so you can understand why I wanted to see the ride.

"See, the first RAGBRAI wasn't nearly the big deal then that it is today. It started as a bet really. These two reporter guys—I forget their names—challenged each other to bike from coast to coast, all the way from the Missouri to the Mississippi. During the trip, they figured they would write columns for the paper talking about Iowa and the small towns they passed through. But a ride across Iowa isn't much of a ride without other folks along for the trip. So, a few weeks before they were to start, they sent out an open invitation in the newspaper to anyone with a bike and a desire to pedal.

"Three hundred people showed up, including one Mr. Clarence Pickard. I remember seeing that first story and thinking how silly the whole thing seemed. No offense, but you gotta admit that it's a bit peculiar to be riding a bike about in the hot summer. That didn't stop these folks, though. And, Mr. Pickard was the best of them all.

"See, he was eighty-three years old, man. EIGHT—THREE. Not thirty. Not fifty. Not even seventy. But eighty-freakin'-three. I don't care what anybody says, that's old, especially if you haven't been riding a bike in years. But they say you never forget. Right?

"Every day there was a new story in the paper about him, and every day he was wearing the same get-up in the pictures, long pants and flannel shirt, high-top sneakers, and this goofy-looking jungle hat. The old codger kept wearing pants—even when it topped a hundred degrees. He might have been the slowest, but he reached Davenport all the way across Iowa alive and well. And that's when I knew."

"Knew what?"

"That I needed to forget about school and get me that Triumph Bonneville. I named her Bertha for my grandmother, God rest her soul. Since '73, my bike hasn't felt another man's hand but my own. She's been just as faithful, too. Nothing is more important than taking care of your horse, whether she's flesh and blood or metal and oil—the only real difference being that you give living horses sugar cubes and the metal variety a squirt of WD-40. But you know that.

"By the winter of that year, I had made my way all the way down to the Gulf of Mexico. The world was a far less scary place than I thought. Sure, people were a bit wary of me with my long hair and beard—this was well before I met my lady, see, and I didn't look nearly as respectable as I do now."

I glanced at the two-day growth scratching across Lance's face, his short but still unkempt hair, his black fingernails.

"If you haven't noticed, see, I'm a pretty friendly sort, and people can tell, too. I've got friends all over the country, and when I finally do marry my lady, we're going to have the wildest wedding ever. It will be the RAGBRAI of weddings, and then we'll ride off together on Bertha. She'll be painted all white and polished bright. My lady and me will be happy and have kids, and they'll even ride around on Bertha someday. Or maybe even in RAGBRAI." He set his pipe down on the table and began walking toward his bike.

"Maybe, it's about time to find my lady and tell her about those letters. Maybe it's time to settle down."

Yes, Mary, maybe it is time. Maybe it is.

Love,
David

DAY 82

....

WITH EYES CLOUDED
BY MAPLE SYRUP

August 4
John A. Latsch State Park
Minneiska, Minnesota

DEAR MARY,

IT'S AMAZING WHAT AN all-you-can-eat French-toast breakfast can do for the weary cyclist's spirit. With the eighteen halves of French toast coated in sticky layers of syrup filling my now rather round belly, I crossed into Minnesota early in the morning and have yet to lose my grin.

Don't get me wrong. I love Iowa. The hills rolled forever, coated in soft golden fur. These mounds were like the sleeping backs of a thousand hibernating bears. As I climbed this pack of bear-like knolls, I felt the excitement of Goldilocks as she snuck into an unknown house. I have never seen land like this. After the monotony of endless corn and soy fields, my eyes ached with Iowa's beauty.

But Minnesota is different. This state of a thousand lakes is refreshing, invigorating, and all those other catchy advertising words used to sell shampoo in commercials. It's like a Key West beach in the deep winter or a hidden swimming hole in the dog days of summer. The land is as vibrant as a forest after a New Hampshire rainstorm. And then there is the Mississippi. The river radiates an ancient power. She is calm, almost sluggish, but instead of a hibernating bear, the Mississippi is a foraging grizzly recently roused from a long winter. She lumbers. She gets distracted. She paws at the earth. Her strength is muted—but incredible—and has seeped into the entire state, nourishing the land.

As I meandered along the river, I could see the Mississippi's bear-spirit in everything. The needled claws of pine trees pawed the sky. Wildflowers nosed through cracked asphalt as bees made honey. Sandy bluffs, eroded by wind and water, tumbled cub-like into the murky Mississippi. Traffic was nonexistent. The world was as it should be.

This day was good.

Minnesota is magnificent.

And, most importantly, I am one state closer to you.

Love,
David

DAY 84, PART I

....

SPIRITS OF SEA AND LAND

August 6
Afton State Park
Afton, Minnesota

Dear Mary,
July 13, 1890. Sunday.

Approximately two hundred people, paying fifty cents a head, frolic and socialize on the decks of the riverboat *Sea Wing* and barge *Jim Grant* as they steam south toward Camp Lakeview for an afternoon of picnicking and military exhibitions performed by the Minnesota National Guard. Captain David Niles Wethern mans the helm with the aide of ten other crew members.

The *Sea Wing* drifts downstream, picking up the bulk of the passengers in Red Wing. After boarding, Randina Olson of that same town and A. O. Anderson of Belmont, North Dakota—hands entwined—discuss their coming marriage on July 16 as they pass Maiden Rock on the left. Mary Leach giggles with a group of girlfriends on deck while flirting with a gang of slightly inebriated young men, one of whom is twenty-six-year-old Martin

O'Shaughnessy whose only fear is water. Nellie Wethern, the wife of the captain, sits in the main cabin trying to restrain the boundless energy of her sons Perley, eight, and Roy, thirteen. At Lake City, the passengers disembark and travel to the fort.

Four days earlier, on July 9, a tornado broke the unbearable heat in Fargo, North Dakota. Nine souls were lost in payment. Two days later, a wandering preacher named Georgas warned the people of Diamond Bluff that the coming journey will be the *Sea Wing's* last. A storm is coming, he said. The End Time is nigh. BEWARE! Georgas preached until about noon on July 13 and then departed, not wanting to witness the coming catastrophe.

At 5:00 p.m., the skies north of Lake City darken. Shortly thereafter, rain suspends the show of the National Guard. Mary Leach and a few friends flee to take cover in an attempt to keep their dresses dry. So lost in the excitement of the storm and being on an adventure, Miss Leach and her companions (some of whom are surely male) neither notice the end of the storm nor hear the call to board sounded by Captain Wethern. As the boat disappears behind the high bluffs, Miss Leach realizes her mistake and weeps for her lost reputation.

Meanwhile, as the *Sea Wing* and *Jim Grant* chug north—lashed together by a rope to make passage between the ships relatively easy—many women and children retire to the main cabin, leaving mostly men—fifty or so—shouting their bawdy songs aboard the smaller barge. The wind gathers force. Then dies sharply. For a moment the singing stops. The paddle wheel cutting the Mississippi breaks the silence.

Suddenly, a huge five-hundred-foot cyclone rises in the path of the *Sea Wing*. Water pounds the hull. Those remaining on deck flee to the already crowded main cabin. In the confusion, Roy Wethern sneaks away from his mother to watch the storm. Captain Wethern begins encouraging the women and children to don life jackets. Martin O'Shaughnessy needn't be told twice as he lashes the preserver tightly to his body.

Aboard the *Jim Grant,* passengers watch with horror as the Sea Wing begins tipping precariously and shout to be cut loose before being dragged to the bottom of the Mississippi. The rope either snaps or is hacked through. The barge drifts free. Now unbalanced, the riverboat tilts forty-five degrees and begins to founder. Containing more than a hundred passengers, mostly women and children, the *Sea Wing* flips over.

In the pilothouse, Captain Wethern struggles fiercely to break the windows before the compartment fills with water. On his second attempt, the glass gives way and he swims to safety. Few in the main cabin are as lucky. Those that do escape the sinking ship are pelted with hail as the Mississippi heaves and seethes. Like many of the women who found the courage to leap off the vessel, Nellie Wethern cannot remain afloat as the weight of her sodden skirts yank her down. Perley, too, is lost within the roiling seas. Roy Wethern is pulled from the water trembling and shouting for his parents. Later that night, the corpse of Martin O'Shaughnessy is found without a life vest. On July 16, after a passing stern wheeler disturbs the waters, Randina Olson's body rises from the depths to be interred in earth beside A. O. Anderson, the man who should have called her "wife" and she "husband."

All told, the Mississippi took ninety-eight lives on that Sunday.

☙ ❧

More than one hundred years later, I found myself in Diamond Bluff, the town that the *Sea Wing* called her home port, reading a weathered wooden sign marking the centennial of the tragedy. A stooped man hobbled toward me, pushing a lawn mower like a walker.

"Terrible shame, that boat wreck. Biggest inland waterway disaster in U.S. history. Or so I've been told."

"It says here that Captain Wethern lived in this town."

"Yup. He did. With his two sons and wife. I carved that sign there with my daughters, so I know a thing or two about the *Sea Wing* and her Captain. In fact, I live in his old house."

"Really?"

"Yes sirree, I do. It's right over thereabouts. That's why me and my daughters made this sign in the first place. The whole thing was Betsy's idea. She wanted to appease the spirits, so to speak."

"The spirits?"

"You know, the ghosts of the dead. She thought they were…uneasy. At least once a week, late at night, she and my other girls would scurry into my bed, claiming they heard all kinds of moaning and groaning. A few times, she even says she talked with little Perley Wethern. I never heard any of the racket or saw any of the goings on that she did. But something was spooking them all right."

He ran a tattered handkerchief across his forehead and continued. "Then one day Betsy says to me, 'Dad, we have to atone.' 'Atone?' I says. 'Atone, Dad,' she repeats looking all serious, like the world will end if we don't. That's when I says, 'For what, dear?'"

The old man crossed his heart and swung his eyes to the sky. "I swear by my Creator, at that moment, the windows began rattling, the lights flickered, and something began beating on the pipes. The Almighty as my witness, the wind stirred the curtains with a name. It was a whisper. Quiet as can be, but no mistaking it. That's for truth. '*Sea Wing*,' we heard. Right then and there my daughters and I began planning that sign."

I reread the wooden monument to the lost vessel.

"Did it work? Are the spirits appeased?"

"To be honest, I can't really say for sure."

◊ ◊ ◊

Later that day, I carried my bike up a set of steps cut deep into a hill hidden far within Afton State Park to a free campsite reserved for canoers. I erected my tent and, exhausted, plopped down at the picnic table. Piles of neatly arranged stones speckled the site. There had to be about twenty mounds of fist-sized rocks. Maybe a troop of Boy Scouts left the piles, perhaps in an effort to obtain a merit badge of some kind or another. Then again, I may have mistakenly wandered onto an ancient Indian burial ground that the state of Minnesota illegally annexed for their park.

The stones certainly looked sacred, and my growing paranoia warned against disturbing the piles. At this point, I glanced to the trees. Branches tied into people shapes dangled from every limb. Scores of these stick figure effigies swung in the wind.

I leapt into my tent.

Mary, I have no idea what is going on nor do I have the guts to pack and leave. I'm too scared to even unzip from my tent; so attempting to drag my bike back down those stairs while avoiding the heaped stones is pointless. All I know is that in my heart and with my actions I will respect what I don't understand and treat these clearly sacred objects with the reverence that they deserve. All I want is sleep, and then I will leave this land as I arrived, in peace. All I can do is pray that any uneasy spirits are in fact appeased.

Please.

David

DAY 84, PART II

....

FRIGHT REDOUBLING

August 6
A Dark and Stormy Night
Afton State Park, Minnesota

Mary,

Have you ever spent the night in a cemetery?

The moon is hidden. The sun is hours away. And the silence, it only grows and grows...

...Until it is shattered by distant snarling and crashing and moaning. Clanking metal accompanies fierce growls and guttural whimpers. The wind howls in anticipation. The witching hour approaches.

I tremble in my nylon cocoon. I'm completely and utterly alone. There are no campers to comfort with human noise, to protect with their bright lanterns, to hear any desperate screams.

I'm trespassing on dead ground. I know it as I know I love you. My only hope is to remain motionless. I must be still. Very still. And silent. Not making a peep. Damn. Even this pen scratching across paper could disturb that which should remain undisturbed.

There is no hope for sleep. No hope for an end to this night. The spirits are awake.

And they are uneasy.

I tried distracting myself from what I know is waiting for me outside with my radio and headphones, but all that cracks the silence is static. I know I need sleep, and yet I also realize that succumbing may lead to my doom. For all my hyperbolic language, Mary, I'm at a loss and honestly don't know what to do. I can't sleep. I can't move. I'm simply…terrified—a grown man terrified, knocked senseless with fear.

I must be vigilant, though. I must be strong. I've biked three thousand miles for Christ's sake! I've done nothing wrong. I respect whatever is out there.

Please, Mary, hear my words even as I write. Lend me the strength to find the morning. Give me the courage to endure this night. The spirits watch, Mary, and they wait…

…Knowing I'm scared something fierce and desperately have to go to the bathroom.

David

P.S. — I couldn't hold it, Mary, and now I've done it because in my rush I tripped over a pile of rocks, scattering them like leaves in the wind, disturbing whatever sacred pattern may have been kept, dishonoring the unknown with my clumsiness. I tried to be careful. I did. But I really had to go and it was dark and I was—no, I am—scared. I pray that whatever spirit's out there watching remembers what it feels like to be terrified and chained to the whims of one's bladder. Please let this night end.

DAY 85

....

THE TRUTH CARRIED
BY DAYLIGHT

August 7
Banks of the St. Croix River
Stillwater, Minnesota

Dear Mary,

That I breakfast along a tributary of the Mississippi once named Hogan-wauke-kin—the River of the Grave—seems appropriate. Burial mounds, a haunted night, the spirits of the damned, and now the grave St. Croix flowing like the Styx toward Hades. There are far more things in heaven and earth, Mary, than are dreamt of in my philosophy. Even by the light of day, when all is said to be made clear, my theories have only been further muddied.

At the first suggestion of dawn—eyes fogged with exhaustion—I gathered the courage to pack and leave the forest deep within Afton Park. The sun warmed the chill from my skin, but still, I refused to allow my eyes to linger on the stones piled about. I pointedly ignored the two mounds I had kicked over when stumbling to relieve myself last night. The hanging stick figures lurked in the periphery, but again, I became like a stoic Spartan and concerned myself with more pressing matters, like getting the hell out of there.

I didn't look back as I dragged my bike back down the rough-hewn stairs, one step closer to civilization and living people.

About fifty feet from the canoe site, a large metal barrel rested on its dented and rusting side. Trash lay scattered around. A few soiled diapers dangled from low hanging branches. Small animal footprints painted the muddy trail with a picture of riotous activity. Not being a Navaho tracker, I can only make an educated guess, but I would say that raccoons love dirty diapers.

Relief washed over me as I made my way back to the ranger station. Sure the stick figures and piled rocks hadn't been explained, but the cause of the racket continuing to fuel that initial blaze of fear at least had a reasonable cause. In the light of day, I was convinced that the ranger knew what was going on and had an equally mundane account for the bizarre state of the site—perhaps they had recreated a Chippewa burial ground for educational purposes or something.

By the time I reached the ranger station, my watch read 5:00 a.m. It would still be two hours before actual living people arrived at their post. After a night of little sleep and constant fear, I needed human noise, signs of human life, a comforting human voice. I tried calling you. No one answered the phone, and when I realized there was only an hour difference, I hung up not wanting to disturb your sleep. The urge to talk was strong though. The residue of my fears needed to be chatted clean, and I craved reassurance that my terror, although extreme, could at least be understandable from another point of view.

So, despite the hour, I phoned my mother and explained the events of the past twelve hours. As I spoke, giggling away my fear with a sort of bravado only suitable for the daylight hours, my mother became more reticent, more concerned, more fearful.

"Dave, I want you to go talk to the ranger. Immediately."

"Come on, Mom. It wasn't that big of a deal. Just some sticks and stones. Besides, the ranger's not going to come in for another hour."

"Wait then. I really think you should. Someone needs to hear about this."

"What's the big deal? Sure, I was scared a bit last night, but I'm positive there's nothing to it all. The ranger's probably already—"

"Listen to me. I just saw this movie, *The Blair Witch Project*, and well—"

"Never heard of it."

"It just came out. Anyway, it's about these college students who investigate the disappearance of seven children in the 1700s, and what you describe is directly out of the movie."

"Yeah, but that was just a movie. It's not real."

"Your sister thinks it's true."

"Well, my sister thinks I'm Satan, so I don't think she's the most reliable source in the universe."

"Listen, it doesn't really matter if the movie is real or not. Because it's scary as hell, and I'm scared as hell, and if someone is trying to screw with people in the woods, the authorities need to be told."

"I still don't see—"

"Just promise me you'll hang out until the rangers show up."

Needing a nap anyway, I stretched out on the grass and watched the clouds as my mind circled around the various possibilities: from mischievous cinema-loving teenagers out for a joke to sinister film-inspiring rituals practiced in the dark corners of our society, from an educational tool for curious anthropology students to a burial ground for the victims of a movie-obsessed serial killer. The unknown prickled my exhausted body with wakefulness, and again, much needed sleep remained elusive.

About an hour and a half later, the ranger walked up smiling.

"Looks like another great day for riding. Hope you had a good night."

"Actually, I have a question. See, I was in the canoe site and well, there were these piles of rocks everywhere—" Silhouetted by the sun, the ranger appeared to stiffen. "And also these sticks tied in the shapes of people were hanging all over the place." I thought I saw his hand drift to his gun belt. "I figured you all were running some kind of program and—"

"Thank you for the information, sir. We'll look into immediately. Good day."

He turned and walked stiff-legged toward the station, walkie-talkie crackling with activity.

My only solace was riding.

Later, while passing through Afton, I stopped at a convenience store to use the bathroom. As I wandered the aisles looking for something sweet, the radio caught my attention.

"...has been missing for three days. She was last seen near the intersection of I-94 and 280 in St. Paul. Be on the lookout for a white van..."

I scurried out of the store.

Pedaling soothed the rising fear. Spinning my cranks as quickly as possible was my childlike attempt to cover my ears and shout to silence bad news. The concerns of riding fully occupied my mind, focusing it away from dreadful thoughts shaping the unknown. Yet just as a child's voice grows hoarse, my brain couldn't be distracted forever from theorizing: a woman had been murdered. Chopped to bits. Pieces of her had been buried beneath my tent. The killer was actually lurking in the shadows, watching me pee on his personal necropolis. I was marked for certain death.

About five miles north of Afton, six police cars roared by, sirens wailing like my own heart. Two miles later, thirty cruisers—Minnesota State Troopers, Washington County Sheriffs, and even a few unmarked Crown Victorias—idled in a field, lights flashing a warning like the preacher

Georgas: Beware! Beware! In the distance, dogs barked. Grouped cops combed the field. There was a shout.

I pedaled faster and faster.

Until now.

My belly has betrayed my legs, and food has become necessary. The fear is there; the memory of last night is still powerful. What had I stumbled upon? Was it just a simple prank or something far more sinister? What action has the ranger taken? Are the police involved? Am I safe even now?

The sun shines, and yet the truth remains as mysterious as this river named after a grave.

David

DAY 86

....

A TALE OF TWO TERRYS ... OR MAYBE THREE

August 8
Father Hennepin State Park
Mille Lacs Lake, Minnesota

D<small>EAR</small> M<small>ARY</small>,
    A<small>S</small> I <small>TWISTED MOISTURE</small> from my dew-soaked sleeping bag, a tiger-striped Boxer pulled a shirtless fellow across the fairgrounds toward me. I dropped my bag and watched the man try to steer his dog around my equipment. Thin-legged, round-bellied, and sway-backed, this man reminded me of a Star-Bellied Sneetch.
"Whoa there, Fifi! I'm coming. I'm coming."
The dog leaped onto my sleeping bag.
"Fifi! Stop that. Get off." The shirtless man, pale skin freckled in a feeble attempt at a tan, jerked the leash. Fifi soared through the air, regained his balance cat-like, and stretched his eager nose toward my crotch. "Sorry about that. Fifi, stop that, damn it!"

He leaned down and stuck his face inches from the Boxer's pug nose. The dog began lapping at his face wildly. The man cackled like a soprano buzz saw.

"Headed off to Sturgis? What are you riding, a Harley?" The dog leaped from his arms and began making figure eights around my legs.

I stepped from the net of the leash. Fifi strained to lick my calf.

"Not quite." Pointing to my bike leaning against the picnic table, I backed away from the dog.

"Now that's something you don't see every day. Bet you have some stories to tell."

"A few. But so does everyone, right?"

"I don't know about that. I'm sure you got all sorts of stories about bears and goats and mad cows. I bet you do. So, where you headed tonight?"

"North. Maybe to around Mille Lacs Lake. Something like that. It depends how I feel."

"Well, in that case, you should have dinner at my house. It's right on the way. Up U.S. 169 in Pease. You got a map? I'll give you directions. Name's Terry. You like chicken?"

When I pulled out the map, Terry showed me how Pease sat directly between where I was and where I was headed. All I needed to do was turn left on CR 8 pass through Pease and then turn right on CR 5, although the sign might say 125th Ave; he couldn't remember. The house number was 22922. I couldn't miss it—big farmhouse set back from the road about a quarter mile down on the right—totally unique.

As Terry pointed out a few pleasant country roads to keep me from heavy traffic, Fifi found the scent of some tasty morsel and began once again walking the walker. "Have a good ride," Terry called as he was dragged away. "I'll see you later. Bring your stories and look for the smoke from the barbeque...Slow down, Fifi, I'm a-coming. The chicken will be waiting for you, too."

The thought of that chicken, basted in sweet barbeque sauce slowly grilled over open flame, tasting pure—of fire and hickory—brought me to Pease in one piece at about half past two. Passing through town, I made a right on CR 5. I rode for about a mile and didn't see the house number. I turned down various gravel roads thinking I may have missed part of the directions. Frustrated, I finally turned around, keeping my eyes peeled for something I may have overlooked. I still couldn't find it. My stomach clenched with the familiar sensation of being hopelessly lost.

Once back at the intersection, I glanced at my odometer to measure out a quarter of a mile. At six-tenths, I came across a big green mailbox, large enough to hold about four loaves of white bread. It's broad side, stenciled in peeling white paint, read:

TERRY & AURALEA SAUNDERS

I had made it. I could practically smell the barbecued chicken hanging heavy in the air. I turned up the gravel drive and headed back toward the farm.

Four mixed breed collies began howling, "Intruder… Intruder…Intruder…" Two children of indeterminate sex, knees dirtied by the wrestling match I had interrupted, scurried to the house shouting, "Grandma. Grandma. There's a funny looking…"

I didn't expect Terry to have kids with all the trouble he had controlling that dog, but the house, although not numerically marked, fit the general description of a farmhouse set back from the road, and according to my none-too-precise calculations, should have numbered about 11911…

…The screen door slammed…

More importantly, the name Terry pretty much assured me I had reached dinner and was thankfully not lost. Wasn't that chicken I was smelling?

Three ostriches, penned behind a twelve-foot high chain-link fence, began squawking and prancing like a high-stepping majorette leading the marching band. The sight of my loaded bike spooked one gangly bird so severely that the poor creature squatted and sprayed streams of urine wildly about as if squeezed by a drunken Scottish piper. Another bird ran in circles, feathers flying, searching, I suppose, for a hole so that it could bury its tiny head and vanquish me from its sight.

An older woman, wiping her hands on her apron and swatting away the two curious children from her skirts, warily approached from the house as if I were a witch craving Hansel and Gretel pie. "Can I help you?" Her tone dipped with suspicion and confusion and fear. She came no closer than fifteen feet.

"Um. Hi there. Terry invited me to dinner early today and said—"

"Terry did that? He didn't say anything about dinner guests."

"Yeah, this morning I met him over at the fairgrounds—"

"You sure about that? 'Cause Terry's my husband and has been with me all day. Only left an hour ago to get some more feed for the birds... Should be back any minute actually."

"Well, he said his name was Terry. He said I should stop over his place in Pease. He said—" I could sense the growing fear radiating from her like heat from hot asphalt. "Look, I'm terribly sorry for the mistake. I didn't mean to cause any trouble. Someone must have been playing a trick on me. I didn't mean to frighten you." I began backing away down the driveway.

"What'd this feller look like?"

"Blondish hair, I guess. Young looking. Sun burned. About my height." She seemed to relax a bit.

"Well, my husband isn't young any more, that's for sure. And he's much much taller than you. And bigger, too. Much bigger. But my son now, I guess you could have met him. His name's Terry, too. But we just call him Junior. He should be coming over in a bit to pick up his kids. I don't know anything about the fairgrounds; he said he was looking at new tractors, but I suppose you could have met him."

She seemed incredibly dubious about that prospect.

"You're welcome to wait for him by that fence there. Just mind the birds. Don't want to stir them all up again. Come on kids, let's go inside now." She glanced at my bike a moment, shook her head, and turned to enter the house. The door creaked and slammed, setting both dogs and birds into another frenzy.

My gut had determined that this could not possibly be the right house. Terry hadn't mentioned his parents, or his kids, or even the huge weak-bladdered birds being raised here. Yet unless I had the directions completely wrong (which was possible), there were no other houses that fit Terry's description. Why someone would essentially strand me, off route in the middle of Minnesota, I couldn't answer, and my heart refused to accept such a possibility. People aren't like that, I kept repeating, despite the evidence to the contrary.

I studied my maps to see how far it was to Mille Lacs Lake. I imagined the grueling time-constrained forty-mile ride ahead, which would have been easy had it not been almost 3:30. But mostly, I pictured Terry arriving to save the day, apologizing to his parents for forgetting to call ahead about his guest.

An old station wagon crackled up the drive. My hope soared. When a long-haired bearded young man, thin and tan, climbed from the car looking at me crosswise, my rising embarrassment brought me to my feet. Who in their right mind would ever guess that a town of a hundred people could contain more than one Terry, let alone three?

"Umm. This is going to sound awfully strange, but I think I just scared the living daylights out of your mother. Could you tell her I'm terribly sorry? Because, clearly, you are not the Terry I met this morning...See I met this guy, Terry, who invited me over for some chicken, and he gave me your address...or at least, his directions lead me here—it was probably some sort of prank though, seeing that you are obviously not the Terry I met this morning— So I'm really sorry...I didn't mean to scare you all...I'll just be on way...again, I'm really sorry. And, tell your mother no harm was meant...I am so sorry."

Before he could say a word, I jumped on my bike and began pedaling as if I had looped around to discover myself once more in Afton Park surrounded by sticks and stones and vans and cops and possible serial killers. The same sort of frenzy that overcame me the other day powered my legs this afternoon—the only difference being that embarrassment rather than fear pushed me onward.

The ride was far from pleasant. Being off route, I kept misjudging the mileage between towns, and because of my desire for speed, I clung to U.S. 169, which is a loud and busy road. Within a four-mile stretch near Milaca, time slowed twice—once as a bottle, tossed from a passing car, shattered two feet from my front tire and then again as a bright pink '57 Cadillac made a right turn without braking, wheels squealing in protest inches from my leg. Relying on the promised chicken, I hadn't eaten the biggest lunch and was down to a single kiwi for my pre-dinner snack. The day had become an utter disaster.

And it hasn't stopped with the ride. Just as dark settled in for the evening, I arrived at the park. Finding a site and setting camp under a moonless sky is far from easy. I kept losing stakes and confusing poles. Then, in a rush to satiate my hunger, carelessness controlled my fingers. Not primed correctly, my stove backfired and spat a ball of fire at my face; once again, it'll be days before my eyebrows return.

It feels like rain, but it's too damn hot and humid for the tent's fly. With it, I'll roast; without, it I'll get soaked. The park is nearly empty but for a bunch of rowdy teenagers, which means sleep will be slow coming. Next thing you know, the police will hold me for questioning about the whole Afton stick fig…

Great! Now my damn pen is running out of ink.

Yours,
David

DAY 87

....

A MAD BEAR

August 9
Walleye Dundee's Restaurant
Wahkon, Minnesota

Dear Mary,

I awoke to rain and, until the patter stopped, decided it best to drift along the outskirts of dream. That state between consciousness and sleep, where great ideas are born and magnificent thoughts are shaped, is my downfall. The glorious and addictive power of bed controls my mornings with a gravity more powerful than the sun's. In those early morning moments, I feel a peace of which monks dream. I am beyond the world and yet deeply a part of it...drifting and floating.

That a car pulled up registered only vaguely. Must be a fisherman, I thought. It didn't matter, though. I was deep.

My tent shook.

"County Sheriff, here. Don't mean to wake you, but we have reports of a mad bear on the loose. You're going to have to pack up and move on."

From floating to sinking in an instant.

"You aren't serious?" I called from my tent.

"Damn serious, sir. This isn't a joking matter. There's a mad bear roaming…"

"All right. I'll be out in—"

A familiar cackle, that loud soprano buzz saw, jolted me upright.

The misplaced Terry had found me!

How exactly, is a story for another letter because Terry is insisting I return home with him. To Pease. For some barbeque.

Love,
David

Letters to Eden

DAY 90

....

KIDNAPPED

August 12
A Sprawling Victorian
Undisclosed Location, Minnesota

Dear Mary,

I apologize for not having written in a few days. I'm intact, though, and in a relatively good mood...despite my kidnapping.

Maybe kidnapping is too strong of a word. I certainly haven't been duct taped and hogtied. No ransom note has been mailed, and the blue-suited FBI agents are still in their offices eating doughnuts. Waylaid seems closer to reality, I suppose. Yes, waylaid.

How I found myself in this situation is a bit strange. It all started with Terry. When I didn't arrive at his house for dinner, visions of twisted bicycles and cracked skulls overcame him with such power that he began calling all the local hospitals. I admit that his reaction seems a tad excessive—being flown into a dramatic frenzy of worry over someone you just met is more than a bit peculiar. As I was to later learn, Terry has the gargantuan spirit of a manic sensualist; so in retrospect, such raging passion fits his character rather well.

But I didn't know that when he found me in Father Hennepin State Park early on that rainy morning. All I knew was that this fellow Terry, a man more stranger than friend, had arrived at my camp some forty miles north of his house and more than a hundred riding miles from where we had originally met.

As he told his tale of anxiety and sleeplessness, of countless phone calls and hours of late night driving to various campgrounds searching for a car-less bicycle, I saw that in some bizarre way I had deeply affected him. Perhaps, it was the uniqueness of adventuring that attracted him so strongly. Or maybe it was that I agreed to his offer of a shared meal so readily, banishing something of his loneliness for a moment. Or maybe, he just envied my tan and wanted to learn its secrets. Whatever the case, something drove him through the night to find me—to make sure I wasn't hurt—to fulfill his promise of barbecued chicken.

Under normal circumstances, a man hunting for me through the night would be classified as stalking. But Mary, I need you to understand something. Crossing the country by bike is far from a normal circumstance. Perception is altered; it must be. To survive the taxing nature of loneliness and the constant ache for home, my eyes have been ripped wide, receiving events with innocence—at least not when fogged by terror in a haunted campsite. Since embarking on this trip, I have allowed myself to be washed from moment to moment, giving little resistance as the currents push me this way or that. I was told recently that if I became any more laid back, I would fall flat on my rear. My butt has been calloused well from the saddle, however, and such a fall would likely cause little damage.

Sure this guy could have been a serial killer, hankering to drag me back Afton-way to filet me in the woods and then pile my grave with stones. Yet how can I explain the power of a new day? The rising sun peaking behind rain clouds. Heavy water drops like liquid diamonds bending grass earthward. Light and gray mixing to color foliage with greens blinding in brilliance. A bicycle washed clean by a nocturnal storm to sparkle. Another day—a new day—to adventure. And this fellow Terry, standing before me, eyes dripping concern and worry and relief and a little mischief.

Something moved me in that moment—yes, I'll have breakfast; yes you can show me Minnesota; yes, I'll come with you.

So began my captivity.

For most of the morning, we drove about the back roads of Minnesota in his black pickup—my bike rattling and rainfly flapping in the bed of the truck—Fifi sitting between us, tongue lolling while the radio blared Madonna and Whitney Houston—his shirtless torso sticking loudly to the vinyl seats every time he shifted to point at another cow or police car or cathedral. The objects he seemed to find interesting were so bizarre that I began to wonder at his stability. The vehemence with which he shouted was startling. We would be mid-conversation about some topic or another, and then suddenly, he would shout "Copper!" as a car passed or yell "Holstein! Holstein!" when seeing cattle or scream "Lordy! Oh Lordy!" at the sight of a steeple. But this peculiar speech oddity wasn't my chief worry.

It was his shirtlessness, if you can believe it. For some reason, it made me extremely uncomfortable. The immodesty of it put me ill at ease, as if his shirtlessness emphasized something lost. What? I wasn't sure. Not at first. At first, I believed that I'd simply found another interesting weirdo to add to the long list of peculiar people I've encountered.

During the drive, between his occasional outbursts, he described his life as a surgical assistant—the joy of seeing patients in recovery flexing once twisted and broken limbs, the disgust he and all the nurses felt at the arrogant doctors, and the inevitable burnout after fifteen years of twenty-two-hour shifts. Three weeks ago, when a doctor had asked for a retractor, Terry stormed from the operating room mid-surgery, never to return. I eventually discovered that he had disappeared for three days, hitchhiking south in an attempt to reach Florida. He got as far as Des Moines before something pulled him back home.

But I learned that later. Right then, in his truck, I only knew for sure that despite my growing unease, Terry had sought me out, had been genuinely concerned, and wanted to show me his house. Yes, I was uneasy, but I didn't feel threatened. I didn't feel eminent doom. I figured I could leave when we arrived at his house. We drove until noon, heading generally south, when he decided we should make a stop at St. Cloud. It was only a bit out of the way, and he really wanted me to see Clemons Gardens.

The strangeness of wandering around Clemons Gardens with a shirtless chap and his boxer named Fifi as a scandalized group of older woman watched his boisterous antics would have been rather amusing if I hadn't been so mortified. Walking beside him was like being at the mall as a child with my father when he would suddenly break into an exuberant rendition of *Blue Moon*—the Marcels' version beginning with all those bom-ba-ba-boms and ding-a-dong dings and dipty-dip-dip blue moons. They saw us standing there, those prim and proper ladies, me the grungy cyclist and Terry the spastic sun-freckled nut, and frowned with disapproval at every loud shout, every excited bark, every petal plucked from the blooming rose gardens.

I wanted to hide. On one hand, I couldn't believe his shenanigans, dancing about like Salome, picking flowers from a public garden, allowing his dog to invade quiet picnics with a curious nose. Another part of me recognized his need for attention—saw the familiar reflection of my dad's behavior—and tried to help, tried to remain calm, tried to guide him back to the truck before the gardens were completely uprooted and the police were called.

Eventually, we left the park a few roses richer and headed to his home.

First, let me say that his house, a large "farmhouse" set back from the road, was a little less than a half-mile from where I had been the day earlier. I had somehow mistaken a right for a left, and ended up going the wrong direction on CR 5. If I had found his house, I certainly wouldn't have missed it. The house was incredible—a grand Victorian with two towers, stained glass, antique wooden doors, and a wraparound porch painted in pinks and purples and maroons.

Upon entering, my jaw unhinged. His place bombarded my senses just as his personality. From a grand double-stair stained by sunlight piercing a reclaimed church window to an actual waterfall singing itself down the walls of his rustic bathroom, the interior stole ideas from a year's worth of *Better Homes and Gardens* read with LSD-clouded eyes.

Each room had a different motif, and each motif a different base color, and each color a different psychological effect—according to Terry, at least. The orange dining room assisted the stomach with digestion. The bright yellow kitchen simmered cooking thoughts rising from the well-regulated spleen. The deep wine boudoir struck the heart with arrows of passion and soothed the fear radiating from the kidneys. The suede walls of the study prodded the hidden masculinity lurking in the liver. The sea green sewing room caressed the medulla oblongata with calming fingers.

Yet the bold colors paled against the artistic clutter scattered about the house. Every exposed surface—every shelf and every table, every chair and every loveseat, every nook and every cranny—had been slathered with the flamboyant designer's equivalent of butter. Thick paisley tapestries draped over leather couches. Accent pillows, flowered with petals like the ones Terry had earlier pilfered, lay scattered about the various rooms. Antique post cards decorated an entire wall in the foyer, and you could almost hear them whispering their tales of foreign journeys to the black and white headshots of Hollywood legends hanging across the hall. The bow of a salvaged rowboat—splintered wood stained green by algae—rocked no more in the mouth of a large fireplace, moored kitchenward. On the mantle battled two armies of delicately painted porcelain figurines wearing homespun aprons. Atop a stack of Barbra Streisand records rested a deer head waiting to be mounted.

Every room contained crated memories that Terry hoped one day to display. Antiques on that table, junk in that corner, pictures and posters, toys and tools, all kinds of things were strewn about with the haphazard touch of an aspiring interior decorator.

"It's not done. But what do you think?" Terry nibbled on his bottom lip.

His home needed to be read like a book, a fat book from which one does not mind the loss of a few weekends. It was packed so densely with interesting tidbits that my eyes ached from constantly darting back and forth.

"Yeah," he continued, "everyone's quiet for a bit after they see the place. It's wonderful for entertaining. We throw great parties here at Christmas. You should come sometime. It's the best party for miles around. And, the eggnog—it's Aunt Hattie's secret recipe—will get you smashed in a flash."

"Where did all this stuff come from?"

"Oh, here and there. But mostly from the shop. I deal in antiques on the side, though I'm getting more heavy into the business since I left work. Anyway, whenever I come across something that catches my fancy, I bring it home. That's why I've got a big house…many things attract my eye—many, many things…as you can tell." He stared at me for a few moments too long and then gestured grandly about his living room.

"It's like a storeroom to a curiosity museum or something. Kinda like where I lived in Annapolis." I ran my hands through my hair, watching shadows move across the cathedral ceiling.

"Hey, can I ask you a question?"

"Shoot." I picked up a stuffed lizard and began tossing it from hand to hand.

"When was the last time you got a haircut—"

"Huh?" I turned to face Terry.

"—I don't mean to be rude or anything like that. It's just that you're looking a bit shaggy around the ears, and the next few days look to be real scorchers. I've got some clippers in the bathroom. I could trim you up real quick. If you want."

It had been awhile—since I was last in Annapolis, I think—and although not of a Samsonian magnitude, my hair was becoming an annoyance. I had been meaning to get a buzz cut in Stillwater, but you know how preoccupied

I had been then, fleeing my fear. Besides, it's not as if I required any high-dollar styling.

"What the heck. Why not?"

"Here comes Delilah." Ripping the air with that buzz saw cackle, Terry led me through the kitchen to the porch.

I write of this haircut for three reasons—first, because that I allowed my hair to be shorn by a shirtless man in the middle of Minnesota seems like an interesting event to chronicle—second, because after the haircut, I was able to shower in a bathroom with a waterfall running down its walls, quite an experience I must say—and most importantly, because, stepping from that bathroom with a towel about my waist, I encountered the perplexed face of a complete and rather muscular stranger.

"Uh, hi."

"Hel-loooo." The man looked at the small puddle collecting around my legs.

"Terry…uh…told me it was okay to take a shower."

"Uh-huh." He grunted and crossed his arms.

"My name's Dave." I reached out to introduce myself as properly as possible while wearing only a towel.

"Charmed." He ignored my hand. "I'm Steve…Terry's…partner."

Ohhhhhhhhhhhhh!

With a twirl, he hurried back down the stairs. "Oh, Terry dear!"

Christ! What had I tumbled into now?

Not knowing exactly how to manage this whole affair, I quickly threw on my dirty clothes and hurried down the stairs to leave.

No sooner had I reached the door when Terry stepped from the kitchen wearing a ruffled apron and asked, "Nice shower?"

"Uh, sure, Terry. Thanks a million. I really needed it. But I—I should really be going soon. It's getting late. I need to log at least a few miles today. You know, the schedule and all. Don't want to fall behind."

"Oh, don't go yet. I still owe you dinner. I insist you stay…you know, with your head shaved like that, your eyes really shine. They're gorgeous."

"Thanks. But really I have to get back on the road. My girlfriend back home is—"

"Dinner's going to be in a few hours. I know after all those miles you've ridden, you have to be starving. You can stay the night afterwards. It's not a problem at all. Besides, your tent needs to dry."

"W—w—what do you mean?"

"Well, it was all dirty and icky so I washed it down with the hose. Probably hasn't been cleaned in months. You don't want to be sleeping in a wet tent now, do you?"

Steve peeked around the corner smiling, the shock surprising him now resolved.

"Please stay. Terry's right. Wet tents are nasty. We've got plenty of food and a great guest bedroom. You can leave bright and early in the morning. It's really no problem."

"I don't want to be any trouble. I—"

"Please," implored Terry. "We won't take no for an answer."

So I stayed and haven't been able to leave yet.

Something is always coming up—the wet tent drying in the afternoon, later Fifi sprayed by an angry skunk with my rainfly caught in the crossfire, then helping Terry haul cans of tomato soup from the store, and finally the messy struggle between dog, man, and soup soak. This day of rest has been greatly appreciated, however, and so long as Steve's around to control Terry's flirtations, I'm generally relaxed. After Steve pulled me aside to explain Terry's breakdown and subsequent attempted flight to Florida, I have parried each coquettish remark with relative good humor. I don't necessarily like the situation, but I certainly understand it.

Terry feels alone and betrayed—even by Steve who only ever tries to help. Through me, though, Steve has been able to soften the paranoia, release some of the anxiety, and perhaps even help Terry begin to heal. After that first dinner together, I saw the pain beneath all those mad antics and recognized them for what they were—symptoms of a deep, soul-rending loneliness. Even in the most committed relationship that monster squats, and Steve understands this. He explained to me that he couldn't provide Terry with everything he needed—that by always being there, he was actually increasing the feelings of desolation. He thought my arrival brought Terry some hope for friendship, a sign that he was not alone. Terry very well may be confusing friendship with something else, Steve granted, but he hoped that was a sign of good things.

So perhaps my kidnapping—I mean waylaying—has somehow ransomed the Terry of old, the Terry Steve deeply loves, from the manic clutches of his broken spirit. I pray for that as I pray for you, Mary. Friends and friendship, love and lovers are keys to the locks clasped shut by our wounded parts. We all have wounds. We all need to mend the soft tissues of our deeper selves. Healing is ever-slow and painful, and things lost are never guaranteed to return. Stepping on that road is hard. And coming home harder.

Love,
David

DAY 91

....

SUCH SWEET SORROW

August 13
South Isle Family Campground
Isle, Minnesota

Dear Mary,

Yesterday evening, I had decided it was time to move on, and over dinner, when I explained the pull of the road and my need to continue, both Terry and Steve understood. They wished me well for the night and hoped the weather would be clear and cool the next day.

It was still dark when my bed began to heave.

"Cock-a-doodle-dooooo!"

I groaned.

"Come on, sleepy head! It's time to get up! Cock-a-doodle-dooooo!"

I peeled away the remainder of my dreams and tried to focus. My limbs hung heavy and dead.

"Terry, what time is it?"

"Time to get up, of course." Terry tossed his head back and began mimicking a rooster again. "Come on. It's time. We have to hit the road. Early bird gets—"

I jerked upright.

"We? What do you mean, *we*?"

"What do you mean, 'what do you mean?' You said we're leaving today. Now stop being silly and get up!" Terry opened a dresser and began pushing clothes into a nylon duffle bag. The garments appeared to have been found by moths many years ago. He held up a white blouse with mother of pearl buttons and a black mesh tank top. "Do you think I should bring this shirt or this other one?"

"You don't wear shirts."

"Too true." He jumped back on the bed. "Now come on! Get up. We have to go!" He tried to roll me onto the floor.

"Terry. Stop!" He backed off like a chastised puppy. "Can I get dressed at least?"

"Oh, sure. You want help?"

"Uh, no thanks. I think I can manage by myself." Terry sat patiently on the edge of the bed. "Uh, maybe in private?"

"Oh, sure. No prob-lem-o. Hurry, though. We need to go."

He left the room; I just sat on the bed. How do you explain to a lonely soul that he's not welcome? How can you just ignore the pleas of new friends after days of hospitality? How could I get out of this situation? I hate confrontation. I hate making a scene. I hate letting people down, even if their demands are absurd.

"Are you ready, yet?" Terry peeked around the door. When he saw me still in bed, he jumped back to rock the mattress. "Come on. We need to go!" Terry reached down, grabbed my shirt, and tried to force it over my head.

"Cut it out." I batted his hands away. "You can't come with me."

"But you said—"

"That I was leaving today. I didn't say we."

"But I have it all planned out. I've got a bike in the garage—"

"Terry, you told me that bike has one speed and two flat tires."

"Yeah, but I'm sure you can fix it. You said you fixed your other bike when it broke."

"Even if I could, which I can't, but even if, it's way too small for you."

"Well, we could raise the seat…Right?" His bottom lip started to tremble.

"You just can't come. This is my trip. Not yours. If you want travel, you need to plan it yourself."

"I did plan it. Last night. All night. It was a good night. I didn't sleep I wink. I have it all planned…"

"That's not planning; that's dreaming."

"Whatever, I'm coming with. I'll follow you in my truck. With Fifi. In the morning, we can decide where we'll meet for the day, and then I'll be there in the afternoon. I can have dinner made. I can set up the tent. Everything will be ready. You wouldn't have to worry about anything. I'll take care of it all."

"No, Terry. I have to go alone. You have to stay here. With Steve."

"Steve hates me. He doesn't love me. Just like all those doctors at the hospital. If he loved me, he wouldn't always be watching me and pestering me and giving me pills. I hate the pills. I hate him! You're the only one who cares. You and Fifi…I'm coming with, and you can't stop me!"

"What are you talking about? Steve loves you more than anything in the world. Why do you think he puts up with all your crap? Christ. Can't you even see that?"

"I hate him. He's like my mother. I hate it. I'm coming with."

"You can't—"

"Please. I need to. You're the only one. The only one."

"Damn it, Terry. You can't come."

"Well, I'll follow you anyway. I'll follow you all the way to San Francisco. I've got a truck. I can keep up. You won't be able to get away. I'll follow you forever."

I grabbed Terry's wrists.

"You need to understand, Terry. You can't come with me. This is my trip. You have your own journey to make. But this—on my bike—is for me alone. You cannot come. You just can't. I have to go alone. Can't you understand?"

"The only thing I understand," Terry said as he yanked his arms away, "is that you aren't my friend. No one loves me. I hate you. I hate you all!"

He tore from the room. A door slammed. Fifi started barking. I put on some clothes and began gathering my things.

"Good morning." Steve stood in the doorway wearing a silk, baby blue bathrobe ruffled around the collar. "Is everything all right? I heard shouting." He yawned. "Damn, it's early. What it is, around 4:30?"

I slammed a pair of dirty socks into my bag and flipped it on the bed.

"Yup."

"What's wrong?"

"Nothing much. Except Terry is insisting he come with me. He's threatening to follow me around the world."

"Christ. You want me to slip him some tranquilizers so you can get away?"

"Not yet. I should talk to him first."

"Well, I'll go start breakfast. If you need something, let me know."

Terry was sitting on the porch, watching the sun rise, shoulders shaking free tiny sobs to mingle with the waking birds. I cleared my throat.

"Leave me alone!"

"Terry, I just—"

"Get away. Leave me be!" He whirled to face me. His face was swollen with tears. "You aren't my friend! Just get away."

"That's not true. It's not. Really. I'm trying to help you. You can't just leave your life here, though. Steve loves you—"

"No he doesn't. Just like you!"

"Listen. We're both trying to look out for you. I know you hurt. I know you don't want me to go. But I have to.

It's time. I have to. I have to finish what I started and get home."

"But why can't I come with? I need to. Or I'll die."

"You won't die. I know that for sure. You're too ornery for that. Besides, who would take care of Fifi?"

"No one, I guess."

"That's right. Your dog needs you—"

"But I need to come with. I need to get away."

"I understand what you are feeling. I really do. But the time just isn't right."

"The time is totally right. I need to start new. I need to get away."

"Why do you think you came back from your trip to Florida?"

"Because I couldn't get a ride farther than Des Moines."

"That's not what Steve told me."

"Well, he's lying. He always lies. He hates me."

"He said that you called him, telling him how much you missed him, how very scared you were, and he came and picked you up."

"But that was before he started hating me."

"I don't think so."

Terry was quiet for a long time.

"You're going aren't you?"

"Yes."

"And I can't come with?"

"No."

"Are we still friends?

"Yes."

"Can I have a hug before you go?"

I paused for a long time, watching the emotions trouble his face.

"Of course."

In my ear he whispered, "Thank you for being my friend."

Love,
David

PART XII

AN INTERLUDE

Itasca State Park, Minnesota

DAY 93

....

THE SOURCE

August 15
Mississippi Headwaters
Itasca State Park, Minnesota

Dear Mary,

A PERFECT MOMENT IS RARE INDEED. It's not so much that these instants of sublimity are infrequent, but rather that we infrequently notice them. Mystics probably live in a constant state of perfect moments strung together like a rosary; so, too, may idiots. But for me, they are sporadic.

During this trip, I have come quite close to experiencing the perfect moment—naked near Breadloaf Mountain, at the foot of the Kancamagus, humming along the Mississippi. It always seems, however, that my monkey brain won't quiet itself enough to fully recognize these moments. Even while watching the Milky Way spin itself through the night sky before bed, my vociferous id and moralizing superego constantly disparage each other, distracting like a gnat bouncing on my eardrums as if they were trampolines. I just can't get out of the way, and the moment disappears before it can be fully appreciated. Just like the bear I saw today.

I had been playing tag with the steadily shrinking Mississippi all morning, every few miles fording what had become a mere crick, when—not fifty feet in front of me—a bear sauntered across the road. To be honest, this bear resembled an enormous dog more than the fearsome embodiment of Ursa Major; it certainly was no giant grizzly, for which I was rather thankful. When a bear strolls across the highway, though, the natural instinct, whether in a car or on a bike, is to slam down the brakes, which I managed to accomplish posthaste.

The squealing of rubber pads against aluminum rims spooked the beast, transforming its leisurely ramble into a fantastic lumbering run toward the Mississippi. By the time I reached the point where the bear had splashed loudly into the shallow trickle, the creature had disappeared.

This bear's quick departure recalls a missed moment in Annapolis a few years ago. The date was July 7, 1995. We were sitting on a bench in State Circle. The air hung thick and heavy. The occasional car passed looking for a free place to park. The lawns before the State House had browned. A large moth banged persistently against a nearby lamp. The old Subway sign flickered neon invitations halfway down Maryland Avenue as we both watched without seeing the Naval Academy guards pace their post. We had stopped talking. The pain was too much.

Across the miles, let's be silent and remember...

...Your eyes were so big and green and beautiful...then they melted...

That had been our chance—a moment almost made perfect by the one thing we were both either unwilling or afraid to give—the ideal kiss. Your uncle had just died. I could sense fear and the need for love at war in you. "She's a friend," whispered my superego. "Your support is all you can offer for her grief despite any deeper feelings you may have." "A tender kiss—she needs it," argued the id. "This is your chance for love. Do it."

With a snap, the instant was gone, like the bear fleeing, and we were still just friends.

Back in Minnesota—today—the road stretched—empty—north and south, connecting horizons and crossing the stream that will journey for some 2,500 miles—this Father of Waters. Tall grasses concealed hidden bogs with waving fingers of green and gold through which the not-so-mighty Mississippi snaked. Tall pines pulled the blue sky down tight like a wool cap on a cold head. Grasshoppers scratched across pavement. The sun tickled my skin taut. For a long time, my entire being was silent.

The moment was perfect.

And as the river that had been my companion for weeks trickled goodbye, touching both its destination in the Gulf of Mexico and its place of birth at Lake Itasca, my imagination spanned the continent—reaching for both ending and beginning like the

Mississippi—only to imagine your eyes melt like they had on that bench.

    The wind calmed to become your lips, and we kissed.

Love,
David

PART XIII

ELEMENTARY NATURE

From White Earth Indian Reservation
to Logan Pass, Montana

DAY 95

....

PENTHOUSE "FORUM"

August 17
Brewer Lake Park
Erie, North Dakota

Dear Mary,

I know you probably never have read any *Penthouse* "Forum", but bear with me for a moment. These types of letters always seem to begin with the writer's complete disbelief concerning the situation being chronicled. They usually begin with phrases like: "I never imagined I would have experienced something worthy of your Forum, but just the other day…" or "I always thought these letters were invented by the editorial staff, but now I know they are true because last week…"

The author will then continue by setting the scene: "on a humid June afternoon, while I was innocently cleaning my neighbor's pool, she sashayed toward me and said…" or perhaps "during lunch hour, when I called my secretary into the office, she locked the door and turned, smiling mischievously…"

So queue up the Barry White, Mary, sit back, and enjoy the ride.

I never thought I would be writing a letter like this to you, but after cycling 110 miles, a strong tailwind pushed me into Brewer Lake Park, which happened to be occupied by a single motor home and a lone woman. The day was sultry, as they must be for these types of letters, and a thin coat of sweat glistened upon my golden skin, further adding to the general seductiveness of the moment. Parking my bike against a tree, I stretched skyward languorously (because in these letters, such languorous stretching is a requirement), loosening the kinked muscles rippling my back. After pouring water over my head to cool ride-heated blood, the refreshing liquid dripped from my shoulder-length hair (for the purposes of this letter, my hair has grown—in fact, my lithe body has become heavily muscled by miles of riding, and if truth be told, I rather resemble a young Antonio Banderas).

So there I am, a celebrity doppelganger, alone in a park as the sun sets…with a woman.

The women of these Forum letters are frequently thirty-three-year-old widows, blonde and still beautiful, hour-glassed to perfection by time. Occasionally, you may come across a substitute teacher whose red hair inflames the hearts of her students, but generally the women seem to be golden haired. When just such a woman interrupted my late afternoon exercise regimen (a series of a hundred one-handed push-ups to maintain my Banderas-like proportions), I couldn't help but remember the Forum letters of my over-sexed adolescence.

"Hey there, big boy, would you like some dinner? I've got plenty in my RV."

She grabbed my elbow and steered me to her camper, which looked as if it hadn't been moved in years. Tall grasses stroked the top of the wheel wells. The rear tire was flat. The crooked screen door slammed my back as I stepped into the darkness.

Dinners in the traditional Forum letters usually consist of candles and merlot, followed by bubble baths and stockings and slow sensual evenings of dancing interrupted by uncontrollable passionate frenzies. Here, there may have been no little sexy red numbers accentuating hips and bust lines, no filet mignon steaks bleeding with some sort of symbolic passion, no satiny sheets on which to cool heated limbs, but nevertheless, there I sat, a plate of Tuna Helper before me and a desperate woman trying to seduce with blunted charms.

"It's a beautiful night," she whispered, gazing at the purple-streaked sky through the dirty windshield of her RV.

I glanced over my shoulder. "Looks like a storm is coming."

"The radio is calling for tornados a few miles west." She turned toward me and pushed her limp bangs from her eyes. "The wind's picking up, too. Going to be a cold night."

I stabbed at some tuna. "Thanks for dinner. I appreciate it. Lately, I've been so sick of trying to light my stove. It's wonderful to have warm food."

She grazed her chipped fingernails across my forearm. "Don't mention it. It's nice to have company."

I coughed and pulled my arm away.

"Do you live out here or something?"

"Yeah. Ever since my ex started pounding on me when he got drunk. I guess, about six months now. Ralph—he's the county Sheriff—keeps an eye out for me. But it gets awfully lonely." She pursed her thin lips, refusing to break eye contact. I coughed again and looked to my plate.

"You smoke?" She asked, reaching into a small bag and pulling out a pack of Lucky Strikes and a Zippo.

"Nah."

"You don't mind…"

"It's your camper."

She grabbed a cigarette from the pack with her teeth, lit it, and took a long drag. She flicked the ashes to the floor. "Nothing beats a cigarette after a meal." Her eyes swung from the smoking ember to capture mine. "Unless it's a cig after sex…"

My fork slipped from my hand.

She reached across the table and handed me my fork.

"You look like a strong man," she said between drags. "I've got some coke. We could do lines and get wild."

Emphasizing her point, she stood and reached across my face to a cabinet above my head. Her lopsided breasts were inches from my nose. Time had distorted the allure of this contemporary Calypso within a bent carnival mirror. I felt trapped in the fun house, yet I didn't feel like having any fun. I squirmed in my seat while she strained to reach her stash. Her leg touched mine. I flinched. A multi-colored, two-foot-long bong tumbled from the cabinet.

She giggled, and I squeezed around her lumpy breasts and scurried to the door. She glanced over her shoulder and grinned, all teeth and animal lust.

And that, Mary, was my *Penthouse* "Forum" moment. I left for my tent before this could develop into another Minnesota kidnapping, and at the point where the traditional Forum letter becomes interesting, mine ends—the juicy bits saved for my dreams of a passionate homecoming.

Love,
David

David Haber

DAY 96

....

RINGERS

August 18
City Park
Cooperstown, North Dakota

Dear Mary,

Imagine this:

You are the coach of the Junior World Horseshoe Pitching Champion. You taught him how to properly grip the shoes on his fifth birthday, and since then you've shown him countless tricks when double flopping and reverse flipping. He is your protégé, the apple of your eye, the Skywalker to your Yoda. This young pitcher had been steamrolling through a tournament in Wisconsin when he finally meets a worthy opponent: your eleven-year-old granddaughter. For whom do you root?

In her first ten throws, she nails eight ringers, and your prized student is forced to play the next twelve innings from behind. The coach in you is worried at the frailty of your apprentice's young ego, but the grandmother in you is bursting proud. Not only is your granddaughter beating the Junior World Champion, but she's also more than holding her own against an older, more experienced boy. You go, girl!

Before a rapt crowd of 150, the two competitors, enthusiastic disciple and close family, take their final throws, tied at thirty-nine. A ringer will win the match, as would a shoe in count (the former being worth three points, the latter, one point). The ringer never comes, and the judge is forced to measure the outcome. Your eyes remain locked shut only to be jimmied open by cheering.

It doesn't really matter who won the match.

What I want you to imagine is being torn in such a manner—feeling ripped apart by conflicting desires. Perhaps, this coach's dilemma was not nearly as stark as I think, but when I heard this story, I couldn't help but relate. I felt the coach's turmoil—the pull of wanting both players to win and succeed—as kin and student battled on the pitching field. There shouldn't have been a loser, but the nature of sport requires it; someone the coach loved would have to be consoled while the other was congratulated.

Such agitation of spirit fills me now, and Mary, I need you to understand it. Like this coach, I am being stretched in opposite directions, one toward San Francisco, the other toward you and home. I want to hurry, to dart through the Rockies and Cascades, zip down the coast, cross over those golden gates, and find an eastward-speeding train. On the other hand, I still feel I must take time, to drink from America's cup and savor each and every drop. There's so much to see, so many stories to hear.

With each tale, I grow in some new way, see some new sight, and more importantly, am allowed to gradually heal.

The wounds caused by Oma's loss and your injury are the most visible and raw, but there are others—deeper scars that have prevented me from crossing the threshold into adulthood. My lack of confidence. My extreme shyness. My inability to express myself as a grown man. Frankly, I still feel like an eleven-year-old kid. All this is to say, despite my almost unbearable desire to find a train or rent a car and return to you—I can't yet. Things have yet to be finished.

If I stop, I will regret, and yet another thing in my life will remain incomplete. How can you love an unfinished person, Mary? And, how can I love you as you deserve? I'm playing horseshoes with my life, tossing experience the forty feet across the sand courts of this country praying to hit a stake. All the innings have to be played; the journey must continue. Just as there must be a winner on the horseshoe court, there are no ties in life.

All I can hope is to pitch a ringer.

Love,
David

Letters to Eden

DAY 99

....

A DEVIL IN THE LAKE

August 20
A Picnic Table Soon to be Floating
Minnewaukan, North Dakota

DEAR MARY,
ABOUT HALFWAY BETWEEN FARGO AND MINOT, there is a lake. Old timers whisper that this lake contains the lost cousin of the Loch Ness Monster. Others claim that after an epic battle between tribes, the victorious Sioux were caught in a fierce storm roiling the waters, killing the entire war party—some say because the lake was rather upset at blood being shed on her shores. This, inevitably, drove a Sioux princess into the depths to reunite with her lost lover. On nights when the moon hides behind the clouds and waves trouble the water, it's told that this princess and her lover can be seen still searching for their lost companions. The Native Americans in the area refused to cross the lake into town until a bridge was constructed in 1897. They called this inland sea Minnewaukan Seche or "Spirit Lake is bad water." Today it is simply known as Devil's Lake.

That this body of water is possessed of spirit became rather obvious as I approached its shores. Over the past six years or so, the lake's water level has risen twenty-one feet, flooding roads and swallowing farms. Each year the lake grows, drowning more telephone poles, encroaching on towns, and causing city councils to reshape century-old infrastructures. A few years ago the village of Minnewaukan had been ten miles from the banks of Devil's Lake; now from a picnic table in the city park, I can toss a stone fifty feet and hit water. The water is swallowing everything.

As I neared the lake this morning, I began to notice an increased volume of truck traffic on the roads. At first, only the occasional big rig would roar by, and I prematurely supposed that my route passed the entrance to a gravel pit. That theory was disproved when I rounded a bend on SR 20 and saw hundreds of dump trucks and tractor trailers idling in a long line, waiting to empty their contents on different portions of the roadway. An orange-clad conductor would point to this truck or that and have the driver dump dirt on the asphalt, which would be followed by a steamroller to pack it down.

In its wisdom, the North Dakota Department of Transportation decided that the only way to save the highways was to raise them above the lake. Tons of rock and earth are hauled from the surrounding states, maybe even from as far as Timbuktu. When one truck leaves to get more dirt, another is there waiting to dump. The cycle is constant and apparently unending.

Over the years, the roads, which had at one time surrounded the body of water, presently cut through its middle in some places; elevated some thirty feet or more from the ground, these stretches slide across the lake's surface like a water-saturated log. As I bounced along the unpaved highway, I could look down and see the tops of telephone poles rippling the surface. If the lake were ever drained, driving along these raised roads would have the same effect as speeding south along the Pacific Coast Highway without the rising mountains on the left to comfort—cliffs plummeting to bogs on either side. The subterranean waters feeding this lake are overflowing, and its spirit continues to grow.

The activity of piling earth ever higher atop these roadways is like constructing a dam across the Atlantic Ocean; there's really no point to such ridiculous effort, but politics and money always have the final word in such matters. The state doesn't want to appropriate funds for new roads that may be washed away in a few years. Farmers want the lake drained so that lost fields can be reclaimed. The town of Minnewaukan is pleased with the current shores because of America's love affair with waterfront property. And the Sioux...well the Sioux pray every day that the cursed lake rises to steal back that which was originally stolen.

The spirit of Devil's Lake is angry, and that anger appears to be growing daily. The waters will continue to rise—to drown everything, so that we will all become mourning Sioux princesses searching for lost loves. It will not stop until all of North Dakota is swallowed. In fact, I best get a move on; otherwise, I'll be forced to build an ark from this picnic table and sail myself to the Pacific.

Love,
David

Letters to Eden

DAY 99

....

ARCHEOLOGICAL RUINS

August 20
City Park
Esmond, North Dakota

Dear Mary,

The town of Esmond is typical of rural North Dakota. Of the 159 residents, sixty-eight are over sixty-two years old. By comparison, the median age in Fargo is thirty. Those remaining struggle on farms that should have been transferred to sons and granddaughters long ago.

Most of the youth have fled. City jobs have become far more attractive than working on the family farm. Higher education has decimated the rural lands of America, making the allure of cities and urban centers that much stronger to the growing class of the highly trained. Big cities provide work that's not only easy to find but also substantially less rigorous than scratching at the dirt in one of the harshest environments imaginable. Given the choice, many opt for a guaranteed paycheck from a law office or a factory or even a telemarketing firm in the city rather than the uncertainty of life on the fields of North Dakota.

The population of rural North Dakota peaked in the 1930s and has been steadily decreasing as families flee to Chicago, Detroit, Minneapolis, and even Fargo. An agrarian existence on the high plains is difficult at best; temperatures fluctuate between negative sixty degrees in the dead of winter and 121 degrees in the summer. With the advent of huge agro-businesses and the subsequent reduction of wheat prices, the small family farm is becoming a dinosaur. The young can read the times as well as anyone.

Just forty years ago, before the youth escaped to cities and the bottom rotted out of farming, Esmond thrived with a population hovering around five hundred. Seven grain elevators cluttered the horizon with prosperity. Five bars and a number of cafés served thirsty farmers coffee or beer depending on the time and the weather. On Main Street, there was even a small hotel, rumored to have boarded John Dillinger or Pretty Boy Floyd or Machine Gun Kelly during their flight from the FBI.

Today, the grain elevators are gone, a single café serves the needs of the community, and the long-vacant hotel has been pulled down only to fester in a rotting pile, taunting the residents with the inevitable future of the town. Earlier today, someone (perhaps one of the eight teenagers still living in Esmond) became disturbed enough by the decay to ignite the remains of the old rooming house in a ceremony of frustration and hopelessness. It still smolders now.

Hidden within this shrinking township, however, another force burns as well. There is life here. There's still a glimmer of vibrancy. At the café, there's still a reason to serve the famous half-inch thick pancakes too big to be contained by the edge of a plate. People still farm; folks still dream, and a new model for rural life is emerging.

Mo8 Designs, a tiny company crafting and selling souvenirs such as jewelry and refrigerator magnets, is actually flourishing in this town. Started as a hobby while Nellie Edwards raised her eight children—"handcrafted between distractions" she claims—her business has grown with her kids, supplying tourist shops in thirty-eight states. Many of her children have become expert in clay molding and miniature painting. With their help, she has created molds depicting Washington's crossing of the Delaware, Lewis and Clark's journey to find the Northwest Passage, bears stealing honey, and turtles just moseying along. Each piece is carefully shaped and fired, hand-painted and glazed, and then sent off to fulfill an order in Minnesota or New Mexico or North Carolina.

What began as a way to bring in a little cash on the side has swelled into a model for Dakotan entrepreneurship. Chrys Edwards, Nellie's Welsh husband, has watched the business expand beyond the confines of their home workshop in amazement. With eight children, space had already been at a premium. But now, as the demand for Mo8-designed products increases, the need for a larger workspace has become apparent.

The sad fact is that both Chrys and Nellie realize their time in Esmond is coming to end. Against the odds, their business is succeeding and requires more space. So, the family plans to relocate to Butte, North Dakota, where they have found a huge house with plenty of room for growth. In a few months, Esmond will be ten residents smaller and that much closer to oblivion. But North Dakota will remain strong.

    The Edwardses give hope to rural America because they refuse to forsake small town life for the allure of Minot or Fargo or Chicago. Although Esmond may eventually fade from the Dakotan landscape, other small towns will survive the fate of becoming but a mark on the map of a future archeological dig—a place where Dillinger once slept. There is the promise of Butte. The hope of Mo8 Designs. And the dream that, someday, the stubborn vibrancy of rural America will welcome our family with its famous pancakes the diameter of a dinner plate.

Love,
David

DAY 100

....

AT THE CENTER OF THINGS

August 21
The Hub of America
Rugby, North Dakota

Dear Mary,

I stand at 48° 21′ 19″ north and 99° 59′ 57″ west—the location designated, in 1931, as the geographical center of North America. Leaning against the fifteen-foot stone obelisk marking the spot, I can't help but thank the heavens that I crossed the geographical center of my journey a thousand miles back.

At least I hope I have.

Love,
David

David Haber

DAY 104

....

THE INVISIBLE FREIGHT TRAIN

August 25
Lewis and Clark State Park
Lake Sakakawea, North Dakota

DEAR MARY,
 IN THE BADLANDS OF NORTH DAKOTA, about twenty miles from civilization, all my water ran out. My throat became as parched as the rippled landscape, wrinkled and carved by eons of fierce weather. Surprisingly, thirst wasn't my chief concern. I was too busy blocking the pounding jabs of the wind to actually care.

 This morning I felt that my spirits had been sufficiently fortified by a large pancake breakfast to pull me through the desolation of western North Dakota. Not until the fat Dakota grasshoppers began kamikazeing my legs—and, assisted by the wind, my eyes and mouth—did any perceived strength crumble like the lands surrounding me.

 The wind's gathering intensity deafened me for three hours. I couldn't hear the grasshoppers pinging between my spokes. I couldn't hear the breath being forced from my lungs in gasps. All that existed was the constant roar from an invisible locomotive riding the spiraled rails of my cochlea.

I was deaf.

I began shouting and yelling, hoping to quiet the wind for even a moment with my voice. The air swallowed all sound but its own. I had been made dumb as well as deaf. My spirit wilted. I stopped riding and just stood straddling my bike, wanting to cry, feeling the thickening in my chest but lacking the moisture to actually form tears.

The dead land matched my spirit.

I screamed. It was a child's scream—a high-pitched wail calling the ghosts of my past to carry me from this country of death. It wasn't even a country, really. It was the stuff to which a country degrades. Red rocks pounded to red dust by red wind.

This has been the worst day of riding ever. And I don't want to feel anything like it again. Yet ending this journey in defeat is a defeat itself. It's one thing to just stop riding, it's altogether different to fail and flee. But those are just words.

Honestly, I'm afraid to wake up tomorrow. I'm afraid to face the wind once again. I'm afraid of being blown away—of losing myself to a powerful gust. The wind has beaten me to the brink, and I don't know how much more I can withstand. I've been rubbed raw to the bone, and the only succor is a sleep troubled by the distant rumbling of the coming freight train.

David

DAY 106

TAG! YOU'RE IT

August 27
Shady Rest RV Park
Glasgow, Montana

Dear Mary,

I heard the Lab rustling around along the side of the road well before I spotted her tail swaying in the grass. As I approached, my panniers creaked, and the Lab's head jerked upright, ears tilted forward, one leg cocked, nostrils flaring. She stood frozen and suspended, waiting for and grinning at what was to come. I shifted and zipped past her. Let the games begin!

Paws against pavement proclaimed her pursuit. I slowed for a moment. She barked once, happy. I turned to see her long tongue flapping in the wind. The Lab was no more than five feet away. I picked up the pace. She matched it. We were going 10.2 mph. I alternately coasted and spun, allowing the dog to feel she had a hope of catching me. With the tailwind I had lucked into, the dog had no chance. I was destined to win this game of canine tag.

A dull thud and prolonged whimpering whirled me in my saddle. The Lab was on its side struggling to regain its feet a few paces behind. I braked, trying to figure out what happened. Had she stepped on a nail? A deep growl raised my hackles as a huge gray wolf–dog beast tore from the tall grass and slammed into my rear pannier. Before even a curse could escape my lips, I took off.

The monster followed and gained.

Jesus!

This huge wolf creature, its gigantic head at waist height, shook the very ground with its loping gait. I could sense the monstrous physical presence gaining. I could smell its fetid breath. Its clear blue eyes reflected unspeakable horrors.

I shifted up. And up. And up. 14.7 mph. 16.3 mph. 19.2 mph. The wolf–dog drew closer. And closer. And yet closer still. A mile had passed. The creature would not tire. My bike suddenly jolted beneath me. The beast had headed butted my pannier! I swerved left and right and back again, trying to confuse.

Which body part could I sacrifice for the greater whole? Which limb would satisfy this beast's hunger? I wish I'd had a steak, or some ribs, or even an entire cow. That would surely slow this devil hound for a moment.

The wind threw me forward, adding its speed to my own, propelling me at 27.3 mph uphill. The dog started to limp, and finally the distance began to increase between us. I shot down the other side of the hill at 45.8 mph, spinning my cranks uselessly as the blessed wind pushed me onward.

I can't say when exactly that wolfhound Hell-beast returned to its doghouse in Hades; it had been behind me one moment then had disappeared in the next. After about five more minutes of maintaining a wind-assisted speed of 22.2 mph—finally confident that the creature would not return—my legs shook me from my saddle, and I collapsed on the road's sandy shoulder, my entire body burning. Never had I ridden so hard, and never will I again. There'll be no more light-hearted games of canine tag on this trip. From now on, I'm going to start carrying prime rib.

Love,
David

Letters to Eden

DAY 107

....

THE BUFFALO SLEEP

August 28
McGuires' Motel
Harlem, Montana

Dear Mary,

A FEW MILES OUTSIDE OF SACO, I leaned against a split rail fence surrounding two boulders, eating my lunch. Called Sleeping Buffalo Rock, these glacial stones were held sacred by the tribes that once roamed the plains. Apparently, the original formation resembled a herd of buffalo—one of the rocks I stood before being the leader. Only having seen a few buffalo from a distance and never having actually observed one sleeping, I can't attest to its likeness. The stones were pale with maroon freckles, not a dark brown, and certainly were not covered in fur, not even moss or lichen; the effort of imagination to find a hidden buffalo seemed extreme. Still, the Plain's tribes saw sleeping buffalo, so sleeping buffalo these stones were and always will be.

A middle-aged couple approached the boulders talking. "They say touching the rocks will give you good luck."

"It's windy out here, Frank. Let's go back in the camper."

"Don't you want to see the buffalo?"

"Doesn't much look like anything but a couple of big pebbles to me. And why the heck are they penned in? They're rocks for cryin' out loud. Seems more like an ashtray with all those cigarette butts scattered everywhere…My hair's a disaster. I'm going back."

"Be right with you, dear." The man looked at me. "Are you going to touch it?"

I shrugged. "Probably."

"That sign over there says the Indians use to leave all sorts of offerings before hunts and things. Looks like now, the only thing people leave behind are Marlboros. Guess that's the way of things."

"Hey, at least, people still stop, though."

"So long as their hair doesn't get ruffled." The man reached into his pocket and tossed a few coins toward the stones. "Can't hurt, right?" He smiled shyly and turned back to his camper, hands buried deep in his pockets, shoulders hunched against the wind.

I reached through the fence and touched the stone. It was cool. The buffalo still slept, even amongst the butts.

Love,
David

Letters to Eden

DAY 108

....

BROKEN SPOKES, DIFFERENT FOLKS

August 29
City Park
Gildford, Montana

Dear Mary,

When I heard the ping, I thought it was just another grasshopper yet again committing suicide between my spokes. After a few hundred feet, however, my cadence dropped. Pedaling became impossible. A quick look to the rear tire revealed the broken elbow and headless shaft of a limp spoke, causing the wheel to rub against the brake pads. Never having changed a spoke before, I have to admit to a bit of trepidation at the whole prospect.

Instead of dealing with the situation along the side of the road, I decided it would be best saved until later. I released the rear brake calipers and wove the broken spoke back into the pattern so that it wouldn't entangle itself with the chainstay and throw me to the pavement.

Climbing back onto my bike, I saw the distant form of two eastbound riders. Thinking a little afternoon conversation might do wonders to get my mind off the spoke, I waited until they neared. One bike pulled a trailer, while the other had panniers. Two six-foot tall caution flags swayed orange warnings at passing cars. The two riders wore matching purple jerseys. They looked loaded for adventure, ripe for swapping tales.

"Hey, where you headed?" I called across the road.

They looked my way and just kept riding. Not even a hello. I stared after them, shocked. Whenever I came across another rider, if traffic permitted, we would stop and chat. I must have stunk something awful. Oh, well, their loss. At least, that's what I tried to convince myself.

Of course, it wasn't their loss but mine. They rode in a pair. I was alone. I'm the one who needed the company—a simple hello, a little eye contact. Still, you would think that upon seeing a two-wheeled compatriot heading in the opposite direction one would at least be curious about road conditions.

Not two minutes later, three riders again approached from the west with the same tall flags. This time I would not be ignored. I swerved to the middle of the road, dismounted, and balanced the frame against my back. When the riders were about ten feet away, I waved and shouted, "Good afternoon! Riding far? The road gets a bit choppy up ahead."

Without a word, they passed.

What the hell? What kind of riders were these? They clearly weren't racers, not with all the bags hanging off their frames and cruising along at about ten mph. I was so irritated that I almost turned to chase after them. I felt like my prom date had just dumped me to dance with Chip Radcliffe, the blonde and handsome Homecoming King, all muscles and straight white teeth.

There's a community in adventuring, whether by bike, foot, or motorcycle; Neale taught me that months ago, and experience has only strengthened his lesson. As wayfarers or pilgrims or whatever it is, we have an obligation to help each other, especially in the small ways. A smile here, a little conversation there, human contact, sharing stories…that's the adventure. Perhaps, these folk were new to riding and didn't yet realize that without help the long hours of loneliness (even in a group) would eventually break the spirit.

I rode on, frustrated and alone.

As the sun began to slide toward the horizon, I stopped in a park for a bit of a nap. Two riders, about fifty-five, relaxed in the shade. A man slept in a tent. His partner, her gray hair pulled back in a tight bun, read a novel at the picnic table. Their equipment had been strewn about in the familiar chaos caused when setting camp.

I smiled. "Good riding?"

The woman slowly looked up from her book, eyed me, and tossed me aside like a crumpled hamburger wrapper. She turned back to her book.

Jesus Christ!

This was crap. Was there something wrong with me? Did I not speak English? Was I too ugly to talk to? Did I seem too needy? What the hell! What fun is riding across the country when nobody will talk with you? I thought about plopping myself down next to the woman and just staring, figuring that eventually an actual living, breathing person would have to be acknowledged.

Instead I hopped on my saddle and rode toward the next town, for the first time wishing my bike was a car so that I could burn some rubber. I pedaled fast, trying to create enough sweat to water my smoldering anger. I would never talk again. Clearly, something in me put people off.

The town of Gildford was quiet as I turned looking for the park. In the distance, I noticed through the heat-rippled air a shaggy pony being led down the middle of the street by a severely bowlegged man. With legs like his, all I would need is a quiver of arrows and some string to go hunting. As I drew nearer, it became clear that this gentleman was about seventy years old, all but two of which had to have been spent on the back of a horse, so splayed were his limbs. If I wanted to back track a few miles, I could have picked up the pair of colorful golf pants discarded on the shoulder, given them to this cowboy, and attached a score of helium balloons to his shoulders. As he floated heavenward, a tiny rainbow would stretch across the sky; he was that bowlegged.

The man waved as I passed. I nodded but refused to say a word. His horse skittered a bit.

"Hey, your tire looks a bit wobbly. You need help fixin' that? There's a playground that a-way."

Finally words. Sweet words. Maybe I didn't smell so bad after all.

"You know how to fix spokes?" I asked as I followed the man to the park.

"Nope. My grandkids say it's tough though, so I reckon you may need a hand." He released his horse to graze near the swing set. He sat on the picnic table, chewing a piece of grass as I unloaded my bags and prepared a space to operate.

My bow-legged friend reasoned that the supposedly difficult conundrum of wheel fixing was overrated so long as you were willing to twist the new spoke into all sorts of unnatural shapes to fit it between the hub and freewheel. He reckoned, in the slow deliberate cowboy way, that it would be far less tedious just to bend the metal shaft and finagle it into place rather than trying to take off the gears; when tension was added to take out the wobble in the wheel, he figured the kinks and bends would straighten, which happened just as he thought.

As he watched me, occasionally suggesting to bend that or twist there, he asked me about my route. When he learned that I planned to swing up to Canada before heading to Glacier National Park, the man spat out the grass stem on which he chewed.

"Why are you goin' to go off and do that?"

"I'm just following my maps."

"Lemme take a peek at 'em."

I pointed to the table. He grabbed one and unfolded it. "If these aren't the darnedest things I've ever seen. How in blazes do you read them? They're all cut up in rectangles."

"Here. Look." I pointed to a section. "Each panel is about a thirty mile area. It's easier than having a whole map wedged in your bag. You get used to it after a while."

He snorted.

"Why in all of Heaven do they have you goin' up that way? Doesn't make any sense. You're better off stayin' on 2 and followin' the High-Line to Browning. Then you could turn on 89 and hit St. Mary's in flash. Or better yet, take 464 to Babb. It's a smaller road. Nothin's up that way, except cattle, but it's real purty." His horse snorted, looking up from the grass. "Hush now, Chester. You just don't fancy goin' up there 'cause it means workin'. I'll tell you straight, you should go to Browning and forget your crazy maps. They take you almost 150 miles out of the way. Canada. Pssshhh. You don't need it. Besides, those small border crossings close this time of year."

"I should head to Browning, then?"

"If it were me, that's what I'd do. You just don't want to spend the night in Browning. Those reservation towns can get awfully rowdy on weekends. But I'm not you, so you can do whatever you want. Although you may get stuck up there in Canada, if you follow those maps. Snow's comin' soon."

"Snow?"

"Yup. Snow. Comes earlier each year."

"Browning it is then."

"Good choice. How's that wheel looking?"

I spun the wheel in its dropouts. There was a slight wobble, but otherwise it looked great.

"Well, I'll have to tell my grandkids about that trick." He scooted off the end of the table and whistled to Chester. "Best git home. Don't want to worry the Missus. Good luck now. That wheel should git you to wherever you're goin'."

Actually, Mary, if I can avoid cranky and silent riders and keep meeting people like Bow-Legged Bob, I won't need any wheels at all to find my way home.

Love,
David

David Haber

DAY 109

....

WRASSLIN'

August 30
She-Oole Lake Park
Shelby, Montana

Dear Mary,

The depression consistently arrives at 1:30 each afternoon. If there were a way for me to jump through time, leaping from 1:29 to 2:31, I'm confident my mileage output would greatly increase. For that hour, I feel so melancholy, so distraught, so alone. The effort required to continue westward is incredible, and each day my reserves are that much more depleted.

When the feelings become the darkest, sometimes I take a nap. Occasionally, I simply stop for the day, frustrated with my swinging moods. Today, I gulped down a milkshake. This ride just doesn't seem to be getting easier.

I know you're tired of hearing about my trials with the wind, so I won't dwell on being tossed off the road to somersault into a gulley—I won't complain about being blinded by the swirling grit carried by the air—I won't obsess over seeing a tractor trailer, hauling the largest

Letters to Eden

ball-bearing ever, tipped on its side across U.S. 2, tumbled by a particularly fierce gust.

It's difficult for me not to talk about the wind a little, though. See, Mary, it's desperately trying to get my attention. There's an actual wrestling match occurring outside my tent—between the west and north winds. I'm not talking about the relative order of a high school wrestling match either, with the protective headgear and Tarzan body suits. What's going on is a full-fledged battle royal between The Mighty Masked Zephyr from the Northern Wastes and Superfly Windy Snuka hailing from the distant west. There is face paint, knee-high red boots, skimpy wrestling trunks, folding chairs, and top turn buckles. It's a steel cage match to the death, and my tent happens to be pitched directly in the center of the ring.

I have pulled in all my equipment, except my bike (which is chained to a tree so it won't blow away). My things are divided and piled into each corner to lend support to the stakes. Still my tent shakes and flexes as if someone is beating it with kicks and punches. I can see the afterglow of the lightning flare the walls blue, yet the wind is so loud I can't hear the thunder rumbling in its wake. Neither can I hear the rain pounding the nylon, but that it's raining I'm certain because of the steady drip leaking through the fly, creating a small puddle at my feet. I can't sleep; I can't think; I can't

Sorry about that.

The Masked Zephyr just leapt from the top rope, smashing into my tent. Hopefully, Superfly will move in for the pin while the Beast from the North is still dazed. Otherwise, I may be the next body slammed during Nature's wrasslin' match.

Love,
David

Letters to Eden

DAY 110

....

REDUCTIO AD ABSURDUM

August 31
Super 8 Motel
Cut Bank, Montana

Dear Mary,

PROPOSITION I:

One is not only an idiot but also completely insane when attempting to bicycle in winds gusting to speeds approaching eighty mph.

DEFINITION I: *Bicycle*—a vehicle comprising two wheels attached in a frame on one plane, propelled by pedals and steered with handlebars fixed to the front wheel.

DEFINITION II: *Insane*—stricken with or indicative of mental derangement.

DEFINITION III: *Idiot*—a human being destitute of common intellectual talent, whether congenital, developmental, or accidental; an individual without comprehension from birth; a natural fool.

Postulate I: A functioning bicycle will move forward when pedaled.

1. Let us first assume that DD (Dumb Dave) rides a bicycle, and furthermore, is neither an idiot nor insane.
2. Let us further suppose that BW (Big Wind) represents winds gusting at eighty mph eastwardly.
3. Being of sound mind and reasonable intelligence, DD heads west into BW.

$$DD \rightarrow BW$$

4. Twenty-five miles is traveled in four hours, and DD is eventually smashed flat by BW.

$$B\underset{DD}{W}$$

5. DD has averaged 5.4 mph over four hours (not including frequent breaks), which by definition appears idiotic,
6. And furthermore, DD has sought his own demise, which is clearly a sign of mental derangement.
7. But it was assumed DD was neither an idiot nor insane, which is absurd.

Therefore, DD is a complete idiot and utterly insane for attempting to bicycle into winds gusting at velocities approaching eighty mph.

Q.E.D.

Love,
David

DAY 111

....

CATTLE CALL

September 1
Chewing Blackbones Campground
Blackfeet Indian Reservation

Dear Mary,

You know you're losing it when you find yourself standing along the side of the road, communicating with cattle. The sad fact is I have become rather proficient in their language. People think that mooing comes by rounding the lips...moooo. Actually the proper call starts with your lips closed and rises from back of the throat, the sound split by a tongue curled toward the roof of your mouth.

Mmmmmmmmmoooooooooaahhhh!

For ten minutes, I called the cows to me, explaining how lonely the road can be and how much I despised hamburgers, much preferring ostrich. It wasn't long before a small herd had clustered near the barbed wire fence to listen in on my bovine orations.

The younger calves huddled close, trying to touch me through the barrier as if I were the lead singer of the

Handsome Heifers and they were my adoring fans. The challenging roar from a rather large bull interrupted my ballad. Becoming suddenly aware of my own frail humanity, I jumped onto my saddle and hauled my rump west before it was roasted. Metaphorically speaking, of course.

Word had spread that there was new bull in town, though—a strange looking skinny fellow with round, spinning legs and no horns. As I climbed higher toward the feet of the Rockies, cattle stopped munching on grass long enough to watch me pass. They, too, had heard rumor of this new bull and were intrigued. Some twenty minutes later, while zooming down a fairly long hill, a small calf leapt through the barbed wire and ran across my path, perhaps to get a closer look.

The thing with rampaging cattle is that they stare at you with such docile eyes, saying nothing, their next action a complete mystery. You can at least read the anger in a bull's gaze. With cows, you just can't tell what in the heck they're thinking. Would she charge me? Would she move from my path? Would she simply stand in the middle of the road and watch me slam into her flank?

Whatever she was going to do, I thought to myself, she had better do quick because I was moving far too fast to stop without killing myself. Just when I decided to swerve to the right and use the grass for padding in case I crashed, the cow lumbered back to the shoulder and mooed a moo of such disappointment as I passed that even a city slicker could have understood.

"Why do you flee," she wailed. "Without even a hello?"

With the cow's fading question chasing me, I vowed never to communicate with cattle again. There are some things that should just remain in the herd.

Love,
David

David Haber

DAY 112

....

SUMMER'S END

September 2
Logan Pass
Glacier National Park, Montana

DEAR MARY,
TO BEGIN THE DAY, I was wearing shorts and a tee shirt. By mid-afternoon, I had bundled myself in every single article of clothing stowed within my bags, including two pairs of dirty socks. In the month of September, it can get mighty chilly atop Logan Pass.

Although the climb didn't seem as steep as the Kancamagus, the ascent up Going-to-the-Sun Highway was far longer, for which, in a strange reversal, I was thankful. The rising grade was a new challenge, a change from the endless weeks trapped upon the flat monotony of the High Plains. The effort of climbing soothed my wind-wearied mind.

I didn't notice the plummeting temperature, just the incredible glory of the Rockies—my vaporized breath thickening the thin air—the glacial ice creeping high above the tree line—the snowmelt tumbling over broken cliffs rising yet higher still, stretching to tickle the hairs in Heaven's nose.

Words are empty when erected next to the works of Nature. The colors are brighter and truer, the cliffs far steeper, the heights simply unimaginable as jagged stones thrust toward eternity. Mary, I must bring you to this park someday, and you will see what I have felt. That I promise; but we must remember to pack warm clothes.

Because at an elevation of 6,664 feet, it is freakin' cold.

While straddling the Continental Divide, I scanned the cliffs for mountain goats...and shivered. I watched tourists step from their cars and scurry back to the heated interiors...and shivered. A freezing mist clung to everything; I shivered still more.

I would have traded my bike for something hot, but there were no concessions atop the pass. No hot chocolate. No hot tea. Nothing that could lend a bit of warmth to my freezing bones. I tried everything to fight the chill. Beneath my orange rain jacket, I layered my fleece shirt atop a turtleneck over my two cycling jerseys. Despite the wool gloves, my hands burned. In desperation, after already having squeezed into my cycling tights, I donned my pair of thin, nylon pants. Still, I leaked heat.

With frozen fingers, I unpacked my stove and found a relatively sheltered spot behind a wall. Huddled from the wind, I simmered water to boil. From the bottom of my pannier, I dug out Neale's crusted jar of brown sauce. It may not have been coffee, but at least the water would have flavor. The stove warmed me just enough to emphasize the chill icing my back. The bubbling water raged, and I imagined coffee grounds, rather than HP Sauce, sinking to the bottom of my pot, disappearing within a fragrant brown murk. How I wished for a cup of cowboy coffee.

I poured my warmed brown sauce water—I'll call it Bloke Coffee—into a cup. Pure heat leeched through my fingers all the way to my numb toes. My teeth relaxed from their persistent chattering. I took a sip. Well, at least the concoction was warm. With Bloke Coffee swelling my tongue, I looked up from my cup, and all my past worries were realized: drifting and swirling to drape Logan Pass with the silence of a new season, snow fell.

Love,
David

PART XIV

....

DOWN FROM THE MOUNTAIN

From Lake MacDonald, Montana,
to Anacortes, Washington

DAY 112

....

THE HIGH LONESOME

September 2
Sprague Creek Campground
Lake MacDonald, Montana

D‍EAR M‍ARY,
 I AM CAMPED between the Euclidean trunks of perfectly straight pines reaching toward the blue and white sheet of the Montana sky. The clouds move quickly, pushed by the speeding jet stream, but for once, I can't feel the wind. The pines protect and shelter while their limbs bow to the breeze, holding their needled hats tightly in place atop their heads.

I have finally descended from the barren Hades of the High Lonesome. The stark sameness of the Great Plains is gone. The air no longer dries my lungs with dust. The Plain's grasshoppers are committing suicide beneath the wheels of some other rider. The horizon is so close that I can almost touch it.

My spirit is free of the High Lonesome.
And I can ride forever.

Love,
David

David Haber

DAY 114

....

THE ADOPTION

September 4
Whitefish Lake Recreation Area
Whitefish, Montana

Dear Mary,

The sun disappeared with a crack as I pulled into Whitefish Recreation Area looking for a place to camp. I had been to two campgrounds earlier in the day, and everything was booked solid. This campground appeared to be full as well. I circled the loop twice trying to find a site, but even the mosquito-infested patch of marshland backing up to a nasty bog was occupied by a large family. Things did not look good when I found the ranger near the bathroom.

"Sorry, we're filled up for the night. You might want to try the KOA a few miles down the road. They may have an opening. But then again, they may not. It's been pretty busy the past few days. It is Labor Day weekend after all. It'll probably be the last nice spell until spring."

"There's no tenting-only sites? Back in the woods or something?"

"Nope. There're all filled with a troop of Boy Scouts. Sorry."

"Look, all I've got is this bike and a tent. Couldn't I just set it up on that grass over there or something?" I pointed to a small area of green next to the bathroom. "I'm sure no one will even notice."

"Sorry, but that's against the rules. I can't allow it. I'm sure you'll be able to find another campground. Somewhere. You'll just have to move on."

"But I'm on a bike. It's dark."

"Sorry. I've got to get back to checking sites. Have a nice—"

"Hector? Is that you?" An older gentleman, wearing tan slacks and a light blue cardigan, lumbered toward us from the restrooms. The ranger and I both stared. "Hector, it is you. I can't believe it. I hoped you would make it. They said you'd be riding a bike, but damn, what a set-up you've got there."

I tried to hide my confusion. I'd never seen this man before in my life.

"Don't you remember me? It's your Uncle Larry. From Missoula. It's been years, I know, but I use to bounce you on my knee. You were only about this high." He gestured to his waist.

I smiled and nodded, glancing at the ranger who watched amused.

"Well, what are you waiting for? Come on over. I'll help you with that tent. Dinner should be ready in a minute. The Uncle Larry special. Your mother loves it."

I wheeled my bike toward his site.

"Hi. The name's Larry Gunthersen," he whispered, shaking my hand. "Call me Uncle Larry, though. I sort of like it."

"Sure thing, Uncle Larry."

And so on this Memorial Day, I had found a place to sleep. Dinner was coming, and I had gained a new family. At least for one night.

Love,
David

Letters to Eden

DAY 115

....

AN UNCLE'S VICES

September 5
Rexford Bench Campground
Rexford, Montana

Dear Mary,

UNCLE LARRY IS A HARD LIVING MAN. His hands tell the story—cracked and broken, twisted and crooked, nicotine-stained and raw, his hands are sorrow and confusion. He had worked in the iron mines of Minnesota most of his life only to retire in Missoula after a messy divorce. Despite her many accusations, he can't quite comprehend why his wife left. Sure, he has a wandering eye, but to appreciate beauty is not such a terrible thing. He never touched, simply watched—and *greatly appreciated*. He knew he wasn't providing the emotional support that his wife craved, yet that doesn't mean he wasn't trying in his own bumbling way.

It may sound as if I'm apologizing for Uncle Larry, but really, he needs no apology. He is what he is—a man whose craft is dying as jobs become more mechanized, whose lifestyle, saturated with cigarette smoke, beer, and gambling, is frowned upon by many, and whose role as provider and protector became challenged when he least expected it.

His wife had come home from what he thought was an afternoon of errands, dressed in a smart little business suit and black pumps. She may have been wearing a tad too much eye shadow, her lipstick may have been a shade too bright, but she felt young again. Alive. Twenty years of raising kids, although wonderful, had worn her down at forty-five. But that day, she remembered what it felt to be excited and starting something new.

Aunt Larry had been hired as a secretary with McClintock Tooling down on Elm Street, a lowly job perhaps, but it was hers. She had won it. She would learn to type, learn to use that Internet thingy, and be the best damn secretary McClintock Tooling had ever hired.

"What do you think?" I can imagine her asking as she pirouetted before her husband.

And I can just as easily hear his confusion as he responds, "Why are you dressed up today? Isn't Thursday the night we normally go to Old Country Buffet?"

"Sure. Sure. But I had an interview today. We need to celebrate. So how do you like the outfit?"

"Pretty fancy. Personally, I like you in skirts better, but I suppose pants are all the rage now-a-days. I didn't know you had that interview today, though. I thought the article about the garden club came out last week."

"It was a job interview. Over at McClintock."

"A job?"

"Yes. I'm going to start working."

Last night, over a dying fire, Uncle Larry explained the hurt. It wasn't that he didn't want his wife to feel valuable, to feel alive, to try something different. He just felt this job of hers directly threatened his manhood, made him somehow obsolete. She didn't need him anymore. She could cook. She could clean. She could even mow grass. Now, she could make money, too.

It wasn't solely about the money, though. To him, it seemed this job made her important—no, vital—to people other than her family in a very visible way. The town would talk. His buddies would razz him. His wife would only have time for the job, and he would spend his golden years alone watching *General Hospital*. That her employer, that old cheat McClintock, was his main poker rival only chapped his hide further.

He tried to support her as best as he knew how, but inevitably, the marriage collapsed around his ears. As her new life was beginning, his was coming to a quick end. Old classmates were moving to Palm Beach, his kids were getting married, and every day, he seemed to get only lonelier. His wife had new friends and greater responsibilities, while his life matched the dark sameness of the mines.

His wife began going to the gym five times a week; she and her girlfriends would spend hours after work laughing and joking at the Ruby Lounge, some newfangled martini bar. She was living Uncle Larry's life in reverse, and he was jealous. He was married to a woman, who on many nights he couldn't recognize, with her frosted blonde highlights and conversations about the World Wide Web. The divorce was inevitable.

On the day she quit smoking, he knew it was over. They had been separated for only two months at that point, but Uncle Larry still clung to the incredible hope that he could somehow win her back. He knew he had treated her poorly; he knew that she felt chained by his very presence. Yet twenty-two years of marriage had to count for something. He would change; he would be better. He would get his life in order. He would join a gym. He would become her exercise partner. He would gain a taste for gin and vodka and vanquish beer from the icebox. With that hope, he knocked on her apartment door with a gift: a new blue pinstriped suit and a sweep-necked blouse with mother-of-pearl buttons. Size ten, he remembered; he knew she would look beautiful.

She glanced at the outfit when she opened her door and said, "I'm a size six now."

Looking at him made her sick. Cracked with deep scars cut in the mines, his was a face of obsolete violence—like a rusting tank half buried in sand. A pitiful face. He could never be her husband again. There were too many years of suffering in silence for her to acknowledge his efforts. It was far too late for reconciliation. She didn't want to talk. She didn't want the outfit.

"You still smoke, right?" She asked. "Do you want to buy my old cigarettes?"

Uncle Larry explained that she had recently ordered seven cartons online from some nefarious Russian company and would be unable to return the shipment. That's 1,400 cigarettes, manufactured overseas, with enough tar and dung and other carcinogens rolled in with the tobacco to paralyze a horse. There was no offer for reconciliation—no offer for a gym partnership—just the chance to buy more than a thousand cigarettes on which my new uncle could slowly kill himself.

I listened to Uncle Larry's story, watching his hands wring and clench as he relived the past year. The embers glowed orange in the fire pit. As the fire turned to ash, the chill Montana evening pulled dark confessions from us both, heating the air with hard truths difficult to admit.

As much as I may wish Aunt Larry her well-deserved freedom and rebirth, I can't help feeling that she should never have left—that Uncle Larry should be forgiven his archaic behavior—that there should have been an opportunity for me to meet her here in Montana. I don't think this because I have a natural sympathy for the male point of view but rather because I see my father in this man, and in my father, I see myself.

What frightens me and makes me suffer with this man is the fear of trying to hold love together and failing, being unable to change, being unable to adapt—like my adopted Uncle Larry, like my father. We are so screwed up, Mary. We try to be strong. We try to be sensitive. We try and try and try, yet fall far short. I wish trying is good enough. I wish trying could re-unite my parents. I wish I could say that all my trying will erase past mistakes and future missteps. I just want a family, a home.

Eden Lane is gone, though. I don't have a whole family anymore. Just like Larry and his ex, my parents can't spend more than a few minutes together. Uncle Larry's story could be my story. We are not so different, any of us. All I know is what I've seen, and what I've seen is that Uncle Larry is alone and still smoking those damn Russian cigarettes.

David

DAY 116

....

THE LUMBERJACK

September 6
Mountain Magic Motel
Libby, Montana

Dear Mary,

I remember writing months ago that once you're wet, you can't get wetter. Well, I think that theory may need amending, because right now I sit with my toes curled beneath the baseboard heater of a small motel room...clearly wetter.

It rained the entire day. My glasses fogged me to blindness. My sodden clothes dissolved into my skin. No matter how hard I pedaled—no matter how often I stared at my odometer willing the miles to turn—rainwater still worked its way through my pores to dilute my very blood.

I don't want to be riding anymore. I don't want to meander across the country. I want to be warm again. I want to be with you. I am tired of this cold and soggy state far beyond the realm of wetter.

My only motivation came from the cryptic words of an overall-wearing farmer sitting two tables away during breakfast. Engrossed with his paper, he had been silent throughout the meal as I chatted up the place. The waitresses seemed to love my tales about the people I've run across. I had the whole café rolling with a reenactment of biking against the fierce plain winds, when the farmer stood up from his breakfast and walked over to my table.

"You've come a long way, son. Wish I could have done something like that."

I nodded.

"But I'm too old for that foolery now. Tell you what, though, I'll pay for your breakfast. That way something of mine will be going with you. Just remember one thing though…" His deep eyes, brown flecked with yellow, held my gaze. "The man who chops wood gets heat twice."

With that, he dropped some cash on the table and left.

"Crazy coot," mumbled the waitress, shaking her head.

While riding through the endless rain later, I realized that that farmer was far from crazy. Biking is like chopping wood. Each spin of the crank is like the swing of an axe, pure physical effort heating the body. Each mile gained is like another log split. The stacked logs assure a crackling blaze to vanquish the chill of night, and the piled miles promise the warm fire of your embrace at journey's end.

I am the Paul Bunyan of bicycle riders, and I have but a few more trees to chop.

Love,
David

DAY 120

....

BOWING AT THE FEET
OF THE CASCADES

September 10
Kamloops Island Campground
Kettle Falls, Washington

Dear Mary,

I FEEL LIKE PUKING. My stomach is agitated; my head is pounding; my skin is aflame. I have been hugging the toilet for the past ten minutes, praying for relief. But none comes. I think I am dying. Or at the very least have the flu.

Which is just wonderful, seeing that in the next four days I have five mountain passes to climb. My legs are weak, my spirit weaker. The Pacific taunts from the other side of the Cascades, so close after so many miles.

All I can do is sleep, hoping that tomorrow will bring a remedy. If my fever refuses to break, I know I should rest. But I can't. I'm so close. Somewhere between Montana and Washington my patience fled. This moseying across America must stop. I need to see the ocean. Soon.

Damn, my stomach is twisting me all up inside.

Despite this flu, I must reach the Pacific, even if that means bowing every mile to empty my stomach. I am so close I can taste…well, I don't want to talk about what I taste.

Your green-tinged lover,
David

Letters to Eden

DAY 122

....

WHEN THE COWS COME HOME

September 12
American Legion Park
Okanogan, Washington

DEAR MARY,
 I AM PASSING THROUGH A DESERT I never expected. Between Wauconda Pass to the east and Loup Loup Pass to the west, weeds tumble, dust swirls, and shadows darken the valley. Migrant workers move from failed orchard to failing orchard as farmers try to make this desert bloom with apple blossoms. Water is pumped from the Columbia River Basin to feed the trees, but frequently that cup does not runneth over. Irrigation is expensive, and cheap apples from China have caused the price per bushel to plunge. Banks foreclose on struggling farmers. The crooked trees, soon to ripen with fruit, are torn from the earth with backhoes, stacked in misshapen piles, and burned along the side of the road. The bonfires mark my progress west through this valley of sadness.

The sadness has been with me for miles. For days. The land is my mirror; I am its reflection. And what I've seen has unmanned me.

I heard it well before I saw it. The dry air trembled with the sound—a bleating, a crying, a wail of such loss, that my heart plunged to my seat. Grief filled the valley as if pushed from a bellows. This howl contracted rhythmically, at one moment stabbing the desert air with sorrow-heavy cries…and in the next moment, ungodly silence.

Around a bend in the highway trembled a calf standing over the slumped form of an unmoving cow. The calf's head was stretched skyward as if trying to block the sight of what sprawled at its hooves along the road's shoulder. It may have been its mother. It could have been its grandmother. The rest of the herd had fled. But for the flies and me, the calf mourned alone.

It wailed, and inside, for the first time, I saw my own fear—my true fear. I'm running, Mary. I've been pedaling out of terror. I'm scared of the new you, of a new home in some unknown place, of the reality of what I have avoided for months. Oma is dead. She is gone. We are alone. Like that lonely calf bleating to the heavens. Oma is dead.

Every time I close my eyes, I see that calf. I see its family stolen by a speeding logging truck. I hear it shake with injustice. I, too, shake. I, too, weep.

I weep for it all.

David

DAY 125

....

CHASED WINDMILLS

September 15
Washington Park
Anacortes, Washington

Dear Mary,

I'm at the highway's end, stopped by the sea. My wheels will spin me no farther west. The road finishes with my tires touching the Pacific. Or rather Puget Sound. Or whatever.

The sky should be an endless blue, not clouded in gray, heavy with rain. I should be able to watch the sun set one final time from my bicycle. I should be able to see the wine dark sea reflect the dusk. Yet I can't. To describe the loneliness at the end of this road is impossible.

Where's the levity, the joy, the accomplishment?

I feel I should philosophize, to sum up the entire trip into a few pithy phrases—the many lessons learned, the countless struggles endured. I should try to describe this many-layered portrait of America painted across my heart. But I can't. I am beyond exhausted. I feel like a corn husk browning along the side of the road. I have ridden almost six thousand miles, and if I never ride another, that's fine.

I want to come home.

I need to come home.

I'm so tired and sad and alone. This adventure is over. That it is time to end, I am positive. Riding my bike into San Francisco Bay is an unimaginable task. My legs can carry me no farther. My heart can't sustain the effort. It's otherwise occupied, watching for the rising sun and reaching east for you.

I have been altered, Mary. Neither wiser nor older, just deeper. I still have fears, I still have doubts, and I still love you. I know it's going to be hard. I'm different, you're different, and in so many ways, our world together is different. We need to re-introduce ourselves—to fall in love all over again.

My letters have told only half the story, Mary. You know that better than anyone. Living will reveal the other. This bike trip is just the asking of a question, and the answer can only be gleaned through time's passage and the next adventure we experience together.

Love,
David

PART XV

....

THE TRUNK OF OUR OLIVE TREE

GENERAL DELIVERY

September 12
Brattleboro, Vermont

DEAREST DAVID,
I HOPE ANACORTES FINDS your legs rested and your heart strong. If not, may this little surprise inspire. Your letters have helped me greatly and have supported me when there was little else. You have carried me with you across the country.

When I last heard from you though, your words scared me a little. I feel like I'm pushing you to end your trip before you want. You said you were going to stop "moseying" and do some serious miles to reach the coast. You may not even go to San Francisco.

I can't help but think that your change in plans is my fault. I need you to understand that I'm okay. I'm sad and living is not easy, but another month apart will make the hug I give you that much tighter. If you want to go on, I really want you to continue. Do you see what I'm trying to say? We have a lifetime ahead of us to practice being one, and I don't want you take a single moment for granted.

Of course, I won't complain if you do decide to end at the Pacific Ocean. Either way, you have done an amazing thing. When I look at a map, I can't believe it. Your will and patience is incredible. And don't think for a moment that you won't need those attributes when you return. Things are different now. You will come to a strange town, to this new tiny apartment in Vermont. I've stocked the cupboard with Fruity Pebbles and pudding snacks and mint chocolate chip ice cream, but I know that it's far from the home we once had. We have to grow into each other again. It will be difficult.

What comforts me though is that I have started seeing our love in my mind as a graceful fluid dance, where each move, each step effortlessly connects with the next. But that's the whole trick with dance; no step ever effortlessly connects with the next. Good dancers just make it appear that way. They have to really practice the moves endlessly. Each day they may master another turn or lift, but the work is very hard to make the dance beautiful.

I want us to be those dancers. Let us show the world what a graceful and gracious dance love can be.

You have won my heart, David. It has become a cavern and what you will find in the deepest most remote part is a large, expansive pool of sweet tenderness. *For you.* That you have chosen me out of the multitude to be the dearest to your heart, I am eternally grateful and humble. That I have chosen you out of the multitude to be the dearest to my heart, I am proud.

Just know, David, that you are the man I was meant for. You have become him. Whatever you decide, I will not stop thinking of you and us and our homecoming.

All my love,
Mary

www.ingramcontent.com/pod-product-compliance
Lightning Source LLC
Chambersburg PA
CBHW032024290426
44110CB00012B/654